Teaching Every Adolescent Every Day

Teaching Every Adolescent Every Day

Learning in Diverse Middle and High School Classrooms

Donald D. Deshler
Jean B. Schumaker
University of Kansas, Lawrence

Karen R. Harris
Steve Graham
University of Maryland, College Park

EDITORS

BROOK
L I N E
BOOKS

ISBN 1-57129-060-5

Library of Congress Cataloging-In-Publication Data
Teaching every child every day : learning in diverse middle and
   high school classrooms / Donald D. Deshler ... [et al.] editors.
       p.   cm. -- (Advances in teaching and learning)
   Includes bibliographical references and index.
   ISBN 1-57129-060-5 (pbk.)
     1. Learning disabled children--Education (Secondary)--United
States.   2. Learning disabled children--Education (Middle school) -
-United States.   3. Social skills--Study and teaching (Secondary) -
-United States.   I. Deshler, Donald D.   II. Series: Advances in
learning & teaching.
LC4704.74.T43   1999
371.9'0473--dc21   99-11951
                                                               CIP

Cover design, interior design and typography by Erica L. Schultz.

Printed in USA
10 9 8 7 6 5 4 3 2 1

Published by
BROOKLINE BOOKS
P.O. Box 97
Newton, MA 02464
Order toll-free: 1-800-666-BOOK

CONTENTS

SERIES FOREWORD

This volume is the fifth in the continuing series Advances in Teaching and Learning. Steve Graham, Karen Harris, and Michael Pressley are the general editors of the series, which focuses on important contemporary topics relevant to school-based achievement and pedagogy.

Each volume in the series focuses on a single topic, bringing together commentary from some of the most important figures contributing to the focus of the volume. The plan at this time is for at least one of the general editors to be involved in the editing of each volume, although often in collaboration with guest editors who are exceptionally expert with respect to the topic of the volume. Those interested in serving as guest editors should contact one of the general editors with a specific proposal for a volume.

INTRODUCTION

Meeting the Challenge of Diversity in Secondary Schools

DONALD D. DESHLER & JEAN B. SCHUMAKER,
University of Kansas, Lawrence

KAREN R. HARRIS & STEVE GRAHAM,
University of Maryland, College Park

Increasingly, educators are expected to teach classes of academically, socially, culturally, racially, economically, and linguistically diverse students. This challenge has been exacerbated in recent years by the calls from state legislatures for more content to be taught to higher levels of proficiency to enable students to meet more demanding outcome standards. The combination of higher outcome standards and increased diversity of classroom membership has placed enormous strains on classroom teachers. These pressures are largely intensified at the secondary level.

While the instructional challenge is enormous, a host of instructional approaches have been designed and validated in recent years that have the potential of significantly altering the instructional dynamic in diverse classrooms. The purpose of this book is to present some of the instructional methods that have been found to be effective in impacting the performance of adolescents in diverse classrooms at the secondary level.

STANDARDS FOR SUCCESSFUL INSTRUCTIONAL PROCEDURES

Instructional routines that teachers report as being most successful in working with diverse classes meet the following criteria (Schumaker, Deshler, & McKnight, 1991). First and foremost, these instructional routines must be considered palatable and usable by the classroom teacher. That is, for any instructional procedure to be employed regularly, it must seen by teachers as readily fitting into their ongoing classroom routines and into their already overtaxed and overburdened lives. Any procedures that require extraordinary amounts of planning time, grading time, material gathering or adaptation generally are not embraced and used on a sustained basis by teachers because more time and commitment are required than they are able to give.

Second, instructional routines must be valued by the average- and high-achieving students in the classroom. Research has shown that classroom teachers are very sensitive to the feedback that average- and high-achieving students give to them about their teaching practices (Bulgren & Lenz, 1996). That is, if average or high achievers indicate displeasure or boredom with a particular instructional routine, teachers generally stop using the routine because they do not want to disenfranchise those students who are the best performers in the class.

Third, instructional routines must be valued by and sufficiently powerful to significantly impact the performance of the low achievers in a classroom. Unless substantial gains can be realized by those students who are at greatest risk for academic failure, they will continue to fall short of meeting standards for acceptable performance. Sustained failure ultimately leads to their withdrawal from classroom engagement and ultimately to dropping out of school altogether.

Thus, in order for instructional routines to be successful in diverse classrooms, they must be sufficiently potent and valued by not only the teacher but by the majority of students in the class. The various instructional procedures discussed in this book have been chosen in light of these criteria.

UNIQUE FACTORS IN MEETING THE NEEDS OF AT-RISK ADOLESCENTS

The collective efforts of professionals in both the public school and research sectors have established several factors as central to quality programming for and the improved performance of at-risk adolescents (Deshler, Ellis, & Lenz, 1996). They are as follows.

1. Adolescence is one of the most difficult and challenging of all developmental stages. The struggle inherent in moving toward independence and establishing a new identity among peers is a significant challenge for any adolescent. For those adolescents who struggle with learning, however, the challenge is doubly difficult. Indeed, coping with the demands of secondary schools, trying to establish independence from home, and gaining acceptance from peers can be a very daunting task for those students who lack fluency in language and comprehension, experience difficulties in noting and responding to the nuances of various social situations, and so on.

2. Quality programming decisions for adolescents who are at-risk for failure must be based on an understanding of the nature of the difficulties with which they must contend. Historically, in attempts to explain the poor performance of at-risk students, the field of education has focused on analyzing the characteristics that define student difficulties. The search for the root of the problem(s) generally has been confined to studying the attributes *inherent in* the adolescents Although understanding an adolescent's learning deficits is important, it is not sufficient. Equally important is understanding the demands of the setting that contribute to the student's problems. For example, the academic and social demands of secondary schools are markedly different from those encountered in elementary settings. Therefore, the effects of these escalated demands on student performance must be carefully considered to arrive at a more complete picture of why a student is functioning in a dysfunctional manner. In short, an adolescent's behavior is understood best when viewed as the result of an *interaction between* the characteristics of the learner and the characteristics of the setting in which the student must adjust and cope.

3. Adolescents must be involved in all aspects of planning and implementing their instructional program, including assessment, program specification, goal setting, monitoring, evaluation, and program modification. At-risk adolescents represent a rich source of information and insight that must be tapped. They should be viewed as highly valued and capable partners in the educational process. To the extent that these students are expected to take an active role in helping to define the nature of their difficulties as well as have a voice in determining the scope and composition of their intervention program, their motivation to be active participants in the learning process will improve.

4. Strategy instruction takes place following a specific sequence so that students master each strategy. Research has convincingly demonstrated that the academic performance of at-risk students improves dramatically if they are taught, in an intensive, systematic fashion, strategies that they can use in learning situations (Harris & Graham, 1996; Hogan & Pressley, 1997; Schumaker & Deshler, 1992). The most effective strategy instruction has been found to be characterized by:

- a careful description of the strategy to be learned;
- a clear model of the new strategy in which the teacher thinks aloud so the students can better understand how good learners think as they solve problems;
- multiple opportunities for practice with the new strategy within a framework in which the teacher carefully scaffolds a set of learning experiences that systematically move the student to mastery;
- well-designed feedback that instructs the student on how to

improve future performance; and
- opportunities to generalize and adapt the strategy to a variety of situations and settings.

In addition to thorough and systematic instruction by any one teacher, a master plan of action should be instituted among the majority of a student's teachers so the strategies taught in one setting get cued and reinforced in other settings. Similarly, efforts should be coordinated across school years and across school sites to build a logical scope and sequence of skill and strategy instruction. In the absence of coordinated and sustained efforts, instruction tends to be sporadic and unfocused, resulting in little if any student gains. In short, the extent to which instruction is *both intensive* (i.e., systematic and focused) during a given instructional session and *extensive* (i.e., presented or prompted in multiple settings and by multiple teachers over time), at-risk students will improve markedly as learners and performers.

The challenge of designing and orchestrating this type of instruction in secondary schools is a major undertaking. Each of the chapters in this volume provides concrete, practical suggestions for operationalizing this type of instruction in secondary classes serving diverse groups of students. Additionally, the chapters in this book collectively address some of the major issues that teachers face who work with at-risk adolescents within the context of highly diverse classes. Our hope is that this book will serve as a valuable resource in helping educators meet the needs of at-risk learners in secondary schools.

REFERENCES

Bulgren, J. A., & Lenz, B. K. (1996). Strategic instruction in the content areas. In D. D. Deshler, E. S. Ellis, & B. K. Lenz (Eds.), *Teaching adolescents with learning disabilities: Strategies and methods* (pp. 409-473). Denver, CO: Love Publishing.

Deshler, D.D., Ellis, E.S., & Lenz, B. K. (1996). *Teaching adolescents with learning disabilities: Strategies and methods.* Denver, CO: Love Publishing.

Harris, K. R., & Graham, S. R. (1996). *Making the writing process work: Strategies for composition and self-regulation* (2nd ed.). Cambridge: Brookline Books.

Hogan, K., & Pressley, M. (1996). *Scaffolding student learning: Instructional approaches and issues*. Cambridge: Brookline Books.

Schumaker, J. B., & Deshler, D. D. (1992). An analysis of a learning strategy interventions for students with learning disabilities: Results of a programmatic research effort. In B. Y. L. Wong (Ed.). *Intervention research with students with learning* disabilities. New York: Springer-Verlag.

Schumaker, J. B., Deshler, D. D., & McKnight, P. C. (1991). Teaching routines for content areas at the secondary level. In G. Stover, M. R. Shinn, and H. M. Walker (Eds.), *Interventions for achievement and behavior problems* (pp. 374-395), Washington, DC: National Association of School Psychologists.

CHAPTER ONE

Closing the Gap to Success in Secondary Schools: A Model for Cognitive Apprenticeship

MICHAEL F. HOCK, JEAN B. SCHUMAKER,
& DONALD D. DESHLER, The University of Kansas

The costs of failing in secondary schools can be devastating. Students who are academically underprepared or who drop out of high school are at a great disadvantage in terms of successful participation in society and attainment of personal hopes and dreams. The instructional agenda for anyone who works with these students is abundantly clear: *we must close the gap between where students are socially and academically and where they need to be in order to be successful in school and life.* Therefore, we must focus our efforts on closing the huge performance gaps between students' skills and what school and the world of work demand of them. Not to do so places many adolescents, *and society itself,* at risk of failure.

THE CHALLENGE OF EDUCATING AT-RISK ADOLESCENTS

The struggle inherent in moving toward independence and establishing a new identity among peers is a significant challenge for any adolescent. For adolescents who are at risk for academic failure, the struggle can be doubly difficult. Indeed, for individuals faced with a learning problem or even a learning disability, the challenges of adolescence—such as coping with the demands of secondary schools, trying to establish independence from one's parents, gaining acceptance from peers, and acquiring sufficient skills to survive in the demanding environment of the post-secondary global economy— often become overwhelming. Such individuals often find that their lack of fluency in language, their problems with comprehension, and their difficulty detecting and responding to the nuances of social situations can be debilitating.

The difficulties confronting at-risk adolescents must be carefully considered when making programming decisions to meet the needs of these students in secondary schools. Such decisions are critical in light of the current trend to educate at-risk students primarily within general education classrooms (Baker & Zigmond, 1995). This trend has been based on literature arguing that students' needs, especially their needs for social integration, can best be met in such classes (Audette & Algozzine, 1992; Gartner & Lipsky, 1987; Stainback & Stainback, 1985; Wang, 1987; Wang & Birch, 1984). However, such arguments have generally focused on implementing inclusionary policies and practices in elementary schools (Schumaker & Deshler, 1988). Few, if any, references have been made to how the organizational structures of elementary and secondary schools differ, how curricula vary from earlier to later grades, or how the gap between the demands of the setting and the abilities of at-risk students to cope with those demands widens as students progress from the elementary to secondary grades.

Many of the proposals that have been advanced in conjunction with the inclusionary education movement call for potentially complex changes in the instructional delivery services to at-risk students, including those with disabilities (e.g., Sailor, 1991). Unfortunately, wholesale application of such proposals to both elementary and secondary schools—without recognizing the key differences in organizational structures, curricula, and learner variables—is a gross oversimplification of a complex set of issues. Clearly, the nature of secondary schools and the characteristics of secondary at-risk students must be considered when changes are made in efforts to better meet the needs of these students (Goodlad, 1983). In this chapter, we propose a set of alternative ways of thinking about and delivering academic services to adolescents who are struggling in secondary school settings. The underlying assumption is that in order to effect meaningful change in the academic and social success of at-risk adolescents, the instructional focus of all teachers and administrators must be on intensive and targeted instruction. This instruction must be aimed at closing the gap that exists between the skill levels of at-risk students and the demands of the secondary general education classroom, as well as the realities of the post-secondary world.

The size and complexity of this gap becomes apparent when we realize that when at-risk students reach the secondary grades, they lack many of the skills considered necessary for success in the general education classroom (Schumaker & Deshler, 1992). Research conducted on adolescents with learning disabilities shows that these students are the lowest of the low achievers: they perform below the 10th percentile on measures of reading, written expression, and mathematics (Warner, Schumaker, Alley, & Deshler, 1980). Furthermore, students with learning disabilities demonstrate a plateauing of basic skills at about the fourth- to fifth-grade skill level when they reach the 10th grade (Rivera, 1997; Schumaker, Deshler, Alley, & Warner, 1983). In addition to these basic skill deficits, at-risk students have been shown to lack proficiency in the use of several higher-order skills and strategies that are required for successful performance in general education classrooms, including paraphrasing, self-questioning, gaining information from textbooks in an efficient manner, critical listening, distinguishing main ideas from details, remembering large amounts of content information, theme writing, error monitoring, and test taking (Hughes & Schumaker, 1991; Lenz, Alley, & Schumaker, 1987; Schmidt, Deshler, Schumaker, & Alley, 1989; Schumaker, Deshler, Alley, Warner, & Denton, 1982).

At-risk students' problems are compounded as they progress through the secondary grades because curriculum demands increase steadily. When students advance to higher and higher grades, they are required to read and analyze larger amounts of printed information, express themselves more in writing, take tests covering larger amounts of content, solve more multiple-step problems, work more effectively in teams, be better self-advocates, and be more socially skilled (Schumaker & Deshler, 1984). As the skill levels of these students plateau and the demands of the setting continue to grow, the performance gap between these students' abilities and what they are expected to do continues to widen (Deshler & Schumaker, 1993).

While the growing size of the performance gap faced by at-risk students across the grades is a significant problem in and of itself, this problem is exacerbated by the fact that each of the skills and/or strategies that must be learned for success in the general education classroom is extremely complex. For example, a student with deficient paraphrasing skills requires remedial instruction in a host of basic skill areas (e.g., differentiating main ideas from details, identifying the most important information, transforming the information into an alternative form, etc.), as well as instruction in strategic application of these skills in order to use them fluently to advantage in the general education classroom.

In addition to the demands present in secondary schooling, certain conditions are inherent at this level of education that differ markedly from those present in elementary schools. First, the classroom pedagogy in secondary schools is based on a teacher-centered instructional focus. Even though student-centered instruction has been espoused by educational theorists for several decades, a study of classroom pedagogy from 1890-1980 concluded that such shifts have historically been resisted by most teachers, and especially those in secondary schools (Cuban, 1984).

Elementary and secondary schools also differ markedly in the complexity and amount of content students face, in the allocation of time for instruction, and in the external pressures imposed upon secondary schools from other institutions (Cuban, 1984). With regard to the complexity and amount to be learned, the content in secondary schools requires more sophisticated skills and strategies than those required in elementary grades; moreover, those skills and strategies are assumed to be in place in order for large amounts of curriculum content to be learned. High school teachers tend to be didactic in the delivery of their content because the large volume of subject matter to be covered often drives the instructional methodology (Goodlad, 1983).

Additionally, the amount of contact time between students and teachers at the two levels differs markedly. Elementary teachers often spend as many as 5 hours per day with the same group of 25 students. In contrast, high school teachers generally spend less than one hour per day with the same group of students, and usually have responsibility for as many as 150 students per day. The amount of a teacher's contact time with a student is an important variable affecting how that teacher might understand and address a specific student's strengths and limitations. Thus, elementary teachers have much more freedom to respond to class or individual student needs than secondary teachers do.

Another difference between primary and secondary schools involves the autonomy secondary teachers have in developing their course offerings (Cuban, 1984). Their autonomous and independent behavior makes the organization and delivery of badly needed skill and strategy instruction extremely difficult to coordinate across teachers and grades. Coordination of content teachers across different subject areas would be the only way to ensure practice and reinforcement of targeted skills/strategies, systematic cueing for their use, and programmed generalization of instruction. But such coordination would add a significant load to content teachers' current responsibilities—especially when most secondary teachers do not view their role as being a teacher of skills and strategies (Scanlon, Deshler, & Schumaker, 1996). And these teachers already feel stressed by the growing amounts of content they are expected to teach (Lenz, Bulgren, & Hudson, 1990).

Closely related to the gap between the skills possessed by adolescents and the demands and conditions present in secondary schools are the heightened expectations young adults face as they enter the world of work. The globalization of commerce and industry has resulted in a dramatic decrease in the industrial jobs that used to employ students not headed for college. As recently as the 1960s, almost 50% of all workers in the industrialized countries were involved in making or moving goods. By the year 2000, however, no developed country will have more than one-sixth of its workforce in the traditional roles of making and moving goods (Pritchett, 1994).

Meanwhile, the explosive growth of technology requires that current and prospective workers have higher levels of skills and new types of skills. The SCANS Report for America 2000 (Secretary's Commission on Achieving Necessary Skills, 1991) insists that high-paying but unskilled jobs are disappearing and that today's workers must be creative and responsible problem solvers who have skills and attitudes on which employers can build.

In summary, those creating educational programs for at-risk students in secondary schools must take into consideration a number of critical factors.

- First, these students have serious deficits that cannot be ignored in light of the demands they must meet in secondary courses. They require instruction in a number of skills and strategies that will enable them to meet complex sets of demands at secondary and post-secondary levels.
- Second, given the conditions under which general education secondary-school teachers work, these teachers cannot be expected to take on the major responsibility for teaching at-risk students the skills and strategies they need to succeed in secondary and post-secondary coursework. Their role in programming for these students must fit within the conditions and pressures they face.
- Third, the ways in which the world of work is changing make secondary programming for at-risk students a "do-or-die" situation. Something drastic must be done for them if they are to be gainfully employed in jobs that will enable them to function independently throughout their adult lives.

AN INSTRUCTIONAL MODEL

Because the problem outlined above is a complex one, it requires a complex solution. The solution must enable teachers like the one highlighted in the following scenario to meet the unique needs of at-risk students like Maurice, a 17-year-old student with learning disabilities.

Ms. Jones is a special education teacher. Maurice is one of the students on her caseload, and an IEP meeting has just been held to plan Maurice's educational program. Ms. Jones felt generally pleased with the results of the meeting. Maurice's parents had attended the conference, as did Maurice, his counselor, and three of his classroom teachers. Consensus was reached on the critical outcomes necessary for Maurice to successfully make the transition from high school to a local community college. Maurice contributed to the planning meeting and shared his goals. He was able to list the academic, social, career, and personal goals he needed to fulfill his hopes and expectations for the future. Everything seemed to be in place.

However, Ms. Jones was still apprehensive. Specifically, she was concerned that she would not be able to deliver the intensive, individualized strategy instruction Maurice needed in order to reach his goal of writing proficiency. Despite good instruction and in-class support from general and special education teachers, Maurice had yet to reach the writing goals he identified as part of his plan to attend community college.

Ms. Jones thought long and hard about Maurice's situation and reviewed the instructional services currently provided to Maurice. Maurice spent his entire day in general education classrooms, and the services he received from special education were delivered in inclusive classrooms. She was thankful for the excellent and accommodating instruction Maurice's teachers presented, but she felt it was not always personalized or intense. For example, in the past, while Maurice had worked hard and received excellent instruction and support in the general education classes he attended, he did not make measurable progress in writing proficiency. Specifically, he could not independently organize, write, and edit well enough to produce acceptable themes and essays. Thus, the gap between his writing skills and the skills necessary for success was not narrowing. In short, Ms. Jones felt she was continuing to put out fires and was not able to provide Maurice with the intensive instruction he needed.

What can the educators in Maurice's school do? How can they find additional *time and opportunity* to support Maurice's development as a writer? How can they find the *time and opportunity* to provide the personalized instruction, guided practice, and corrective feedback Maurice needs while helping him to benefit from the instruction in all of his required secondary courses? How can a situation be created such that content instruction is not sacrificed for skill instruction?

Clearly, a comprehensive instructional model needs to be put in place for at-risk secondary students like Maurice. The remainder of this chapter will focus on just such a model, based on validated instructional procedures, that takes into account the characteristics of at-risk students and the realities of secondary schools and post-secondary environments. The philosophical foundations for the model, the parts of the model, and the conditions necessary to make it a reality will be described and discussed.

Philosophical Foundations

Our instructional model for at-risk adolescents is based on the notion of apprenticeship. Typically, the term *apprenticeship* is associated with the mastery of craft skills such as typesetting, auto mechanics, and electrical construction. However, the apprenticeship method can also be used to train novices in such scholarly fields as law, medicine, journalism, and education. Educators use an apprenticeship model to mentor student teachers and teach them the skills, strategies, and knowledge necessary for success as teachers (Collins, Brown, & Newman, 1989; Rogoff, 1990).

For at-risk adolescents, a *cognitive apprenticeship* must be made available. A cognitive apprenticeship establishes a teaching and learning relationship in which interactions between "expert" learners and "novice" learners support the movement of the novice toward the expert end of the learning continuum (Pressley & McCormick, 1995). The notion of a cognitive apprenticeship is based on the belief that people learn to be good learners. That is, students are not innately endowed with the skills and strategies to approach learning tasks in appropriate ways; they *learn* them. Rogoff (1990), for example, has stated that "children's cognitive development is inseparable from their social milieu in that what children learn is a cultural curriculum; from their earliest days, they build on the skills and perspectives of their society with the aid of other people" (p.190).

The goal of a cognitive apprenticeship is to support the development of expert learners who know how to learn independently and interdependently and do so at appropriate times to produce positive learning outcomes for themselves (Hock, Deshler, & Schumaker, 1993; Hock, Schumaker, & Deshler, 1995). Such expert learners have been called "good information processors" by Pressley, Borkowski, and Schneider (1989). They defined good information processors as individuals who:

a. know a large number of useful learning strategies (i.e., efficient and effective ways to approach learning tasks);
b. understand when, where, and why these strategies are important;
c. can select and self-regulate strategy usage wisely;
d. are reflective and planful while learning;
e. believe in carefully deployed effort;
f. are intrinsically motivated to learn; and
g. know a great deal about many topics and have rapid access to their knowledge.

To help produce good information processors, expert learners work cooperatively with novice learners. They help the novices to problem-solve, to create and select strategies, to apply strategies to authentic tasks, and to self-regulate learning activities (Collins et al., 1989; Hock, Deshler, & Schumaker, 1991; Palincsar & Brown, 1984; Scardamalia & Bereiter, 1983; Schoenfeld, 1983). The role of the expert learner is to:

- Assess the skills and strategies a novice has already acquired;
- Co-construct strategies with the novice that meet the novice's needs and that are efficient and effective for completing learning tasks;
- Describe new strategies and parts of co-constructed strategies fully, taking care to address when, where, why, and how the strategies are appropriately used;
- Model use of cognitive and metacognitive strategies for the novice; and
- Guide the novice's practice and generalization of the strategies.

To guide the novice's practice and generalization of the strategies, the expert engages in *scaffolded instruction* during practice sessions (Rogoff, 1990). In other words, the expert learner establishes a "scaffold of support" around the student as the student applies strategies to acquire new knowledge, remember critical information, and demonstrate understanding of acquired knowledge. The expert provides just enough support and structures practice sessions so that the novice learner moves beyond his or her existing comfort level. The expert encourages the novice to stretch and move to a higher level of learning with each practice attempt. Scaffolded instruction also gives the expert learner additional opportunities to provide models of the cognitive and metacognitive features of strategies currently being learned (Hogan & Pressley, 1996; Pressley & McCormick, 1995).

Students who have participated in a cognitive apprenticeship approach learning tasks independently with confidence, knowledge, and skill in applying effective learning strategies. The following is an example of how an student who has engaged in a cognitive apprenticeship might think:

"Okay. I have an essay to write for English. I can do this and do it well! The essay is due in five days, and I have 30 minutes right now to get started. Since this is a formal essay, I think I'll use the Theme Writing Strategy [Schumaker, 1997]. Yes, I think that strategy will work for this assignment.

"Let's see ... How do I get started? Well, I know the strategy is called 'TOWER' for short. Hmm. . . The letters in 'TOWER' remind me to *Think* about the topic, *Organize* the information, *Write* the theme, *Edit* it, and *Rewrite* it. All right then, in the time I have, I can start the *T* step.

"'Think about the topic' means I need to do some brainstorming about what I know about the topic. I can also do some research if I need more information. Hmm ... I don't know anything about this topic. Let's see. Maybe I can find some information about this in my textbook. I'll read the material and jot down some notes as I read. Then I'll spend some time thinking about what I've learned. Once I know what I intend to write about, I'll visit with my teacher to see if I'm on the right track. Yes, this sounds like a good plan for now ... Yes, here's a section in the textbook about the topic. I'd better get started if I'm going to get this done."

PARTS OF THE MODEL:
AN ANALOGY FOR SERVICE DELIVERY

The service delivery model for the cognitive apprenticeship must, of necessity, be comprehensive and permeate a student's education. It must allow for individual needs and personalized instruction.

The cognitive apprenticeship model, in essence, is similar to the service delivery model encountered by a couple about to have a baby. Such a model typically has three major components. The first component involves an *individualized assessment of needs and the development of a personalized plan*. A multidisciplinary team gathers information concerning family history and the medical condition of the expectant mother, and explains the delivery options to the couple.

Then, together with the prospective parents, the team develops a personalized service plan detailing the present condition, individualized goals, and specific interventions. The personalized plan lists *where* services will be delivered, *what* interventions will be used, the hoped-for *outcomes*, and the *individuals responsible* for each outcome.

The second component of the service delivery model is *general instruction*. General instruction typically consists of a series of large-group classes designed to inform expectant parents about child development and the birthing process. For example, 12 couples might learn about the Lamaze method and proper prenatal nutrition. Instruction is presented to the group by a knowledgeable staff. Nurses introduce new information, concepts, and skills to the diverse group of learners. They model new skills and schedule practice opportunities. They teach expectant partners how to work as a team and provide scaffolding support as prospective parents practice the skills to proficiency. They circulate among the couples, providing help where needed and noting those that may need additional help.

After a period of instruction that lasts 9 weeks, most couples in the group feel prepared for the upcoming event. When the time for delivery arrives, a couple checks into the maternity ward. Other expectant parents are there, and the multidisciplinary staff monitors progress and provides support to the group. The prospective parents have the sense that they are all part of a group with common experiences and hoped-for outcomes. General instruction continues until the baby is delivered—or until circumstances require the third component of the model to be operationalized.

The third component of the model is *intensive personalized service.* This component of the model is used when a mother or baby needs additional help. For example, in the case of fetal distress, an alternative service delivery becomes necessary for the hoped-for goal to be achieved. The staff immediately responds to the need for personalized service. The team grows. Surgeons, surgical nurses, a pediatrician, and an anesthesiologist join the team. The place of delivery changes. The prospective parents are moved from the general obstetric ward to a surgical operating room. Thus, as needed, service delivery changes from routine monitoring and preparation for normal delivery by the obstetrician and her staff to comprehensive, multidisciplinary crisis intervention.

The surgical team does its job efficiently and well. Specialists work together in a well-orchestrated effort with common outcomes in mind. For example, some members of the team perform a Caesarean section. Others immediately step in to ensure the well-being of the baby. Within an hour, the parents and newborn are together in the maternity ward, and they rejoin other families in the general service area. The personalized and intensive services are effective and supportive of the general service plan. More importantly, each family's personalized needs are met as required by the circumstances.

AN EDUCATIONAL SERVICE DELIVERY MODEL FOR COGNITIVE APPRENTICESHIP

To create a cognitive apprenticeship within schools, instruction might be delivered as it is delivered within the service delivery model described above. The educational version of this model is designed to support the inclusion of all students in the general education experience and to meet the needs of individual students as they arise to ensure their attainment of critical outcomes necessary for optimal participation in society. This approach to service delivery is called *Supported Inclusion* (Joint Committee on Teacher Planning for Students with Disabilities, 1995). Like the model described above, the Supported Inclusion Model has three components (see Figure 6-1 on the next page).

Individualized Assessment and Personalized Plans

First, the model includes an *individualized assessment and development of a personalized plan*. In order to obtain an accurate portrait of each student's skills and abilities, curriculum-based measures of the student's strengths and needs are gathered (Rivera, 1997). In addition, an

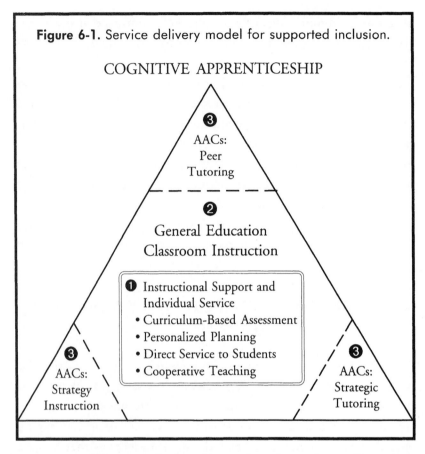

Figure 6-1. Service delivery model for supported inclusion.

assessment of the general education settings the student will encounter is conducted to determine what demands are inherent in those settings. Both assessments are designed to determine exactly what instruction is needed in order for the student to be successful in the general education setting and curriculum. A personalized educational plan is developed by the student and educators working as a team, based upon the assessment information and the targeted outcomes. The plan includes a report of the student's present levels of performance, his or her individualized goals, and the planned instructional interventions.

A set of instructional methods has been developed and validated to aid educators and students in preparing such personalized educational plans. Through these procedures, students are taught a strategy, called the Self-Advocacy Strategy (Van Reusen, Bos, Schumaker, & Deshler, 1994), that enables them to inventory their strengths and weaknesses, assess the demands they will be facing, create goals focusing on their weaknesses, develop plans for learning, and communicating their findings to others. Through learning this strategy, students become empowered to guide their own educational programs and to plan for transitions into the world of work and into future educational settings.

The Self-Advocacy Strategy has been successfully taught in whole-school efforts. Whitaker (1997), for example, taught the Self-Advocacy Strategy to 72 seventh-grade students. These students were prepared to conduct their own parent-teacher conferences while learning the strategy. Prior to the initiation of Self-Advocacy instruction, the students' school had 41% parent attendance at parent-teacher conferences. After the Self-Advocacy instruction had taken place and students began conducting the conferences, there was 76% attendance. Thus, the Self-Advocacy Strategy can be taught in such a way as to empower students to become involved in their education and to involve their parents in it as well.

General Instruction

The second component of the model is *general instruction*. The foundational assumption underlying this component is that educational services for all students, including those with mild disabilities or low achievement, must be provided in general education classrooms to the fullest extent possible. Within these classrooms, general educators share the responsibility for the success of all students. They have the assistance of special and other educators who work with them, as needed. They cooperatively plan, deliver, monitor, and manage instruction in such a way that all students achieve important and socially valid outcomes. A guiding principle is that all students will be successful in general education classrooms and will maintain a presence in general education.

In order for success to be achieved by all students, instructional methods for achieving that success and for creating a cognitive apprenticeship in general education settings must be used. A new approach to instruction in general education settings has been developed and validated for these purposes. Called the Content Enhancement Approach (Lenz & Bulgren, 1995; Lenz et al., 1990), it enables teachers (expert learners) to share new ways of learning content with large groups of diverse students (novice learners). When teachers use this approach to content instruction, they *plan* and *deliver* instruction in such a way as to enhance student understanding and retention of the content and to share methods of thinking about and learning subject matter content.

The emphasis of the *planning* process used by Content Enhancement instructors is on (a) identifying which content is most important to teach and (b) transforming that content into easily understood and motivating formats. Planning for diverse classes of students, including students with mild disabilities, entails thinking deeply about the content, choosing the information that students truly need to know, separating the central concepts from the details, identifying critical relationships among the concepts and details, and selecting and constructing instructional devices that make the content easy to understand and memorable. These instructional devices are designed to depict, in concrete form, both the critical pieces of information (i.e., concepts and details) and the ways those pieces of information are related.

The emphasis of the *teaching* process used by Content Enhancement instructors is on the partnership created between the teacher (the expert) and the students (the novices). Students are seen not as vessels to be filled with facts by the teacher, but as partners who are guided to discover information and identify relationships among the pieces of information. In the process, both teacher and students learn and understand information in new ways.

To guide students in this process, Content Enhancement teachers use a set of teaching routines specifically designed to engage students in the learning process in a continuously active way. Each routine has a specific purpose within the instructional process and entails several steps in which the students' participation is enlisted in co-constructing the instructional device. The routines are used routinely and in combination with each other to create a powerful synergy. (For a detailed explanation of Content Enhancement planning and teaching routines, see Bulgren & Lenz, 1996; Lenz, 1997; Lenz, Bulgren, Schumaker, Deshler, & Boudah, 1994; Lenz, Marrs, Schumaker, & Deshler, 1994).

The Content Enhancement Approach was developed through a series of research projects over the past 14 years with the help of teachers and students. It is based on several validated instructional principles.

- First, students learn more when they are actively involved in the learning process. The Content Enhancement Approach requires that they think, listen, speak, and write during the instructional process.
- Second, students learn more when abstract, complex concepts are presented in concrete forms. The Content Enhancement Approach involves the use of various concrete devices (e.g., content maps, graphic devices) to represent information.
- Third, students learn more when the structure or organization of information is made apparent to them and when relationships among pieces of information are made explicit. The concrete devices used in the Content Enhancement Approach show students the structure of information so that they can easily understand such relationships between different pieces.
- Fourth, students learn more when important information is distinguished from unimportant or less important information. The Content Enhancement Approach involves carefully choosing the most important information to present and presenting it in organized ways so that students can make this distinction.
- Finally, students learn more when new information is tied to

previously learned information. The Content Enhancement Approach involves students in a continuous review process to make connections between the information they are learning and the information they have previously learned. Additionally, certain routines, such as the Concept Anchoring Routine (Bulgren, Schumaker, & Deshler, 1994), directly connect new information to information in students' experiences.

An important cornerstone of the Content Enhancement Approach is the "less is more" notion. The research cited above clearly indicates that if teachers are selective in choosing the most important information for students to learn and presenting that information using the Content Enhancement principles, students learn more than if they are presented with lots of information in traditional ways. This does not mean, however, that large amounts of meaningful content are sacrificed. The Content Enhancement routines have been designed to be integrated into the instructional milieu of the class routine in such a way that the integrity of the content is maintained. They allow the content teacher to present information to the class as a whole while reaching individual students to improve their learning. In short, enhanced content instruction involves choosing important content, deeply thinking about the best ways to present the content, inventing devices that make the content "come alive" for students, and working with students in partnership to identify the important information and the relationships among that information.

Intensive Personalized Instruction

The third component of the model involves *intensive personalized instruction*. This component provides expert learners and apprentices the time and opportunity to address individual learner needs in the same intensive way that the medical profession responds to the unique needs of patients in crisis situations. This component is carried out using school-wide educational "emergency rooms"—called Academic Achievement Centers (AACs)—in which all students, including normal achievers and those students with disabilities or low academic achievement, can receive the personalized service they require.

While AACs are closely related to what are currently called resource rooms, they differ from resource rooms in several key ways. First, AACs are not restricted to students with identified special education needs. AACs are open to all students regardless of academic skill level. Any student can access instructional support within the AAC for almost any content area as the need arises. For example, students with successful academic records can access instructional support in an area in which their performance is not as strong as they would like. Students with multiple academic needs can receive support in a variety of areas. Both students with relatively high grade-point averages intent upon earning even higher averages and those who struggle with academics in general can receive personalized instruction in skills and strategies in the AAC by working with experts, including peers, to become as proficient in learning as possible.

AACs also differ from resource rooms in terms of staffing patterns. While a resource room is usually staffed only by special education teachers, an AAC is staffed by special educators, general educators, para-educators, and adult volunteers. Special educators in the AAC provide intensive instructional services, teaching small groups of special and general education students strategies to help them meet the demands of their general education classes. Instead of supervising the hallways or a study hall, general educators staff the ACC on a regularly scheduled basis. They provide drop-in assistance in their content area(s) to any student who requests additional content clarification, thereby providing parts of a cognitive apprenticeship in the subject areas. Para-educators and adult volunteers also staff the AAC. Like the general educators, they are specially trained to provide elements of the cognitive apprenticeship. For example, they provide supplementary strategy practice and content drill and review to individuals or small groups of students (Welch, Richards, Okada, Richards, & Prescott, 1995).

Finally, the AAC is different from a resource room with regard to hours of operation and accessibility. An AAC is open before and after school as well as during school hours. Students can go to the ACC during study-hall hours, seminar times, and lunch time during school hours. The AAC is centrally located so that all students can access it readily. It can be a large room, several rooms in one location, or several rooms spread throughout a school, but it must be readily available for student attendance.

In sum, the AAC is designed to provide the *time, opportunity,* and *expertise* for intensive personalized services that are aligned with the goals of the general education curriculum and the cognitive apprenticeship (see Figure 6-2). To provide these services, the AAC offers three unique interventions: (a) small-group strategy instruction, (b) strategic tutoring, and (c) peer tutoring.

All three interventions are focused on teaching students how to learn and perform within the general education curriculum. Specifically, all three focus on teaching students *learning strategies*—strategic approaches to academic tasks. This focus has been chosen for the AAC because strategic instruction has been validated as an effective intervention for students with disabilities and low achievement (Schumaker & Deshler, 1992). A learning strategy has been defined (Deshler & Lenz, 1989) as

> an individual's approach to a learning task. A strategy includes how a person thinks and acts when planning, executing, and evaluating performance on a task and its outcomes (p. 205).

A learning strategy is a complex combination of several cognitive and metacognitive strategies and overt behaviors. One example of a learning strategy is the Sentence Writing Strategy (Schumaker & Sheldon, 1985), designed to help students write a variety of sentences. Each of the steps in the Sentence Writing Strategy involves the use of a cognitive strategy (such as mentally choosing a sentence formula from a menu of formulas and exploring words that fit the formula), the overt behaviors involved in mechanically writing the sentence, or

Figure 6-2. Academic Achievement Centers At A Glance

WHAT are Academic Achievement Centers (AACs)?

- AACs are academic "emergency rooms" in which students receive intensive one-on-one or small-group instruction designed to close educational gaps.

WHERE are AACs located?

- An AAC may be an area identified as a school-wide learning center. An AAC may also consist of a series of smaller areas or classrooms located throughout the school. Generally, an AAC may be any area in a building in which a teacher or para-educator could meet with a student or small group of students.

WHO staffs AACs?

- An AAC could be staffed by special and general educators, administrators, counselors, para-educators, and/or adult volunteers.

WHEN are AACs open?

- The AAC could be available before, after, and/or during the school day.

WHAT activities occur at AACs?

- Students learn task-specific strategies for completing a variety of academic tasks.

- Students acquire content knowledge, complete class assignments, and create unique strategies that address current academic demands.

- Students study and learn content with peers as they complete class assignments.

a metacognitive strategy (such as checking the structure of the sentence against the chosen formula). When used in combination, these steps are very powerful in enabling learners to write a variety of sentences.

Instructional procedures for teaching a variety of at-risk adolescents several learning strategies have been designed and validated over the past 17 years. These methods comprise the *Learning Strategies*

Curriculum, an instructional methodology for teaching students information processing strategies to take in information from the environment, transform and manipulate that information in such a way that they can remember it, and express the information in ways that demonstrate their competence. The strategies that focus on taking in information are those involved with decoding long words, gaining meaning from reading passages, and dealing with long reading assignments (e.g., textbook chapters). The strategies that focus on transforming and manipulating information are those related to taking notes from lectures and written materials, creating study cards, creating memory devices, and testing oneself. The strategies that focus on expressing information are those related to writing sentences, paragraphs, and themes, and those related to taking tests. Thus, the strategies students can learn create a conceptual "whole" with regard to the major types of information-processing functions they must use to be successful in secondary and post-secondary settings (Deshler & Schumaker, 1986; Deshler & Schumaker, 1988).

The strategies in the Learning Strategies Curriculum can be taught to mastery through an eight-stage instructional process (Ellis, Deshler, Lenz, Schumaker, & Clark, 1991) to create an intensive and personalized cognitive apprenticeship. In Stage 1, a pretest is given to determine each student's strengths and weaknesses in the targeted area and to create commitment to learn a new strategy. In Stage 2, the new strategy is described. Students become aware of the steps of the strategy and where, when, why, and how the strategy can be used. In Stage 3, the strategy is modeled for the students in such a way that they see and hear how a person thinks about and uses each of the strategy steps. In Stage 4, students become proficient in speaking about the strategy. They learn to name and explain each of the strategy steps. In Stage 5, they begin to practice using the strategy within circumstances that are easy to navigate. For example, they apply a reading strategy to materials written at their ability level. Instruction is scaffolded such that students experience success through a sequence of guided practice and independent practice activities. After each practice attempt, individual students receive specific and corrective feedback about what they did well and how they might improve the next attempt. In Stage 6, students practice using the strategy under circumstances that approximate those of the general education curriculum. For example, 10th-graders apply a reading strategy to materials written at the 10th-grade level. Again, corrective feedback is provided after each practice attempt. In Stage 7, a posttest is given, and students' achievement is celebrated. Finally, in Stage 8, students learn how to generalize their use of the new strategy to a variety of circumstances and learning situations. The sections below outline each of the three forms of strategy instruction that are offered in an AAC.

Small-group strategy instruction. Strategy instruction is best implemented in small-group or one-on-one instructional arrangements. Although it has been successfully implemented in large inclusive classes (Ellis, 1992; Beals, 1983), the circumstances within those classes included several factors such as the presence of a specially trained teacher—e.g., a special education teacher with special training, or a specially trained assistant for the general education teacher (Deshler & Schumaker, 1993). While many students benefit from strategy instruction in secondary general education classes when these conditions are not present, students with disabilities and other low achievers tend not to benefit from the instruction (Fisher, Schumaker, & Deshler, 1995).

The Academic Achievement Center is an optimal setting for strategy instruction for students with disabilities or low achievement. In the AAC, students can access small-group strategy instruction that will enhance their ability to succeed in the general education classroom. For example, students who need to learn to write sentences can participate in small-group intensive instruction on the Sentence Writing Strategy. Students who need to learn how to study for vocabulary tests can participate in small-group instruction in the Vocabulary Learning Strategy (Ellis, 1992). Small instructional groups can be organized for a relatively short period of time until students master the targeted strategies, and then other groups might be convened as needed across a school year.

To provide a more concrete example of how strategy instruction might be carried out in the ACC, let's look again at Maurice, the student who needs some intensive writing instruction. Let us assume that in order for Maurice to become a proficient writer, he needs instruction in all the writing strategies, beginning with the Sentence Writing Strategy. Ms. Jones, Maurice's teacher, talks with Maurice about his schedule and determines that he can come to the ACC on a regular basis during fifth hour, when he has a study hall scheduled, and after school two days a week. She also finds six other students who need the same instruction during fifth hour and sets up intensive writing instruction to take place during that time. All of the students, including Maurice, start instruction in the Sentence Writing Strategy together. They take a pretest, are introduced to the strategy, watch a model of the strategy, learn to name and explain the strategy steps, and begin to practice the strategy together.

As they progress, however, some students learn faster than others. At this point, the instruction become more individual and personalized. Maurice receives individual feedback after each practice attempt and then moves on to the next appropriate lesson. As Maurice begins to learn to write, he gets excited about the process and comes into the ACC after school so that he can complete more lessons. He works with the fifth-hour teacher to decide what lessons he should complete after school, and the teacher who staffs the ACC after school gives him feedback after each practice attempt in the same way the fifth-hour teacher does. As Maurice masters a strategy, he begins to use it as he completes his assignments in his classes. His strategy instructors work with his general education teachers to ensure that they prompt Maurice to use each strategy and recognize Maurice's attempts to improve his writing. In this way, Maurice and other students like him learn the skills they need to be successful in high school and beyond.

Strategy instruction has been found to be very effective in providing students with learning disabilities and other low achievers with the skills they need for success in high school. Studies have shown that secondary students with disabilities who learn writing strategies are able to write at levels comparable to or higher than those of their peers without disabilities (Schmidt, Deshler, Schumaker, & Alley, 1989). On high-school tasks such as reading a textbook chapter and taking a test over the content, they earn average (C) or above average (B) grades (Bulgren, Hock, Schumaker, & Deshler, 1995; Schumaker et al., 1982).

Strategic tutoring. The second type of strategic intervention available in the ACC is strategic tutoring—an instructional process in which the expert learner (the teacher) teaches novice learners strategies *while* tutoring the subject-matter content. During strategic tutoring sessions, teachers and students respond to the demands of the general education curricula by co-constructing, learning, and applying strategies (Hock et al., 1995).

Four key factors (see Figure 6-3) define the role of the expert learner in the strategic tutoring process: (a) content knowledge and content transformation, (b) knowledge of strategies, (c) strategic teaching skills, and (d) mentoring skills. First, strategic tutors recognize that students with disabilities and low achievement may need immediate help with pressing course assignments. Since they are expert learners, they can quickly sort out what needs to be done on an assignment, and they can work with the content in ways that will help students understand it. Second, strategic tutors know a number of learning strategies and the steps to those strategies, plus they know how to guide students through a co-constructive process to create strategies "on the spot" that will be appropriate for the assignment or task at hand. Third, they know how to quickly teach students to use a spontaneously generated learning strategy using an abbreviated form of the eight-stage methodology described above. Finally, they know how to advise students in a mentoring capacity to give them a feeling of connection to people in their world.

Strategic tutoring is different from traditional tutoring in several ways. Most importantly, the emphasis of strategic tutoring is on the cognitive apprenticeship and on teaching students strategies that they can apply both to the task at hand and to similar future tasks. In

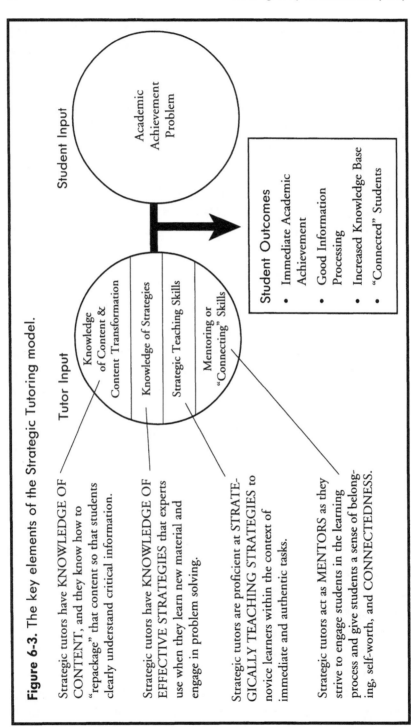

Figure 6-3. The key elements of the Strategic Tutoring model.

Student Input

Academic Achievement Problem

Tutor Input

Knowledge of Content & Content Transformation

Knowledge of Strategies

Strategic Teaching Skills

Mentoring or "Connecting" Skills

Student Outcomes

• Immediate Academic Achievement

• Good Information Processing

• Increased Knowledge Base

• "Connected" Students

Strategic tutors have KNOWLEDGE OF CONTENT, and they know how to "repackage" that content so that students clearly understand critical information.

Strategic tutors have KNOWLEDGE OF EFFECTIVE STRATEGIES that experts use when they learn new material and engage in problem solving.

Strategic tutors are proficient at STRATE-GICALLY TEACHING STRATEGIES to novice learners within the context of immediate and authentic tasks.

Strategic tutors act as MENTORS as they strive to engage students in the learning process and give students a sense of belonging, self-worth, and CONNECTEDNESS.

contrast, the emphasis of traditional tutoring is solely on completing the task at hand. Often, traditional tutors actually resort to completing the task *for* the student (Hock, Schumaker, & Deshler, 1995). In addition, strategic tutoring focuses on creating independent information processors. Unfortunately, the products of traditional tutoring are often students who have become dependent upon tutors for help when completing assignments (Carlson, 1985). Furthermore, strategic tutoring involves a specified sequence of instructional methods based on the eight instructional stages, whereas traditional tutoring has little structure or organization. Strategic tutors engage in systematic instruction that includes: (a) assessing the student's strategy needs and obtaining the student's commitment to learn a strategy for the task at hand and similar tasks; (b) creating or co-constructing a strategy appropriate to the task at hand; (c) giving a direct explanation of the strategy; (d) modeling the strategy; (e) checking to see that the student fully understands the strategy and when, where, and how to use the strategy; and (f) structuring student practice of the strategy with constant guided support (Hock et al., 1995).

In addition, strategic tutors structure independent practice of the strategy on the task at hand, provide positive and corrective feedback on student use of the strategy, and guide the student to generalize the strategy to future tasks. Figure 6-4 (pp. 28-30) presents an example of a checklist that the strategic tutor might use to guide the tutoring process through the guided practice stage.

In contrast to subject-matter tutors, the role of the strategic tutor is multifaceted. Strategic tutoring requires that the tutor act as a model expert learner and thinker responsible for organizing situations for learning. The tutor transforms the subject matter and engages students with the content to increase both the students' understanding of content and their ability to use learning strategies to act independently on the curriculum in the future (Hock et al., 1993; Hock et al., 1995).

Let's take a look at how the strategic tutoring process might benefit Maurice, who is currently receiving writing strategy instruction in the AAC. Although Maurice is now able to write some simple

Figure 6-4. The strategic tutoring checklist.

STAGE 1: DURING THE **ASSESSMENT &**
COMMITMENT PHASE, DID THE TUTOR:

____ 1. Ask about the assignment?
("Exactly what is it that you are supposed to do? Explain the
assignment to me.")

____ 2. Review previous performance?
("How did you do on the last assignment/test?")

____ 3. Determine the student's current strategy?
("How did you approach this type of task in the past? What
steps will you take in order to complete this assignment? When
and why would you use this strategy?")

____ 4. Ask if the strategy works?
("Do you think you might need to add something to your
strategy? Did this approach work for you last time?")

____ 5. Provide a rationale for creating a new strategy
("What will the result be if you get a better grade on this type
of assignment? Others who have used this strategy have
received B's on their themes.")

____ 6. Gain the student's commitment ("Would you be willing to
create or expand a strategy which will result in improved
performance in this area?")

STAGE 2: DURING THE **CREATE & EXPLAIN** PHASE,
DID THE TUTOR:

____ 7. Create a strategy?
("What if we add this step to the strategy you are currently
using? This is a proven approach to this task. Let me explain
the steps to you What else could we do?")

____ 8. Explain each step for the alternative strategy?
("OK, our new strategy says we should _____ first, next we
_____, next ____," etc.)

____ 9. Compare and contrast the new strategy with the old one?
("How is this different from what you used to do?")

____ 10. Ensure that the student has taken notes on the strategy?
("What are the steps of the new strategy? Write down the steps
of the strategy we've constructed so that you can refer to them
later.")

Figure 6-4 (Continued)

STAGE 3: DURING THE **MODEL** PHASE, DID THE TUTOR:

____ 11. Set student expectations for the modeling activity?
("Watch me carefully as I model for you. I'll be asking you to take over so watch me use the strategy we developed")

____ 12. Model the strategy?

____ 13. Involve the student?
("What is the next step? What should I do next? OK, you complete the example.")

____ 14. Review and/or modify the strategy?

STAGE 4: DURING THE **CHECK FOR UNDERSTANDING** PHASE, DID THE TUTOR:

____ 15. Have the student explain the strategy?
("Explain to me how you would describe this strategy to another student.")

____ 16. Have the student discuss *what* the strategy is designed to do, *why* it is important, and *when and where* the strategy could be used?

____ 17. Ask the student to name the steps of the strategy?
("OK, explain to me exactly what you do when you take lecture notes and use the strategy we've been working on.")

____ 18. Allow the student to customize the strategy?
("What do you think about the strategy? Do you think it might need to be modified to work better for you?")

STAGE 5: DURING THE **GUIDED PRACTICE** PHASE, DID THE TUTOR:
*CUE**

____ 19. Establish what will happen during the session?
("What are your goals for this session? OK, according to your plan, it looks like we need to cover ____ during the session.")
DO

____ 20. Review academic goals and any persistent error patterns?
("Remember, the last theme you wrote contained comments

* From Lenz & Bulgren (1995).

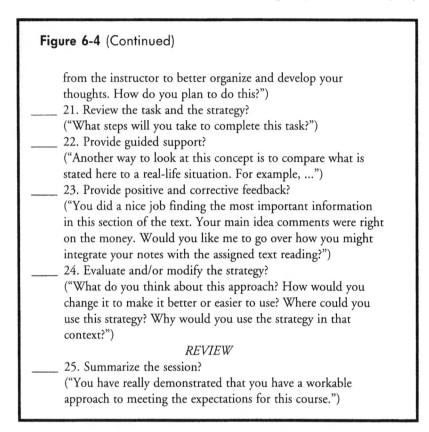

Figure 6-4 (Continued)

from the instructor to better organize and develop your
thoughts. How do you plan to do this?")
____ 21. Review the task and the strategy?
("What steps will you take to complete this task?")
____ 22. Provide guided support?
("Another way to look at this concept is to compare what is
stated here to a real-life situation. For example, ...")
____ 23. Provide positive and corrective feedback?
("You did a nice job finding the most important information
in this section of the text. Your main idea comments were right
on the money. Would you like me to go over how you might
integrate your notes with the assigned text reading?")
____ 24. Evaluate and/or modify the strategy?
("What do you think about this approach? How would you
change it to make it better or easier to use? Where could you
use this strategy? Why would you use the strategy in that
context?")

REVIEW

____ 25. Summarize the session?
("You have really demonstrated that you have a workable
approach to meeting the expectations for this course.")

sentences, he notices that each time he answers questions on written homework assignments in history class, his teacher circles the verbs and writes notes on Maurice's papers that Maurice is having trouble with subject-verb agreement. As a result of this problem, Maurice is earning low grades. He has a history homework assignment due tomorrow and wants to earn a better grade. He stops by the AAC after school and asks the on-duty history teacher to help. The teacher looks at Maurice's past papers and notices that Maurice uses singular verbs with plural subjects. She asks Maurice to show and tell her the steps he has been following so far to check a sentence for subject-verb agreement. Maurice indicates that he does not understand what to do. The teacher explains that verbs and subjects must match in number in a sentence, draws him a chart of examples, and then works with Maurice to co-construct a strategy for checking his sentences once he writes them. The resulting strategy has three steps: (a) Determine if the subject of the sentence is singular or plural, (b) Select the proper formula card (from the example charts), and (c) Check your sentence with the formula card. Maurice and the teacher discuss where and when Maurice might use these steps to improve his work. The teacher models use of the strategy on one of Maurice's sentences. She asks Maurice to explain how he will use the strategy. When he is able to do so, she asks him to check and correct several of his sentences on past papers. She provides feedback to him until he checks and corrects several sentences correctly. Then she asks him to work on his latest assignment while she works with another student. She reminds him to check each sentence using the three-step strategy as he works. Finally, she reviews Maurice's final product and provides feedback. She encourages Maurice to use the strategy each time he writes and to stop by the AAC to have someone provide him with feedback on his next written assignment.

Maurice also decides to approach his math teacher, who is available to help students at the AAC during fifth period. Maurice is struggling with the concept of order of operations, and his grades on math homework and quizzes are low because of this problem. Following the same instructional procedures outlined above, Maurice and his math teacher create a strategy to help Maurice apply the order of operations to his math assignments. In one tutoring session, they create the MATH Strategy (see Figure 6-5 on the next page). Below, Maurice demonstrates his knowledge of the strategy.

TUTOR: Maurice, now that we've created, discussed, modeled, and practiced this strategy, why don't you apply the MATH Strategy to your algebra homework. Think aloud as you work through the problem, so I can see how well the strategy works. I'll answer any questions you have and help if you get stuck.

MAURICE: OK. Here's the problem... $[16–5^2 \text{ x } (5–4)] \text{ x } (4^2–18)$. Let's see, I'll use the strategy note cards I made to remind me of the MATH Strategy steps. So first, I need to MOVE FROM LEFT TO RIGHT and remember to solve from left to right. Also, I need to look for parentheses, brackets, and exponents. OK, I did that and I see the problem has brackets, parentheses, and exponents.

Now, I need to figure out what to do next. The next step of the strategy is to ALWAYS SOLVE WITHIN PARENTHESES AND BRACKETS FIRST. OK. Oh! This step also has three rules that say to do exponents, multiply or divide, and then add or subtract in that order.

Let's see. There's the first set : $[16–5^2 \times (5–4)]$ multiplied to the second set $(4^2–18)$. So, I'll solve each by using the rules under Step 2:

- Exponents first, working left to right
- Multiply or Divide, working left to right
- Add or Subtract, working left to right.

Well, in the first set of brackets, I see an exponent, 5^2, which makes 25. And then in the second set of brackets, 4^2, which makes 16. I better rewrite this:

$$[16–25 \times (5–4)\,] \times (16–18)$$

Well, those are done. Let me move on to finishing the work *inside* the parentheses: (5–4), that equals 1, and (16–18) equals -2.

Figure 6-5.
"MATH": A Co-Constructed Strategy for the Order of Math Operations.

STEP 1: **Move** from Left to Right

STEP 2: **Always** Solve *Within* Parentheses & Brackets First

- Solve for any Exponents

- Multiply or Divide

- Add or Subtract

STEP 3: **"Tackle"** All Other Parenthetical Exponents

STEP 4: **"Handle"** the Math

- Multiply or Divide

- Add or Subtract

Better rewrite it again ...

$$[16–25 \times 1] \times (-2)$$

OK ... Now let's work on that big bracket. I did the exponent, and I worked out what was in the parentheses. Now I guess the next step is multiplying or dividing, moving from left to right. Well, there's only a sign to multiply, and it will have to be 25 x 1, which makes 25.

$$[16–25] \times (-2)$$

OK ... Now I have one set of brackets, but only one thing left to do. Since there are no exponents outside the parentheses, I can skip Step 3 of the strategy. Great! OK, There is no multiplication or division within, so I'll add or subtract ... That would be 16–25, which is -9.

$$[-9] \times (-2)$$

Let's see, Step 4 of the MATH Strategy is HANDLE THE MATH. I'm almost done. Now I only have 2 numbers to work with, -9 and -2, and I have to multiply them ... So my answer is ... 18.

TUTOR: Maurice, that was excellent! You used the strategy correctly, monitored how well it was working, and used your notes when necessary. Are you ready to do more homework?

MAURICE: Yes. This isn't so tough once you know what to do.

Strategic tutoring that embodies the process exemplified here has been shown to be effective with college students. For example, college students at risk of academic failure who have learned strategies for writing themes and comprehending literature from strategic tutors have earned higher scores on quizzes, tests, and themes in English composition and literature classes than students with similar or better academic profiles who did not participate in strategic tutoring. More importantly, their overall course grades in these classes have been, for the most part, C's or higher (Hock, Flynn, Schumaker, & Deshler, in prep; Hock, Deshler, & Schumaker, 1991).

To summarize, the ultimate goal of strategic tutoring is to ensure that students can independently complete the tasks necessary for them to succeed in educational settings. Critical outcomes include meeting the immediate demands of general education curricula, an increased knowledge base, proficiency in using a wide variety of cognitive and metacognitive strategies, and the skills and desire to participate as a contributing member of a learning community.

Peer tutoring. A third intervention provided within the ACC is peer tutoring, in which students instruct other students (Maheady, Sacca, & Harper, 1988). Peer tutoring has been shown to be successful in providing at-risk students time and opportunity to gain knowledge, improve skills, participate more fully in general education, and require fewer special education placements (Fisher et al., 1995; Greenwood, 1991; Greenwood & Delquadri, 1995; Greenwood, Delquadri, & Hall, 1989; Pressley & McCormick, 1995; Slavin & Madden, 1987). Some peer-tutoring programs have involved students in teaching each other strategies for learning content, like summarization of reading passages (e.g., Simmons, Fuchs, Fuchs, Mathes, & Hodge, 1995; Welch et al., 1995); other programs have focused on engaging students in practice and immediate feedback with content information and basic skills such as spelling words, math facts, or social science facts (Delquadri, Greenwood, Stretton, & Hall, 1983; Maheady et al., 1988; Pomerantz, Windell, & Smith, 1994). Peer tutoring has been shown to be effective at the elementary (Slavin & Madden, 1989), secondary (Greenwood, Terry, Utley, Montagna, & Walker, 1993; Maheady et al., 1988), and college levels (Fantuzzo, Riggio, Connelly, & Dimeff, 1989). Thus, it is a robust intervention that appears to work across settings and age groupings.

Peer tutoring programs have been implemented in a variety of ways. The program most appropriate for AACs is one in which students pair up and one student tutors the other outside the general education setting. Hock, Deshler, and Schumaker (1993) have described a college peer tutoring program in which tutors and tutees engage in tutoring activities at a learning center.

Effective peer tutoring programs incorporate a structured approach to preparing tutors to conduct tutoring sessions and have clear procedures for tutors and tutees to follow. Therefore, the peer tutoring program within the AAC is, of necessity, based on a cadre of trained peer tutors who know how to help students complete a variety of tasks. Some advanced peer tutors might be able to use strategic tutoring methods to help students in certain subject areas. Others might be specifically trained to help students review and practice certain learning strategies. Still others might be trained to lead study groups of students preparing for a test, or to help prepare an individual student for a test through a verbal quizzing process.

Let's take a final look at how Maurice might benefit from some peer tutoring support in the AAC. Let's say, for example, that Maurice has learned all the writing strategies and he has just written a 15-page paper for his science class. The paper is worth 25% of his grade for the quarter, and Maurice wants to hand in a polished product. He knows that peer tutors are available in the AAC to check papers for errors in capitalization, punctuation, spelling, and other areas. He stops by the AAC before school and asks for a peer tutor to help him edit his paper. The peer tutor agrees to read the paper and provide feedback after school. Maurice also knows that peer tutors are available for helping to ensure that students master information for tests. He has a test coming up in civics class at the end of the week and is currently working to complete the study cards he needs to get ready for the test. He figures that he will have all the study cards ready by the next day. He sees a notice on the bulletin board in the AAC that a group of students will meet the next day to compare study cards. He adds his name to the list and makes an appointment to meet with a peer tutor after school the next day to quiz him with his study cards.

Summary

The three-part instructional model described here—which includes assessment and planning, general instruction, and intensive personalized instruction—is a blueprint that can be varied as needed. Some educators have chosen to incorporate strategy instruction within general education classes instead of having a special setting in which strategy instruction takes place. For example, in some schools, the writing strategies are taught across the secondary English classes (e.g., the Sentence Writing Strategy in English I, the Paragraph Writing Strategy in English II, etc.). In other schools, strategy courses are offered for credit. In still others, strategy instruction is offered in cooperatively taught class-within-a-class (Hudson & Klamm, 1989) arrangements or team-teaching arrangements (Boudah, Schumaker, & Deshler, 1997). Regardless of where the instruction takes place, safeguards must be in place to ensure that students receive instruction in a variety of strategies across all the information-processing functions and that they master these strategies. If these safeguards are in place, the performance of students like Maurice can improve at a rate that will close the gap between the students' current skills and the skills expected of them in college and other post-secondary settings. Students like Maurice, their families, and their teachers can feel good about the students' chances for success in high school and can look forward to potential success in postsecondary educational settings.

CONDITIONS FOR PUTTING THE MODEL IN PLACE

In order to make the service delivery model outlined in the previous section a reality, certain conditions need to be present within secondary schools. These conditions include factors related to the mindset of the educators within the school as well as instructional arrangements that must be present. Several of the essential conditions are described below.

Policy-Level Support

The chances of at-risk students becoming independent, effective learners increases dramatically when they receive more than isolated experiences with strategy instruction and when critical concepts are emphasized across classes. Regrettably, many students receive only sporadic or isolated exposure to any one kind of instruction—

especially instruction that is strategy-based. The success rate and magnitude of change that students show as information processors are directly related to the amount of instruction they receive:

- in *multiple strategies* within and across various academic areas (e.g., reading, writing, organizing, remembering, etc.);
- across *multiple settings* (i.e., in the majority of a student's classes);
- from multiple teachers (when all of a student's teachers emphasize strategic learning and prompt strategy use, it becomes a prevailing expectation, and student performance improves);
- across multiple schools and grade levels (i.e., when receiving and feeder schools coordinate efforts by specifying a logical scope and sequence of strategy instruction); and
- in multiple instructional target areas (e.g., in academic and affective domains).

In order to successfully implement this type of coordinated instruction on behalf of at-risk students, teachers need favorable instructional conditions within which to teach. Foundational policy-level support would include:

- *Planning times* that are conducive to teachers' collaborating with key building staff (and when teachers work in team teaching arrangements, it is essential that they have *joint* planning time);
- *Sufficient budgetary support* for supplies (folders, posters, photocopying, tapes, etc.) and personnel (paraprofessional support, substitutes so teachers can participate in staff development and peer-coaching experiences, etc.); and
- *Ongoing staff development opportunities* so teachers can continually learn new components of the model and refine existing skills.

When multiple components and dimensions are considered in educational planning, at-risk students are more likely to become strategic learners and not merely the learners of a few isolated strategies.

Learning Communities and Partnerships

While policy-level supports are important, unless there is a prevailing commitment among a building staff to continuous learning and improvement, there will not be sufficient synergy to markedly impact the performance of all learners. One of the greatest challenges facing school staffs today is how to effectively work together to improve the quality of instruction offered to students. Given the diversity and generally large size of secondary school staffs, this problem is especially challenging in these settings. Sergiovanni (1994) contends that community building is at the heart of school improvement; teachers and administrators must view their roles in helping students as being interrelated. While personal growth and development is critical to professionals' being at their best, they must also view their growth *as a team* to be a critical task. Senge (1990) has argued that through team learning and collective thinking, groups of people can develop a level of wisdom and insight that surpasses the sum of individual members' talents in the group.

Secondary schools have long been characterized as disconnected organizations in which teachers are very isolated and have few reasons or opportunities to collaborate with each other (e.g., Fullen with Stiegelbauer, 1991; Rosenholtz, 1991). Additionally, in the absence of training and practice in team learning, the teaching process can be frustrating and can reinforce isolated work rather than collaborative work. Senge (1994) has outlined a set of guidelines that facilitate team learning, including the following.

- Teams should specify rules for conversations. These may include agreements to tell the truth as each person knows it, bring relevant information immediately to the team, or limit the time that everyone speaks.

- Teams should clarify how decisions will be made and by whom, and establish ways to safely check and challenge each other.
- Once rules are set by consensus, teams should discuss how to deal with violations of the rules.

At the foundation of a learning community within a school staff is a shared vision of what staff members want to create and build together. Extended conversations among teachers and administrators about the broad array of issues that influence the performance of academically diverse classes—such as the roles of different teachers, what curriculum to teach, how to deliver instruction, and how to team together for optimal instructional impact—can have an enormous effect on the overall quality of instruction that takes place within secondary schools, because they help teachers to view problems and solutions within the context of a system in which responsibilities and rewards are shared.

Teacher-Driven Staff Development Activities

In order for a comprehensive model of educational programming for at-risk students to be created within a school, the staff development opportunities available to teachers must address their needs and be driven by the problems they face in implementing innovative practices. They need to take part in a planned series of training activities that cycle through several phases (Schumaker & Clark, 1990). Each phase must include an analysis of needs, introduction of innovative and validated practices, discussion of anticipated problems and potential solutions, implementation, discussion of encountered problems and their solutions, and evaluation of outcomes (Knight, in press).

An Instructional Focus

Educators who create successful cognitive apprenticeships focus their efforts on delivering instruction in such a way that their students can make maximal gains, instead of on "fighting fires." The overwhelming majority of their time is spent in contact with students as they deliver instruction to those students. They do not waste time making structural changes in students' educational programs (e.g., changing a disruptive student's class schedule) or by working with distal variables (e.g., tracking, retaining, or classifying students); they know that the real differences are made in children's lives through high quality instruction (Wang, Haertel, & Walberg, 1993). Due to the quality of their instruction, students are highly attentive and productive, and there is little need for disciplinary action.

Intensive Instructional Delivery

One of the greatest challenges facing secondary teachers who work with at-risk adolescents is the shortage of time that they have to address the often large list of learning problems the students present. Compounding this problem is what Goodlad (1983) called the "we want it all" mentality that characterizes the prevailing approach to secondary education in America; rather than targeting a limited number of curricular and skill components to teach to students, educators try to teach *everything*. Often, such instruction merely skims the surface and fails to give adequate attention to those parts of the curriculum that are especially important to master. Worse, the drive to cover all the content often ignores the needs—and the actual learning—of the students.

Given the shortage of instructional time available, teachers who work with at-risk students must carefully select the content, skills, and strategies that are taught. The material that students learn must result in significant payoffs in terms of usable and marketable skills and knowledge. Our focus must be to intensively teach those curricular and skill/strategy competencies that will close the gap between where at-risk adolescents are currently performing and where they need to perform in order to compete with their normally achieving peers. Indeed, Meyen and Lehr (1980) have argued that *the* primary factor contributing to significant student growth is not the amount of instructional time, but rather the intensity of instruction over a sustained period of time. They have conceptualized intensive instruction as consisting of the following:

- Consistency and duration of time on task;
- Timing, frequency, and nature of feedback to students based on their immediate performance and cumulative performance;
- Regular and frequent communication by teachers to students of their expectations that students will master targeted skills and demonstrate continuous progress; and
- A pattern of pupil-teacher interaction in which the teacher responds to student initiatives and uses consequences appropriate to students' responses.

Additionally, engaging students in thinking about and setting goals that are meaningful to them (Seabaugh & Schumaker, 1981) and teaching them how to be effective self-advocates with regard to achieving those goals (Van Reusen, Deshler, & Schumaker, 1989) aid in promoting intensity of instruction. In other words, students who are actively engaged in achieving their own goals will be more likely to become engaged in the instructional process.

The Long View

Educators who create successful cognitive apprenticeships use the framework of their students' future lives to guide their programming decisions—working to ensure that their students succeed in the long run rather than get by in the short run. They have specified the outcomes that they want to achieve with their students, and they keep those outcomes in mind. They strive for student attainment of a critical mass of knowledge, skills and strategies that they can use independently throughout their lives. These instructors also ensure that instruction emphasizes student independence, insisting that students do for themselves what they are capable of doing, and avoiding methods and ways of interaction that foster dependence on the part of their students.

For example, teachers of students with learning disabilities do not tutor students on content so that they can barely pass the next test; nor do they read tests to their students. They teach students how to study for tests and take tests by themselves so that they can independently prepare for and take any test that they might encounter throughout their lives. Since research has repeatedly demonstrated that at-risk students can and do learn complex skills, these instructors hold high expectations for their students, and they communicate and teach according to those expectations.

Validated Practices

As they deliver instruction, teachers within cognitive apprenticeships use materials and procedures that have been shown, through research, to be effective for the kinds of students they serve. For example, they provide explicit instruction on skills they want students to use, model those skills in a variety of ways, provide numerous opportunities for students to practice the skills, provide positive and corrective feedback after practice attempts, and require students to reach mastery. They do not waste precious instructional time on methods that have no empirical foundation. They are critical consumers of curriculum materials and methods, and they choose only those products that can be used to create socially significant progress in their students. For example, they choose programs that help students learn the skills to earn B's instead of F's in general education classes, rather than choosing programs that produce minimal gains of a few percentage points. They do not discard programs that are working well in order to substitute the latest educational "fad." They do not get sucked in by the latest myth being espoused within the field of education.

Programming Success

Educators arrange situations within cognitive apprenticeships where children can succeed rather than fail. They place youths in settings and situations that offer a high probability of success for those youths. They do not place them in situations where they might be viewed by themselves or others as failures and/or where they might be rejected by their same-age peers. They make prior arrangements for the success of youths through instruction and other types of intervention. For example, if they are planning to place a youth within a general education classroom where cooperative group structures are in use, they take time to teach that youth the basic social skills necessary for successful group participation.

Student-Centered Focus

Teachers involved in cognitive apprenticeships focus on student needs and student outcomes. Although focusing on each student's needs is difficult, especially for secondary teachers who see as many as 150 students or more per day, there are ways of ensuring that the needs of different groups of students are met within the curriculum. These methods must be used if positive student outcomes are to be achieved for all students. Students who need intensive instructional arrangements in order to achieve these outcomes are provided such arrangements. Additionally, the outcomes that are to be achieved are explicitly identified and targeted as a part of each educator's vision of his or her role in the educational process. These outcomes must be socially significant ones—such as graduation, gainful employment, and ability to succeed in post-secondary learning environments—that are related to life success and quality of life factors for all students.

Clearly Defined Roles

Mutual understanding and respect are critical factors that serve as a foundation for working partnerships within schools. Educators who enjoy the respect of their colleagues also respect those colleagues. They understand the enormous pressures that all educators face today, and they avoid making recommendations or demands on their colleagues that fly in the face of those pressures. For example, special educators do not ask general education teachers who teach 150 students per day to spend an hour every day planning or modifying instruction for one student, or filling out paperwork that those teachers consider meaningless. They understand what general educators can accomplish within the context of their classes and the numbers and types of students who are enrolled in those classes, and they tailor their recommendations to fit those circumstances. They respect and celebrate general educators' knowledge, skills, and expertise, and they believe in their interest in helping children learn. Likewise, general educators understand the pressures facing special education teachers and those teachers' roles in preparing students to succeed in general education classes. They celebrate these teachers' expertise as learning specialists who can teach students the necessary skills and strategies needed for success at the secondary level.

Growth of Mind

Educators engaged in cognitive apprenticeships participate in a serious process of lifelong learning and espouse principles related to the growth of minds. They understand that the fields of education and special education are continually changing, that new methods are continually being developed, and that the only way to keep abreast of the "latest" is to be students themselves. They seriously engage themselves in the process of learning about and trying out new methods. They also are critical evaluators of how well new methods work and the kinds of gains that can be achieved through their use. They refer to themselves as learners in the presence of their students, model good learner behaviors constantly, and talk about how individuals can continuously strive to grow as learners.

Evaluation

Educators engaged in cognitive apprenticeship are self-evaluators. They take a hard look at the outcomes they are achieving. They compare the gains their students make against standards that have been determined as acceptable for those students. They monitor the progress of different groups of students within their classes—looking not only at how well the high-achieving students are progressing, but also at how well the average-achieving students, low-achieving students, and students with disabilities are progressing). When programs are not working, and students are not making gains, they look for and try new ways of teaching that will work better and that will help them achieve the desired outcomes. They accept failure as a stimulus for learning new ways of educating students, and they strive to eliminate failure wherever it occurs.

CONCLUSION

A comprehensive service delivery model to support the success of at-risk students in general education at the secondary level and beyond is possible if it is carefully set up across educational settings, if it is based on validated instructional practices, and if certain conditions are present to ensure its effectiveness. Within this new model, general education teachers provide cognitive apprenticeships as they teach their general education classes through the use of Content Enhancement methods. At-risk students are enrolled in these classes and receive support for their work in an Academic Achievement Center.

Strategic teachers and tutors located in Academic Achievement Centers not only help students to learn the necessary content, but also teach them the strategies they need to make the learning of content meaningful, integrated, and transferable. In addition, strategic teachers and tutors assume the role of mentors for the student in an attempt to connect the student within the learning community. The efforts of strategy teachers and strategic tutors is directly supported by peer tutoring practice sessions. Thus, strategy instruction and strategic tutoring provide support for students, including those with disabilities, by delicately balancing content acquisition, instruction in strategies required for attaining content knowledge, facilitating students' learning experiences through strategy instruction, and building supportive mentoring relationships. As a result, students become independent information processors, capable of lifelong learning and success in any educational environment.

In the chapter that follows, Fisher provides a detailed explanation of the Content Enhancement Approach, which is supportive of the service delivery model described in this chapter. Specifically, Fisher proposes that general education programs can effectively mediate learning in diverse classrooms through interventions that (1) revise curriculum, (2) focus on content planning, (3) enhance classroom instruction, (4) guide the adaptation of textbooks, (5) utilize peer tutoring, and (6) teach students how to learn. Readers should find this chapter particularly helpful in putting into practice a general education environment that is responsive to the instructional needs of all learners.

REFERENCES

Audette, B., & Algozzine, B. (1992). Free and appropriate education for all students: Total Quality and the transformation of American public education. *Remedial and Special Education, 13*(6), 8-18.

Baker, J.M., & Zigmond, N. (1995). The meaning and practice of inclusion for students with learning disabilities: Themes and implications from the five cases. *Journal of Special Education, 29*(2), 163-180.

Beals, V.L. (1983). *The effects of large group instruction on the acquisition of specific learning strategies by learning disabled adolescents.* Unpublished doctoral dissertation, University of Kansas, Lawrence.

Boudah, D.A., Schumaker, J.B., & Deshler, D.D. (1997). Collaborative instruction: Is it an effective option for secondary inclusion? *Learning Disability Quarterly, 20*(9), 281-304.

Bulgren, J.A., Hock, M.F., Schumaker, J.B., & Deshler, D.D. (1995). The effects of instruction in a paired associates strategy on the information mastery performance of student with learning disabilities. *Learning Disabilities Research and Practice, 10*(1), 22-37.

Bulgren, J.A., & Lenz, B.K. (1996). Strategic instruction in the content areas. In D.D. Deshler, E.S. Ellis, & B.K. Lenz (Eds.), *Teaching adolescents with learning disabilities: Strategies and methods*. Denver, CO: Love Publishing.

Bulgren, J.A., Schumaker, J.B., & Deshler, D.D. (1994). *The concept anchoring routine*. Lawrence, KS: Edge Enterprises, Inc.

Carlson, S.A. (1985). The ethical appropriateness of subject-matter tutoring for learning disabled adolescents. *Learning Disability Quarterly, 8,* 310-314.

Collins, A., Brown, J.S., & Newman, S.E. (1989). Cognitive apprenticeship: Teaching the craft of reading, writing, and mathematics. In L.B. Resnick (Ed.), *Knowing, learning, and instruction* (pp. 453-494). Hillsdale, NJ: Erlbaum.

Cuban, L. (1984). *How teachers taught: Constancy and change in American classrooms, 1890-1980*. New York: Longman.

Delquadri, J.C., Greenwood, C.R., Stretton, K., & Hall, R.V. (1983). The peer tutoring spelling game: A classroom procedure for increasing opportunity to respond and spelling performance. *Education & Treatment of Children, 6*(3), 225-239.

Deshler, D.D., & Lenz, B.K., (1989). The strategies instructional approach. *International Journal of Disability, Development, and Education, 6*(3), 203-244.

Deshler, D.D., & Schumaker, J.B. (1986). Learning strategies: An instructional alternative for low-achieving adolescents. *Exceptional Children, 52*(6),583-590.

Deshler, D.D., & Schumaker, J.B. (1988). An instructional model for teaching students how to learn. In J.L. Graden, J.E. Zins, & M.J. Curtis (Eds.), *Alternative education delivery systems: Enhancing instructional options for all students* (pp. 391-411). Washington, DC: National Association of School Psychologists.

Deshler, D.D., & Schumaker, J.B. (1993). Strategy mastery by at-risk students: Not a simple matter. *Elementary School Journal, 94*(2), 153-167.

Ellis, E.S. (1992). *LINCS: A starter strategy for vocabulary learning*. Lawrence, KS: Edge Enterprises, Inc.

Ellis, E.S., Deshler, D.D., Lenz, B.K., Schumaker, J.B., & Clark, F.L. (1991). An instructional model for teaching learning strategies. *Focus on Exceptional Children, 23*(6), 1-24.

Fantuzzo, J.W., Riggio, R.E. Connelly, S., & Dimeff, L.A. (1989). Effects of reciprocal peer tutoring on academic achievement and psychological adjustment: A component analysis. *Journal of Educational Psychology, 81,* 173-177.

Fisher, J.B., Schumaker, J.B., & Deshler, D.D. (1995). Searching for validated inclusive practices: A review of the literature. *Focus on Exceptional Children, 28*(4), 1-20.

Fullan, M.G., with Stiegelbauer, S. (1991). *The new meaning of educational change.* New York: Teachers College Press.

Gartner, A., & Lipsky, D.K. (1987). Beyond special education: Toward a quality system for all students. *Harvard Educational Review, 57*(4), 367-395.

Goodlad, J.L. (1983). *A place called school.* New York: McGraw-Hill.

Greenwood, C.R. (1991). A longitudinal analysis of time, engagement, and academic achievement in at-risk vs. non-risk students. *Exceptional Children, 27,* 453-465.

Greenwood, C.R., & Delquadri, J. (1995). Classwide peer tutoring and the prevention of school failure. *Preventing School Failure, 39*(4), 21-25.

Greenwood, C.R., Delquadri, J., & Hall, R.V. (1989). Longitudinal effects of classwide peer tutoring. *Journal of Educational Psychology, 81,* 371-383.

Greenwood, C.R., Terry, B., Utley, C.A., Montagna, D., & Walker, D. (1993). Achievement, placement, and services: Middle school benefits of classwide peer tutoring used at the elementary school. *School Psychology Review, 22*(3), 497-516.

Hock, M.F., Deshler, D.D., & Schumaker, J.B., (1991). *Annual report on the GOALS program.* Lawrence, KS: Institute for Research in Learning Disabilities.

Hock, M.F., Deshler, D.D., & Schumaker, J.B. (1993). Learning strategy instruction for at-risk and learning disabled adults: The development of strategic learners through apprenticeship. *Preventing School Failure, 38*(1), 43-49.

Hock, M.F., Flynn, G.C., Schumaker, J.B., & Deshler, D.D. (in prep). *The effectiveness of a literature comprehension strategy with at-risk college students.* Lawrence, KS: The Center for Research on Learning.

Hock, M.F., Schumaker, J.B., & Deshler, D.D. (1995). Training strategic tutors to enhance learner independence. *Journal of Developmental Education, 19*(1), 18-26.

Hogan, K., & Pressley, M. (1996). *Scaffolding student learning: Instructional approaches and issues.* Cambridge, MA: Brookline Books.

Hudson, F.G. (1993). *Class within a class: A shared responsibility of regular and special education.* Kansas City, KS: The University of Kansas Medical School.

Hughes, C.A., & Schumaker, J.B. (1991). Test-taking strategy instruction for adolescents with learning disabilities. *Exceptionally, 2,* 205-221.

Joint Committee on Teacher Planning for Students with Disabilities (1995). *Planning for academic diversity in America's classrooms: Windows on reality, research, change, and practice.* Lawrence: The University of Kansas, Center for Research on Learning.

Knight, J. (in press). *Teacher-driven professional development.* Lawrence, KS: The University of Kansas, Center for Research on Learning.

Lenz, B.K. (1997). *The course organizer routine.* Lawrence, KS: Edge Enterprises, Inc.

Lenz, B.K., Alley, G.R., & Schumaker, J.B. (1987). Activating the inactive learner: Advance organizers in the secondary content classroom. *Learning Disability Quarterly, 10*(1), 53-67.

Lenz, B.K., & Bulgren, J.A. (1995). Promoting learning in content classes. In P.T. Cegelka & W.H. Berdine (Eds.), *Effective instruction for students with learning disabilities* (pp. 385-417). Boston: Allyn & Bacon.

Lenz, B.K., Bulgren, J.A., & Hudson, P. (1990). Content enhancement: A model for promoting the acquisition of content by individuals with learning disabilities. In T.E. Scruggs & B.L.Y. Wong (Eds.), *Intervention research in learning disabilities* (pp. 122-165). New York: Springer-Verlag.

Lenz, B.K., Bulgren, J.A., Schumaker, J.B., Deshler, D.D., & Boudah, D.A. (1994). The unit organizer routine. Lawrence, KS: Edge Enterprises, Inc.

Lenz, B.K., Marrs, R.W., Schumaker, J.B., & Deshler, D.D. (1993). *The lesson organizer routine.* Lawrence, KS: Edge Enterprises, Inc.

Maheady, L., Sacca, M.K., & Harper, G.F. (1988). Classwide peer tutoring program on the academic performance of mildly handicapped students. *Exceptional Children, 55*(1), 52-59.

Meyen, E.L., & Lehr, D.H. (1980). Evolving practices in assessment and intervention for mildly handicapped adolescents: The case for intensive instruction. *Exceptional Education Quarterly, 1*(2), 19-26.

Palincsar, A.S., & Brown, A.L. (1984). Reciprocal teaching of comprehension-fostering and monitoring activities. *Cognition and Instruction, 1,* 117-175.

Pomerantz, D.J., Windall, I.J., & Smith, M.A. (1994). The effects of classwide peer tutoring and accommodations on the acquisition of content area knowledge by elementary students with learning disabilities. *LD Forum, 19*(2), 28-32.

Pressley, M., Borkowski, J.G., & Schneider, W. (1989). Good information processing: What is it and what education can do to promote it. *International Journal of Educational Research, 13,* 857-867.

Pressley, M., & McCormick, C. (1995). *Cognition, teaching, and assessment.* New York: Harper Collins.

Pritchett, P. (1994). *New work habits for a radically changing world.* Dallas, TX: Pritchett & Associates.

Rifkin, J. (1995). *The end of work: The decline of the global labor force and the dawn of the post-market era.* New York: Putnam.

Rivera, D.P. (1997). Mathematics education and students with learning disabilities: Introduction to a special series. *Journal of Learning Disabilities, 30*(1), 2-19.

Rogoff, B. (1990). *Apprenticeship in thinking.* New York: Oxford University Press.

Rosenholtz, S.J. (1991). *Teachers' workplace: The social organization of schools.* New York: Teachers' College Press.

Sailor, W. (1991). Special education in the restructured school. *Remedial and Special Education, 12*(6), 8-22.

Scanlon, D.J., Deshler, D.D., & Schumaker, J.B., (1996). Can a strategy be taught and learned in secondary inclusive classrooms? *Learning Disabilities Research and Practice, 11*(1), 41-57.

Scardamalia, M., & Bereiter, C. (1983) Child as co-investigator: Helping children gain insight into their own mental processes. In S. Paris, G. Olson, & H. Stevenson (Eds.), *The psychology of written language: A developmental approach* (pp. 67-95). London: Wiley.

Schmidt, J.L., Deshler, D.D., Schumaker, J.B., & Alley, G.R. (1989). Effects of generalization instruction on the written language performance of adolescents with learning disabilities in the mainstream classroom. *Reading, Writing, and Learning Disabilities, 4*(4), 291-309.

Schoenfeld, A.H. (1983). Problem solving in mathematics curriculum: A report, recommendations and an annotated bibliography. *The Mathematical Association of America,* MAA Notes, No. 1.

Schumaker, J.B. (1997). *The theme writing strategy.* Lawrence, KS: The University of Kansas.

Schumaker, J.B., & Clark, F.L. (1990). Achieving implementation of strategy instruction through effective inservice education. *Teacher Education and Special Education, 13,* 105-116.

Schumaker, J.B., & Deshler, D.D. (1984). Setting demand variables: A major factor in program planning for the LD adolescent. *Topics in Language Disorders, 4*(2), 22-40.

Schumaker, J.B., & Deshler, D.D. (1988). Implementing the regular education initiative in secondary schools: A different ballgame. *Journal of Learning Disabilities, 21*(1), 36-42.

Schumaker, J.B., & Deshler, D.D. (1992). Validation of learning strategy interventions for students with learning disabilities: Results of a programmatic research effort. In B.Y.L. Wong (Ed.) *Contemporary intervention research in learning disabilities: An international perspective.* New York: Springer-Verlag.

Schumaker, J.B., Deshler, D.D., Alley, G.R., & Warner, M.M. (1983). Toward the development of an intervention model for learning disabled adolescents. *Topics in Learning and Learning Disabilities, 3*(2), 15-23.

Schumaker, J.B., Deshler, D.D., Alley, G.R., Warner, M.M., & Denton, P.H. (1982). Multipass: A learning strategy for improving reading comprehension. *Learning Disability Quarterly, 5,* 295-304.

Schumaker, J.B., Nolan, S.M., & Deshler, D.D. (1985). *The error monitoring strategy.* Lawrence, KS: The University of Kansas.

Schumaker, J.B., & Sheldon, J. (1985). *The sentence writing strategy.* Lawrence, KS: The University of Kansas.

Seabaugh, G.O., & Schumaker, J.B. (1981). *Effects of three conferencing procedures on the academic productivity of LD and NLD adolescents.* Research Report #36, University of Kansas Center for Research on Learning.

Secretary's Commission on Achieving Necessary Skills (1991). *What work requires of schools: SCANS report for America 2000.* Washington, DC: U.S. Department of Labor.

Senge, P. (1990). *The fifth discipline.* New York: Doubleday.

Senge, P., Roberts, C., Ross, R.B., Smith, B.J., & Kleiner, A. (1994). *The fifth discipline fieldbook: Strategies and tools for building the learning organization.* New York: Doubleday.

Sergiovanni, T.J. (1994). *Building community in schools.* San Francisco: Jossey-Bass.

Simmons, D.C., Fuchs, L.S., Fuchs, D., Mathes, P., & Hodge, J.P. (1995). Effects of explicit teaching and peer tutoring on the reading achievement of learning-disabled and low-performing students in regular classrooms. *The Elementary School Journal, 95*(5), 387-408.

Slavin, R.E., & Madden, N.A. (1987). *Effective classroom programs for students at risk* (Report No. 19). Baltimore: The Johns Hopkins University, Center for Research on Elementary and Middle Schools.

Slavin, R.E., & Madden, N.A. (1989, February). What works for students at risk: A research synthesis. *Educational Leadership,* 4-13.

Stainback, S., & Stainback, W. (1985). *Integration of students with severe handicaps into regular schools.* Reston, VA: The Council for Exceptional Children.

Van Reusen, A.K., Bos, C.S., Schumaker, J.B., & Deshler, D.D. (1994). *The self-advocacy strategy for education & transition planning.* Lawrence, KS: Edge Enterprises, Inc.

Van Reusen, A.K., Deshler, D.D., & Schumaker, J.B. (1989). Effects of a student participation strategy in facilitating the involvement of LD adolescents in the IEP process. *Learning Disabilities, 1*(2), 23-34.

Wang, M.C. (1987). Toward achieving educational excellence for all students: Program design and student outcomes. *Remedial and Special Education, 8*(3), 25-34.

Wang, M.C., & Birch, J.W. (1984). Effective special education in regular classes. *Exceptional Children, 50,* 391-398.

Wang, M.C., Haertel, G.D., & Walberg, H.J. (1993). Toward a knowledge base for school learning. *Review of Educational Research, 63*(3), 249-294.

Warner, M.M., Schumaker, J.B., Alley, G.R., & Deshler, D.D. (1980). Learning disabled adolescents in the public schools: Are they different from other low-achievers? *Exceptional Education Quarterly, 1*(2), 27-36.

Welch, M., Richards, G., Okada, T., Richards, J., & Prescott, S. (1995). A consultation and paraprofessional pull-in system of service delivery. *Remedial and Special Education, 16*(1), 16-28.

Whitaker, M. (1997). Unpublished doctoral disseration, University of Kansas, Lawrence.

CHAPTER TWO

Mediating the Learning of Academically Diverse Secondary Students in Content-Area Courses

JOSEPH B. FISHER, Grand Valley State University

As the class bell rings, the hallways empty, and students filter into Ms. Nichols' fifth-hour world history class. While the students settle, Ms. Nichols takes attendance, calling the names of her 32 students one by one. Ms. Nichols is a good teacher. She cares for her students and knows her content well. Nevertheless, she is very concerned that she is not meeting her students' needs. This is understandable given the diverse abilities of the students enrolled in her classes. Of the students in her fifth-hour class alone, one is mildly mentally handicapped, one is gifted, four are learning disabled, seven are at risk for dropping out of school, and six are on the honor roll. As she reads these students' names aloud, she wonders how she can possibly help all of them to learn.

Teachers like Ms. Nichols are not alone. Over the past several decades, the diversity among students in America's classrooms has increased dramatically (Hodgkinson, 1991). Today's students are not only more ethnically, culturally, and economically diverse than students just 10 or 20 years ago; they are also more academically diverse. Unfortunately, like Ms. Nichols, many secondary content-area teachers have not been prepared to mediate the learning of academically diverse groups of students (Deshler & Schumaker,

1988). However, as underscored by Hock, Schumaker, and Deshler in Chapter 7 of this volume, if secondary schools are to prepare *all* students to participate successfully in society and to attain personal hopes and dreams, content-area teachers must be able to provide instruction that is responsive to the educational needs of *each* of their students.

Fortunately, in recent years, much has been learned about how content-area teachers like Ms. Nichols can mediate the learning of academically diverse groups of students (Fisher, Schumaker, & Deshler, 1995). Specifically, teachers of academically diverse groups can: (a) revise the curriculum, (b) redirect content-area planning, (c) enhance content-area instruction, (d) adapt content-area textbooks, (e) engage students in peer tutoring, and (f) teach students how to learn. This chapter describes these six methods in detail.

REVISING THE CURRICULUM

Conventional secondary content-area curricula are designed to expose students to large amounts of information and emphasize the memorization of isolated facts (Carnine, 1991). This fact is problematic given that many students in academically diverse classes have difficulty storing and retrieving information (Deshler, Schumaker, Alley, Warner, & Clark, 1982). In recent years, several new content-area curricula have been researched and developed. These new curricula are predicated on the proposition that curricula can enhance students' learning by de-emphasizing memorization of isolated facts and emphasizing reasoning and problem solving (Cawley, 1994). Two of these curricula are the Big Ideas Curriculum and the Shared Context Curriculum.

The Big Ideas Curriculum

The Big Ideas Curriculum (Carnine, 1994) is comprised of generative principles and concepts that underlie content-area information; it highlights the "big ideas" that link content-area information into networks. The purpose of identifying these unifying ideas is to help students develop holistic understandings of content, rather than knowledge of isolated bits of information (Woodward, 1994). When information is linked into networks, it becomes easier to learn, remember, and apply. To better explain this curriculum, examples from history, science, and mathematics are described below.

Big Ideas in History. A big idea that helps explain major events in history is the problem-solution-effect model (Kinder & Bursuck, 1991); this model forges explicit relationships between events, facts, and concepts, making them easier to understand and remember. For example, unlike traditional history curricula that merely list series of acts imposed by the British (e.g., the Wool Act, Hat Act, Iron Act, Navigation Act, Sugar Act, etc.) as the causes of the Revolutionary War, the problem-solution-effect model connects these regulations, making them easier for students to understand and learn. It helps students understand that prior to the Revolutionary War, England was importing raw materials for industries that were not turning a profit, and that the English government had incurred massive debts from the French and Indian War. To solve these two problems, the English government passed several revenue-producing laws that required the colonists to buy manufactured goods from England, to sell raw materials only to England, and to tax items brought into the colonies. As a result of these laws, many colonists became angry, boycotted the purchase of English goods, and pushed for their independence.

The problem-solution-effect model can be applied to help understand numerous historical events. For example, it could be used to explain that in the early 1800s, the Mormons were faced with the problem that others did not approve of their religious beliefs. After the murder of two prominent Mormon leaders in Illinois, many Mormons moved to Salt Lake, a remote area where they would not be confronted by disapproving others. The result of this migration was the establishment of a community committed to representative government and religious freedom. The problem-solution-effect model could also be used to explain that the development of the cotton gin reduced the expense of removing seeds from cotton, making it possible for southern farmers to grow and sell more cotton, which increased their need for slaves.

Big Ideas in Science. A big idea that helps explain major events in science is the model of the *convection cell* (Woodward & Noell, 1991). This model is introduced to students through the example of heating water in a pan. When a cold pot of water comes into contact with a hot burner (placed, for example, beneath the pot on the right side), the temperature of the water molecules increases, and they begin to move faster and become less dense. These less dense molecules move up the right side of the pan and create an area of high pressure in the upper right corner of the pan. They then move from areas of high pressure to areas of low pressure—hence, from the upper right corner of the pan to the upper left corner. Here, as the molecules cool, they move more slowly and become denser; they sink to the lower left corner of the pan, and the process begins again (see Figure 2-1 on the facing page).

Like the problem-solution-effect model in history, the convection cell model can be applied to a variety of science phenomena. For example, it helps explain the movement of the earth's mantle, the formation of land and sea breezes, and the development of hurricanes and tornadoes (Woodward, 1994).

Big Ideas in Mathematics. A big idea in mathematics is that the volume of a three-dimensional figure equals the area of the base times some multiple of the height (Carnine, 1991). This simple fact is obscured in many existing mathematics curricula, in which students are expected to memorize seven different formulas to calculate the volume of seven different three-dimensional figures:

- prism: $l \cdot w \cdot h = v$
- wedge: $\frac{1}{2} \cdot l \cdot w \cdot h = v$

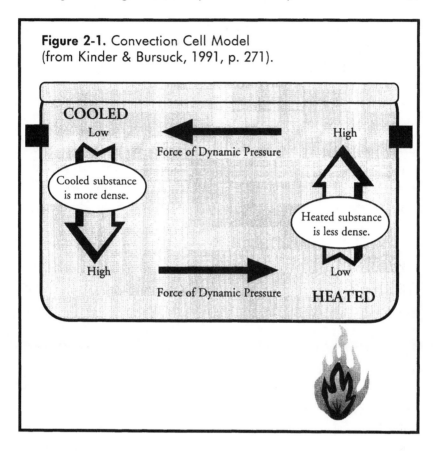

Figure 2-1. Convection Cell Model
(from Kinder & Bursuck, 1991, p. 271).

- cylinder: $\pi \cdot r^2 \cdot h = v$
- triangular pyramid: $\frac{1}{6} \cdot l \cdot w \cdot h = v$
- rectangular pyramid: $\frac{1}{3} \cdot l \cdot w \cdot h = v$
- cone: $\frac{1}{3} \cdot \pi \cdot r^3 = v$
- sphere: $\frac{4}{3} \cdot \pi \cdot r^3 = v$

When these formulas are examined to identify a unifying big idea, the number of formulas students must learn can be reduced from seven to slight variations on *one* ($B \cdot h = v$).

- prism: $B \cdot h = v$
- wedge: $\frac{1}{2} \cdot B \cdot h = v$
- cylinder: $B \cdot h = v$

- triangular pyramid: $B \cdot \frac{1}{3} \cdot h = v$
- rectangular pyramid: $B \cdot \frac{1}{3} \cdot h = v$
- cone: $B \cdot \frac{1}{3} \cdot h = v$
- sphere: $B \cdot \frac{2}{3} \cdot h = v$

This big idea significantly reduces the number of formulas students need to memorize; it also helps to clarify their conceptual understanding of calculating volume. "Big ideas" that have been identified in other areas of mathematics include fractions, multiplication, division, and word problems (Engelmann, Carnine, & Steely, 1991).

The Shared Context Curriculum

The Shared Context Curriculum was designed to enhance students' abilities to understand new content and use that information as a tool to solve problems. Developers of this model emphasize that students learn to understand and use knowledge to solve problems in *contextualized learning environments* (Cognition and Technology Group at Vanderbilt, 1993a)—environments in which teachers and students share a common frame of reference for interpreting information. Moreover, the tasks students perform in such environments are authentic and meaningful. Unfortunately, traditional classroom environments are often decontextualized. As a result, students may view the information being taught as unrelated to their world and not useful for solving real-world problems (Brown, Collins, & Duguid, 1989). To bridge the gap between decontextualized and contextualized learning environments, this curriculum uses videodisc-based simulations; the simulations provide students and teachers with a common frame of reference and create authentic problems for students to solve. To explain this curriculum, examples from mathematics and science are explored below.

Shared Context in Mathematics. To create shared contexts in secondary-level mathematics, a series of 12 videodisc-based simulations called *The Adventures of Jasper Woodbury* (Cognition and Technology

Group at Vanderbilt, 1993b) have been developed. Each videodisc in this series focuses on a particular area in mathematics (e.g., geometry, statistics, algebra, etc.) and contains a video adventure that ends in a complex challenge that the students must resolve. Each adventure also contains teaching episodes that model particular problem-solving approaches and the information needed to resolve the complex challenge.

For example, at the end of the adventure titled *Rescue at Boone's Meadow,* students are challenged to develop a plan for saving an injured bald eagle by flying it from a remote location to an animal hospital; the plane must arrive at the animal hospital within a limited amount of time. The adventure provides the information students need to solve this distance-time-rate problem: the distance from the animal hospital to the injured eagle, and the top speed at which the plane can fly. It also presents multiple models of how to solve similar distance-time-rate problems.

Once solutions to an adventure's challenge have been created, students then engage in "what if" thinking: they revisit the original adventure from a new point of view and apply what they have learned to other problems. For example, in *Rescue at Boone's Meadow,* students are asked to rethink how the presence of headwinds or tailwinds could have affected their proposed solution. Students are also invited to compare their plans for saving the eagle with Lindbergh's plans for flying from New York to Paris.

Shared Contexts in Science. To create shared contexts in secondary-level science, a second series of videodisc-based simulations called *Scientists in Action* (Cognition and Technology Group at Vanderbilt, 1995) has been developed. Similar in framework to that of the *Jasper Woodbury* series, this series teaches both information and problem-solving strategies that are applied to resolve science challenges. Each videodisc in the series focuses on a particular area in science (e.g., ecology, biology, archeology, etc.). Each adventure also emphasizes conceptual understanding of larger principles of science (e.g., data collection, data analysis, problem formulation, and hypothesis testing).

The Effectiveness of Curriculum Revision

Curriculum revision is a developing area. Nevertheless, research studies suggest that the implementation of revised curricula can improve the achievement of academically diverse groups of students. For example, research has indicated that application of the Big Ideas Curriculum significantly impacts the achievement of academically diverse groups of students in secondary science and math classes (Hofmeister, Engelmann, & Carnine, 1989; Kelly, Gersten, & Carnine, 1990). In another research study, academically diverse classes of students who received mathematics instruction through the *Jasper Woodbury* series scored significantly higher on a standardized math test than similar classes of students who received a more traditional mathematics curriculum (Cognition and Technology Group at Vanderbilt, 1993a). This study also indicated that the *Jasper* students were less anxious about mathematics and more likely to see mathematics as relevant to everyday life.

REDIRECTING CONTENT-AREA PLANNING

Teachers can also mediate the learning of academically diverse groups of students by redirecting their content-area planning—especially when they must deliver large amounts of complex content (Bulgren & Lenz, 1996). Usually, secondary teachers' planning focuses only on the content to be delivered and the classroom activities to take place. However, if teachers are to meet the needs of all the students in their classes, their planning must also focus on the needs of different kinds of learners (Joint Committee on Teacher Planning for Students with Disabilities, 1995). Two approaches developed to help secondary teachers rethink their planning to include the needs of students, as well as on the content to be delivered and on the activities to take place, are the Planning Pyramid and ReflActive Planning.

The Planning Pyramid

The Planning Pyramid (Schumm, Vaughn, & Leavell, 1994) is a visual device developed to help secondary teachers make decisions about the curriculum they are required to teach in light of their students' varying educational needs. This approach is based on the premise that although all students are capable of learning, not all students will learn all the content presented in a course. The Planning Pyramid (see Figure 2-2) is used to guide teachers to attend carefully to what content *all* of their students should learn, what content *most* of their students should learn, what content *some* of their students will learn, and how their students' learning will be directed.

The bottom level of the Planning Pyramid represents information that the teacher believes is essential for *all* students to understand. The information at this level may be conceptually broader and more general than that at higher levels. The middle level of the pyramid represents information the teacher believes is important for *most* students to learn. This level includes facts and information about the ideas and concepts at the base of the pyramid. The top level of the pyramid represents information the teacher considers to be supplementary. This information is more complex and will be acquired by only a *few* students who have added interest in and desire to learn more about the topic being studied.

The developers of the Planning Pyramid caution that students should *not* be assigned to learn information from a particular level of the pyramid based on their ability. All students should have equal access to information from the middle and top levels of the pyramid if they have interest in learning that information. Moreover, they indicate that activities at the base of the pyramid should be just as interesting as those at the top. The information from all levels should be taught in an engaging and meaningful way (Vaughn, Bos, & Shumm, 1997).

Planning Units with the Planning Pyramid. The Planning Pyramid can be used to plan a unit of instruction. In determining what

Figure 2-2. The Planning Pyramid (from Joint Committee on Teacher Planning for Students with Disabilities, 1995, p. 8).

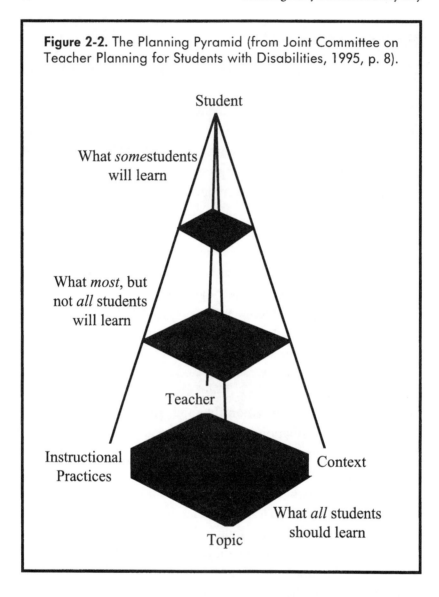

concepts to teach in a unit, and where various concepts will lie on the pyramid, teachers often find it useful to use a self-questioning process. Questions pertaining to the *topic* include:

- Is the material new or review?
- What prior knowledge do students have of this topic?

- How interesting is the topic to individual students?
- How many new concepts are introduced?
- How complex are the new concepts?
- How clearly are the concepts presented in the textbook?
- How important is this topic in the overall curriculum?

Questions pertaining to the *teacher* include:

- Have I taught this material before?
- What prior knowledge do I have of this topic?
- How interesting is the topic to me?
- How much time do I have to plan?
- What resources do I have available?

Questions pertaining to the *students* include:

- Will students' communication skills make comprehension of a particular concept difficult?
- Will students with reading difficulties be able to function independently while learning about the concept from text?
- Will students with behavior or attention problems be able to concentrate on this material?
- Will there be students, of any ability level, with high interest in or prior knowledge of this concept who would be anxious to explore it in greater depth or share their knowledge with classmates?
- Will my students have the vocabulary they need to understand this concept?
- What experiences have my students had that will relate to this concept?
- Is there some way to relate this concept to the cultural and linguistic backgrounds of my students?

Once teachers have decided what concepts to teach, they can record this information on the Unit Planning Form (see Figure 2-3).

Figure 2-3. Unit Planning Form (from Joint Committee on Teacher Planning for Students with Disabilities, 1995, p. 9).

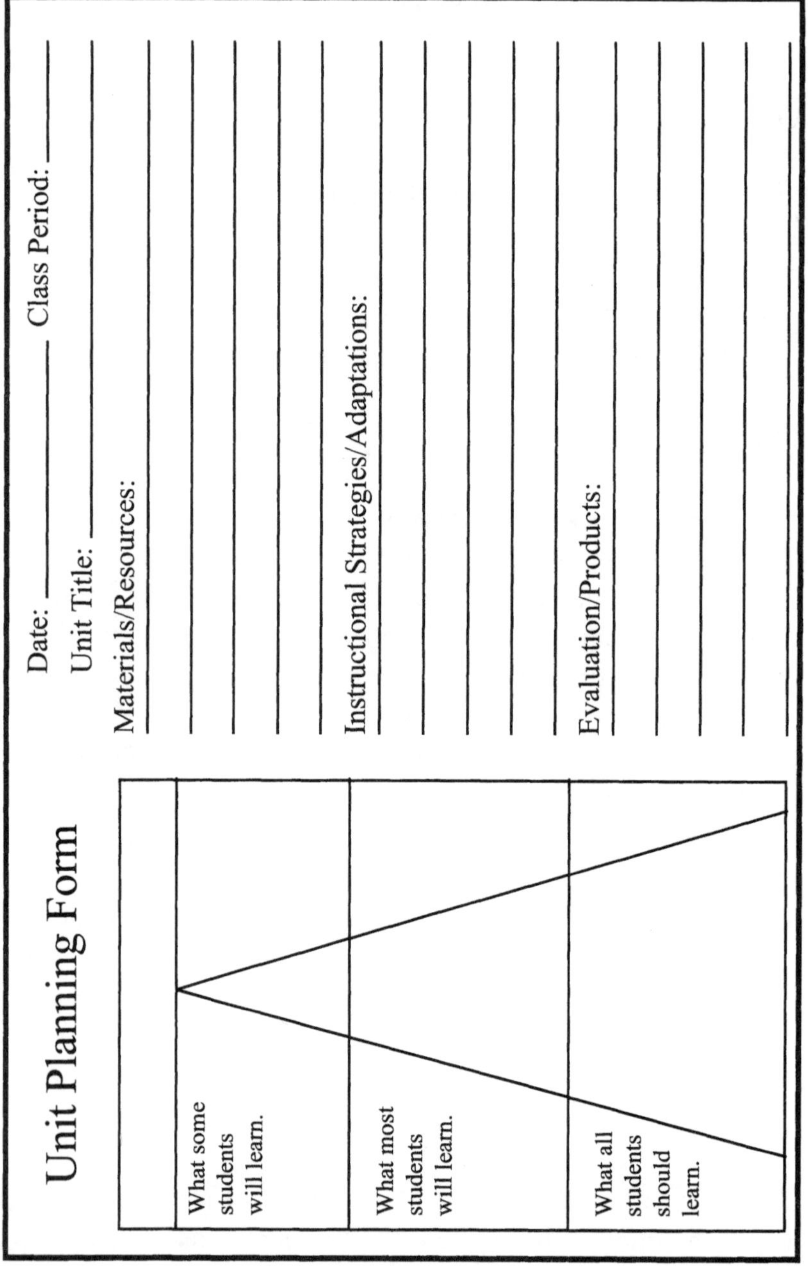

Unit Planning Form

Date: _____ Class Period: _____

Unit Title: _____

Materials/Resources:

Instructional Strategies/Adaptations:

Evaluation/Products:

What some students will learn.

What most students will learn.

What all students should learn.

This form also contains space to record the materials and resources needed for instruction, the instructional strategies and adaptations they will use to aid students' learning, and the evaluation procedures and projects they will use to monitor students' understanding.

Planning Lessons with the Planning Pyramid. Teachers can also use the Planning Pyramid to plan an individual lesson. As with planning units, planning lessons using the pyramid guides teachers to be more explicit about what they want all, most, and some students to learn. However, when planning lessons, teachers consider not only questions pertaining to themselves, to their students, and to the topic, but also those pertaining to the environment in which they teach and the instructional strategies they will use. Questions pertaining to the *learning environment* include:

- Are there any holidays or special events that are likely to distract students or alter instructional time?
- How will the class size affect my teaching of this concept?
- How well do my students work in small groups or pairs?

Questions pertaining to instructional strategies include:

- What resources do I have to teach this lesson?
- What methods will I use to motivate students and to establish a purpose for learning?
- What grouping pattern is most important?
- What instructional strategies can I implement to promote student learning?
- What instructional adaptations can I implement to assist individuals or subgroups of students?

Using the Lesson Planning Form, teachers can make an agenda listing the instructional strategies to be used during instruction (see Figure 2-4 on the next page). This form also contains space for the teacher to record the materials needed for instruction, the evaluation

Figure 2-4. Lesson Planning Form (from Joint Committee on Teacher Planning for Students with Disabilities, 1995, p. 11).

Date: _____ Class Period: _____ Unit: _____
Lesson Objective(s): _____
_____
_____

Materials	Evaluation
In Class Assignments	Homework Assignments

Lesson Planning Form

Pyramid	Agenda
What some students will learn.	1 _____ _____ 2 _____ _____
What most students will learn.	3 _____ _____ 4 _____ _____ 5 _____ _____
What all students should learn.	6 _____ _____ 7 _____ _____

procedures to be used, and the assignments students will need to complete.

ReflActive Planning

Another way teachers can make decisions about the curriculum they teach in light of their students' needs is by using ReflActive Planning (Lenz & Bulgren, 1994). The basic premise of this method is that all courses contain critically important content that every student should learn. The seven steps of ReflActive Planning guide teachers to select that critical content and choose instructional practices that enhance students' learning of the content. The acronym "SMARTER" is used to help teachers think through these steps and to engage in the following behaviors:

- *Select* critical content outcomes;
- *Map* the organization of the critical content in a way that will be meaningful to students;
- *Analyze* why the critical content might be difficult for students to learn (e.g., consider the quantity, complexity, student interest and background, relevance, organization);
- *Reach* a decision about enhancing the content by selecting instructional practices to promote learning;
- *Teach* using these practices;
- *Evaluate* students' mastery of the critical content; and
- *Reevaluate* planning and teaching decisions.

Once teachers have identified what information is critically important to teach, that content can be organized and shared in advance of instruction to help students recognize how it fits together into a "big picture." Framing the content in advance of instruction can enhance students' ability to recognize relationships between pieces of content, to understand content that has already been presented in relation to content that remains to be taught, and to self-monitor the content they have learned.

For framing to be most beneficial, teachers must frame content in cooperation with students. Three organizational routines have been researched and developed for this purpose: the Course Organizer Routine (Lenz, Deshler, et al., 1994), the Unit Organizer Routine (Lenz, Bulgren, Schumaker, Deshler, & Boudah, 1994), and the Lesson Organizer Routine (Lenz, Marrs, Schumaker, & Deshler, 1993).

The Course Organizer Routine. The Course Organizer Routine is used by teachers to introduce students to the critical content-area information they will learn during a course and the ways that information is organized. The teacher uses a two-page visual device called a Course Organizer to display:

- the name of the course;
- a statement summarizing what the course is about;
- a list of the questions that all students should be able to answer by the end of the course;
- a graph for charting progress throughout the semester;
- the names of concepts underlying the course content;
- a map organizing the units of content to be studied;
- a list of the strategies and routines students will use to process course content; and
- a list explaining how members of the class will interact.

An example of a completed Course Organizer is shown in Figure 2-5. A teacher does not launch a course with a completed Course Organizer, however; he or she completes a blank Course Organizer in cooperation with the class. To begin, the teacher describes to students what the course is about and outlines the questions all students should be able to answer by the end of the semester. Second, the teacher identifies the units that will be studied throughout the course and shares the key concepts that underlie the course content. Finally, the teacher and students decide how all members of the class will interact with one another and what routines and strategies will be used to guide learning.

Figure 2-5a. Course Organizer (page 1).

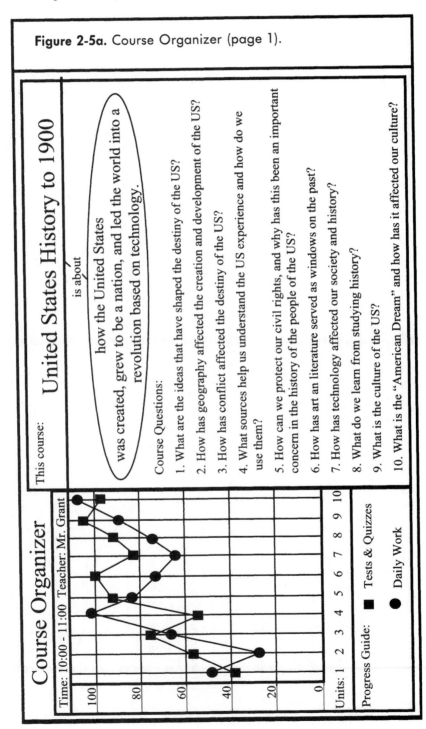

Course Organizer

Time: 10:00 - 11:00   Teacher: Mr. Grant

This course: **United States History to 1900**

is about

how the United States was created, grew to be a nation, and led the world into a revolution based on technology.

Course Questions:

1. What are the ideas that have shaped the destiny of the US?

2. How has geography affected the creation and development of the US?

3. How has conflict affected the destiny of the US?

4. What sources help us understand the US experience and how do we use them?

5. How can we protect our civil rights, and why has this been an important concern in the history of the people of the US?

6. How has art an literature served as windows on the past?

7. How has technology affected our society and history?

8. What do we learn from studying history?

9. What is the culture of the US?

10. What is the "American Dream" and how has it affected our culture?

Units: 1 2 3 4 5 6 7 8 9 10

Progress Guide: ■ Tests & Quizzes

● Daily Work

Figure 2-5b. Course Organizer (page 2).

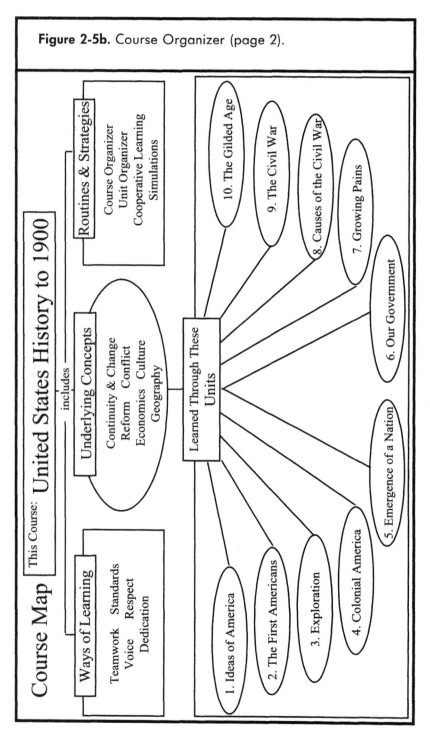

After each unit of study, the teacher and students revisit the Course Organizer to summarize the content they have learned and to survey the content they will learn next. After all the units of study have been completed, the Course Organizer is used to review the critical content that all students in the class should have learned.

The Unit Organizer Routine. The Unit Organizer Routine is used to introduce students to the critical content to be taught during a unit of study. This routine is built around a teaching device called a Unit Organizer. An example of a Unit Organizer completed by a teacher and students is provided in Figure 2-6. Specifically, this organizer includes:

- the title of the current unit of study, previous unit of study, and next unit of study;
- the main idea connecting the units together;
- a map depicting how the information in the unit is organized;
- terms describing the relationships between the contents of the unit;
- a list of questions that students should be able to answer at the end of the unit; and
- a schedule highlighting the names and dates of required tasks, activities, and assignments.

To engage students in the construction of a Unit Organizer, the teacher first provides the titles of the current unit, the previous unit, and the next unit, and discusses with students how these three units are connected. Second, the teacher explains how the contents of the current unit fit together, and depicts that information in a unit map. The center of this map includes a statement paraphrasing what the unit is about. Once the unit map is completed, the teacher and students generate a list of self-test questions about the unit. Finally, the unit schedule is outlined and recorded on the Unit Organizer.

The Lesson Organizer Routine. The Lesson Organizer Routine is

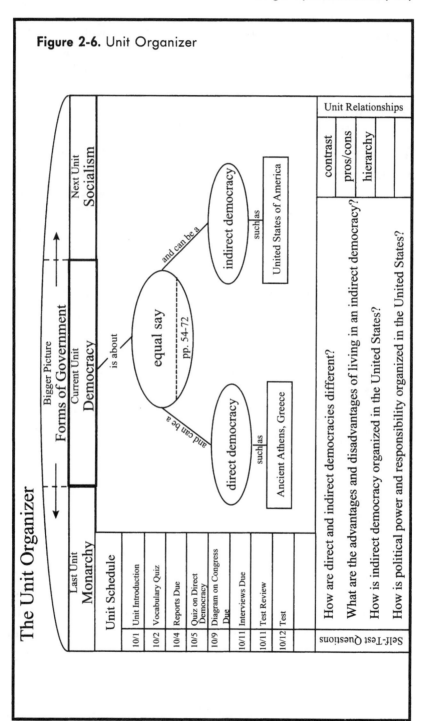

Figure 2-6. Unit Organizer

used at the beginning of a lesson to familiarize students with the content to be taught. It is built around a teaching device called the Lesson Organizer. An example of a completed Lesson Organizer is provided in Figure 2-7. Specifically, this organizer includes:

- the topic of the lesson;
- a statement paraphrasing what the lesson is about;
- a term or terms describing the relationships present within lesson content;
- a term or terms specifying one or more strategies students should use to gain, store, and express lesson content;
- a map depicting the relationship between the lesson topic and the unit of study;
- a map depicting the organization of the lesson content; and
- a list of questions students can ask themselves to check their understanding of the lesson content.

To construct a Lesson Organizer with students, the teacher first names the lesson topic, paraphrases the topic in language students will understand, and identifies important relationships between different aspects of the lesson content. (Common relationships within lesson content include cause/effect, problem/solution, and sequence of events.) The teacher also discusses with students how specific cognitive and metacognitive strategies they have learned can be used to process the lesson content more efficiently and effectively. Next, the teacher and students review how the lesson topic is related to the unit of study and depict the relationship between the lesson and unit in a map. Then the teacher explains the basic concepts, ideas, and vocabulary to be taught and depicts this information in a lesson map. Finally, the questions students should be able to answer by the end of the lesson and the tasks students must complete as part of the lesson are identified.

Figure 2-7. Lesson Organizer

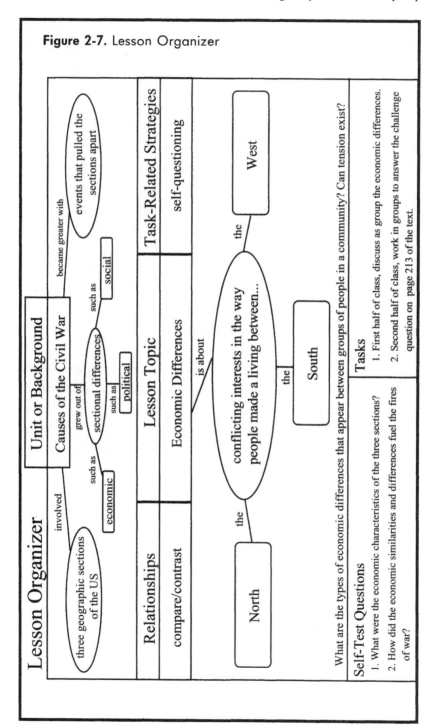

The Effectiveness of Redirecting Planning

Research studies have indicated that rethinking content-area planning does help teachers to mediate the learning of academically diverse groups of students. For example, a research study on the Planning Pyramid (Schumm et al., 1994) indicated that this approach enabled teachers to be explicit about what they want all of their students to learn and to be more proficient in planning units and lessons for academically diverse groups. Likewise, research studies on ReflActive Planning (Lenz, Alley, & Schumaker, 1987; Lenz, Deshler, et al., 1994; Lenz, Bulgren, et al., 1994) indicated that applying each of the organizational routines helps teachers more clearly explain what students are expected to learn. These studies also indicated that application of each routine improved the performance of average-achieving students, low-achieving students, and students with learning disabilities on academic tasks, including tests. Not surprisingly, additional research has indicated that the academic performance of students improves even more when their teachers use these routines in combination. Teachers who participated in these studies also reported that they found the Course, Unit, and Lesson Organizer Routines useful and easy to apply.

ENHANCING CONTENT-AREA INSTRUCTION

A third way secondary teachers can mediate the learning of academically diverse groups of students is by enhancing their content-area instruction. Teachers can transform content-area information that is difficult for students to learn into easy-to-understand formats. This information can then be presented to students in memorable ways using content-enhancement routines (Schumaker, Deshler, & McKnight, 1991), sets of instructional procedures that help teachers control and coordinate their instruction to minimize students' difficulties and maximize their learning. These procedures also help engage students as active participants in the learning process.

Several content-enhancement routines have been developed to help secondary teachers mediate the learning of academically diverse groups of students (Bulgren & Lenz, 1996). This section describes two routines for improving students' comprehension of text material, three routines for helping students understand complex concepts, and two routines for helping them recall important information.

Text Comprehension Routines

Text comprehension routines have been designed to enhance secondary students' understanding of passages in content-area textbooks that are important, yet difficult to understand. Beginning in middle school, textbooks are one of the primary means through which new information is presented to students (Armbruster, 1984). This fact is problematic, given that many students in academically diverse classes lack the skills required to read and comprehend complex text (Deshler et al., 1982). Even for skilled readers, the information in textbooks can be difficult to process because it is often poorly organized (Kantor, Anderson, & Armbruster, 1983). The Survey Routine and Semantic Feature Analysis were developed to help students better understand materials in content-area textbooks.

The Survey Routine. The Survey Routine (Schumaker et al., 1989) was developed to prepare students to process passages of text more effectively. Used before students read a passage independently, this routine helps them focus on the organization of the passage, the key pieces of information in a passage, and the relationships among these pieces of information. It is built around a teaching device called a TRIMS Learning Sheet. An example of a completed Learning Sheet is provided in Figure 2-8. This sheet is used to display:

- the *Title* of the textbook passage and a statement predicting what the title is about;
- statements indicating the *Relationships* between the current passage and other passages within the unit;

Figure 2-8a. TRIMS Learning Sheet (page 1).

TRIMS Learning Sheet

<u>T</u>itle

1. Title: <u>Senses and Behavior</u>

2. This is about <u>How our senses relate to our behavior</u>

<u>R</u>elationships

3.

| Animal Systems Controlling Life |
| Unit |

| Support and Locomotion | Senses and Behavior | Drugs |
| Last | Current | Next |

4. The relationship of current passage to the unit:_____

<u>The senses are one type of animal system that controls life.</u>

5. The relationship of passages within the unit:_____

<u>Like the senses, support and locomotion are animal systems.</u>

<u>Drugs affect our senses and how we move.</u>

<u>I</u>ntroduction

6. • <u>Senses affect behavior from birth.</u>

   • <u>Behavior is how a person acts.</u>

   • <u>Senses - tell what is going on around us.</u>

<u>M</u>ain Parts

7. (Fill in next page)

<u>S</u>ummary

8. • <u>This is about the sense organs and how they work.</u>

   • <u>How does each sense affect how you behave?</u>

   • _____

Figure 2-8b. TRIMS Learning Sheet (page 2).

Main Part #1 ___ The Eye

| Questions |

- What are the parts of the eyes and their jobs?
- What are the four steps of the light pathway?
- _____

| Parts & Job | Diagrams |

Outside parts: Inside parts: Lens Muscle _____ P. 24
Eyelid   Iris   Cornea   Retina _____
Sclera   Pupil   Lens   Optic Nerve _____

Main Part #1 ___ The Tongue and Nose

| Questions |

- What are the four types of tastes detected by the tongue?
- What are the seven types of smells detected by the nose?
- Why are the tongue and nose grouped together?

| Neuron Types | Diagrams |

Tongue Neurons: Nose Neurons: _____ P. 29
Bitter   Salty _____
Sour   Sweet _____

Main Part #1 ___ The Ear

| Questions |

- What are the parts of the ear and their jobs?
- What are the steps of the sound pathway?
- What are sound waves?

| Parts & Job | Diagrams |

Outer Ear   Ear Bones _____ P. 34
Ear Canal   Oval Window _____
Ear Drum   Spiral Tube _____

- statements paraphrasing the *Introduction* of the passage;
- information depicting the structure of the passage and the *Main* parts (most important information) it contains; and
- a statement highlighting the main points made in the *Summary* of the passage.

To complete this sheet prior to reading, the teacher and students first locate the passage's title and predict what the passage may be about. Next, the teacher and students review the relationships between the current unit of study and the previous and following units of study. They also clarify how the text passage they are about to read is connected to the current unit of study and how all the passages within the unit are related. Highlighting these relationships helps students to connect what they are learning to what they have already learned. The teacher and students then skim the passage's introduction and paraphrase the main ideas. Afterward, they examine each heading within the passage (e.g., "The Eye," "The Ear," etc.), and formulate questions about each. They then skim the summary of the passage and underscore its main points. Finally, once the Learning Sheet has been completed, students read the text passage. To be actively engaged while reading, they work to answer the questions they formulated.

Semantic Feature Analysis. A second text comprehension routine, called Semantic Feature Analysis (Bos & Anders, 1992), was designed to help students understand important vocabulary terms, ideas, and/ or concepts introduced in textbook passages. This routine is built around a teaching device called a Relationship Chart. An example of a completed Relationship Chart is provided in Figure 2-9. Vocabulary words from the text are displayed along the vertical axis of the chart, and conceptual features of these vocabulary words are displayed along the horizontal axis of the chart.

Before completing a Relationship Chart with students, the teacher examines the text passage to identify important vocabulary words students should learn and the critical features of these words. The

Figure 2-9.
Relationship Chart (from Bos & Anders, 1992, pp. 81-95).

Relationship Chart: Fossils

Important Ideas

Key relationship + no relationship - uncertain ?	Types of Life		Location			Extinct?	
	Plant	Animal	Sea	Land	Lake	Extinct	Not Extinct
Trilobites							
Crinoids							
Giant cats							
Coral							
Bryozoans							
Guide fossils							
Dinosaurs							
Fish							
Brachiopods							
Small horses							
Ferns							
Winged bugs							
Trees							

vocabulary words are listed down the vertical axis of the chart, and the critical features are listed across the horizontal axis. A copy of this chart is then provided to students. Next, the teacher introduces students to the terms and the features that characterize them. The students and teacher make predictions about the relationships between each term on the vertical axis and each feature on the horizontal axis. Each pair of terms is noted as either related (+), unrelated (−), or unknown (?). After making predictions, students read the passage and either confirm or disprove their predictions. They then amend their predictions based on what they have learned.

Concept Understanding Routines

Routines have also been designed to enhance students' understanding of important content-area concepts. The teaching of concepts is heavily emphasized in content-area courses, especially in science and social studies (Bulgren & Lenz, 1996). However, many of the concepts secondary teachers are required to teach are abstract, complex, and unfamiliar to many students in academically diverse classes. To enhance teachers' instruction of such concepts, the Concept Anchoring, Concept Comparison, and Concept Mastery Routines were developed.

The Concept Anchoring Routine. The Concept Anchoring Routine (Bulgren, Schumaker, & Deshler, 1994a) was designed to introduce students to a new concept by relating it to a concept that they already know and understand. This routine is built around a teaching device called an Anchoring Table. An example of a completed Anchoring Table is presented in Figure 2-10. This table is used to display:

- the name of the new concept;
- the name of the known concept;
- a list of items and descriptions indicating what students know about the known concept;
- a list of characteristics of the known concept;

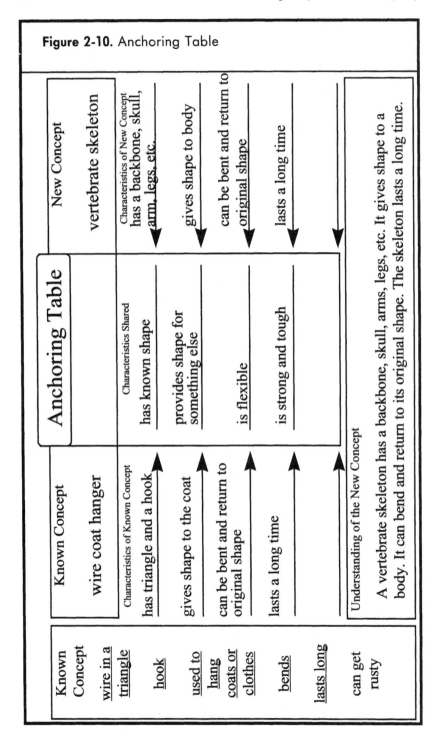

Figure 2-10. Anchoring Table

- a list of characteristics of the new concept;
- a list of the characteristics both concepts share; and
- a statement defining the new concept.

When constructing an Anchoring Table with students, the teacher first names both the known concept and the new concept that will be learned. The known concept must be familiar to all students in the class if the routine is to be effective. (In our example, the familiar concept of a wire coat hanger is used as an "anchor" for learning about the new concept: the vertebrate skeleton.) Second, the teacher and students list what they know about the known concept. From this list, they identify the important characteristics of the known concept. The teacher then guides students to list characteristics of the new concept that parallel those of the known concept and highlights how the parallel characteristics form an analogy. Finally, the teacher and students forge a statement expressing their understanding of the new concept.

The Concept Comparison Routine. The Concept Comparison Routine (Bulgren, Lenz, Deshler, & Schumaker, 1995) was designed to enrich students' understanding of two or more concepts by exploring and organizing their similarities and differences. This routine is built around a teaching device called a Comparison Table. An example of a completed Comparison Table is presented in Figure 2-11. This table is used to display:

- the names of two or more concepts;
- the name of the category or class into which the two or more concepts fit;
- a list of the characteristics of each concept;
- a list of characteristics both concepts share;
- phrases explaining how the characteristics are alike;
- a list of the characteristics the concepts do not share;
- phrases explaining how the characteristics are different; and
- a summary of how the two concepts are alike and different.

Figure 2-11. Comparison Table

Comparison Table

Overall Concept
Vertebrates

Concept
Birds

Concept
Mammals

Characteristics
Most fly
Warm-blooded
Live worldwide
Backbone
Young hatch from eggs

Characteristics
Most travel by foot
Warm-blooded
Live Worldwide
Hair
Backbones
Most young born alive

Like Characteristics

Warm-blooded
Live Worldwide
Backbones

Like Categories

How body temp is
regulated
Where they live
How their bodies are
supported

Unlike Characteristics

Most Fly
Feathers
Young hatch from eggs

Unlike Characteristics

Most travel by foot
Hair
Most young born alive

Unlike Categories

How they travel
What Covers their
bodies
How young are born

Summary

Birds and mammals are two vertebrates that are alike with regard to how their body
temperature is regulated, where they live, and how their bodies are supported. They
are different in terms of what covers their bodies and how they travel from one
place to another. They are also different in terms of how their young are born.

To complete a Comparison Table with students, the teacher follows a set of established procedures. To fully participate, students must have some prior knowledge of the concepts being compared. To begin, the teacher names the two concepts that will be compared and reviews the characteristics of each with students. The teacher and students then determine which of these characteristics are alike and which are not alike. Next, with the teacher's assistance, the students fit the like and unlike characteristics into broader categories. Finally, the teacher and students draft a summary statement that describes the similarities and differences among the two concepts being compared.

The Concept Mastery Routine. The Concept Mastery Routine (Bulgren, Deshler, & Schumaker, 1993) is another routine designed to clarify and consolidate students' understanding of important content-area concepts. The teaching device on which this routine is built is called a Concept Diagram. An example of a completed Concept Diagram is presented in Figure 2-12. This diagram is used to display:

- the name of the concept being taught;
- the name of the category or class into which the concept fits;
- a list of key words relating to the concept;
- a list of characteristics the concept sometimes, always, and never possesses;
- names representing both examples and nonexamples of the concept; and
- a statement defining the targeted concept.

Following the instructional procedures for the Concept Mastery Routine, the teacher constructs a blank Concept Diagram in collaboration with students. As with the other concept understanding routines, students must have some prior knowledge of the concept in order to participate in a meaningful way. To begin, the teacher conveys to students the name of the concept and a category or class into which it fits. Next, students brainstorm key words and informa-

Figure 2-12. Concept Diagram

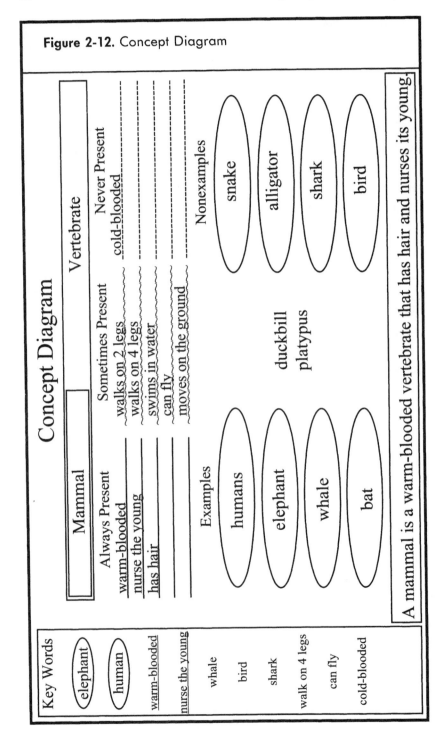

tion they know about the concept. The teacher and students then identify characteristics that are always present, sometimes present, and never present in examples of the concept. Finally, the teacher and students examine several examples and nonexamples of the concept and write a succinct definition.

Content Remembering Routines

In addition to comprehending both text material and complex concepts, students in secondary classes are also required to store and recall large amounts of information (Deshler et al., 1982). This fact is problematic because memory deficits are among the characteristics most commonly associated with academically diverse groups of students (Scruggs & Mastropieri, 1992). To enhance students' storage and recall of information, Elaborative Interrogation and the Recall Enhancement Routine were created.

Elaborative Interrogation. Elaborative Interrogation (Scruggs, Mastropieri, & Sullivan, 1994) is a routine teachers can use to improve students' recall of content-area information. Unlike the previously described routines that are built around visual devices, Elaborative Interrogation is built around a verbal device called Structured Questioning. Structured Questioning is simply the systematic use of questions to guide students to generate rational explanations for important content-area facts.

Before Elaborative Interrogation can be used, the teacher needs to target important facts that students should learn. Once one of these facts has been shared during instruction, the teacher uses Structured Questioning to guide students to generate an explanation for the fact. For example, after indicating to students that penguins carry their eggs on top of their feet, the teacher would ask, "Why would penguins care for their eggs in this way?" If students were unable to respond, the teacher would ask further questions: "Where do penguins live? What is the temperature like in that area of the world? What conditions are required for eggs to hatch?" This line of questioning would continue until it guided students to explain, "Penguins live in a cold and icy world. So that they will hatch, penguins carry their eggs off the ground to keep them warm." This type of elaborated thinking makes the original fact—that penguins carry their eggs on their feet—more meaningful to students, and therefore easier to remember.

The Recall Enhancement Routine. The Recall Enhancement Routine (Bulgren, Schumaker, & Deshler, 1994b) was also designed to enhance the meaningfulness of important content-area information. The central component of this interactive routine is the construction of a mnemonic device (a technique to assist memory) by a teacher and students. There are many types of mnemonic devices, including:

- *Acronyms.* Acronyms are formed by using the first letter of each word in a list to form a new word. An example of an acronym for the five Great Lakes (Huron, Ontario, Michigan, Erie, and Superior) is "HOMES."
- *Acrostics.* Acrostics are formed by using the first letter of each word on a list to form a sentence with the same initial letters. An example of an acrostic for remembering the names and order of the planets (Mercury, Venus, Earth, Mars, Jupiter, Saturn, Uranus, Neptune, and Pluto) is "My Very Educated Mother Just Served Us Nine Pizzas."
- *Rhymes.* Storage of information can also be enhanced by putting it into the form of a rhyme. A famous example of a rhyme for remembering information is "In 1492, Columbus sailed the ocean blue."

Following the procedures for the Recall Enhancement Routine, the teacher targets a portion of content critical for students to remember. Then, during instruction, the teacher introduces the targeted content to students, underscoring the importance of remembering this information and working with students to construct a mnemonic device to aid their memory. For example, after presenting a lesson on newspaper editors' code of ethics, the teacher and students would review the content and identify all four parts of the code—be *Fair,* be *Accurate,* be *Impartial,* and be *Responsible.* Next, the teacher could explain that the first letter of each part can be isolated to form the acronym FAIR. Together, the teacher and students might construct the sentence "Newspaper editors have to be FAIR" to make the code more memorable.

The Effectiveness of Content Enhancement

Many research studies have measured the effects of the content-enhancement routines described above. Overall, the results of these studies have indicated that each routine positively impacts the achievement of academically diverse groups of students. For example, in one study, students who were taught using Semantic Feature Analysis scored substantially higher on a passage comprehension test than students who were taught using direct vocabulary instruction (Bos & Anders, 1992). In another study, students who were taught using the Concept Comparison Routine understood significantly more about concepts than students who were taught using traditional concept instruction (Bulgren, Lenz, et al., 1995). And in still another study, students who were taught using Elaborative Interrogation recalled significantly more facts than students who received traditional content instruction (Scruggs et al., 1994). In addition to reporting positive effects on students' academic performance, many of the teachers who participated in these studies also reported that they found the content-enhancement routines easy to use and would recommend them to other teachers.

ADAPTING CONTENT-AREA TEXTBOOKS

A fourth way teachers can help mediate the learning of academically diverse groups of students is by adapting content-area textbooks. As mentioned previously, beginning in middle school, textbooks are the primary means through which new information is presented to students. However, many textbooks are poorly organized, and many students lack the skills required to comprehend complex text. And although text comprehension routines have been developed to help, teachers do not always have the time or the opportunity to provide this level of support to their students. Fortunately, students' comprehension of textbook passages can still be mediated without the direct support of their teachers, by using study guides, graphic organizers, and vocabulary drill sheets.

Study Guides

A study guide is a set of teacher-developed statements or questions that students answer to improve their recall and understanding of information from a passage of text (Lovitt & Horton, 1988). These statements and questions are written to direct students to focus on the most important information in the passage.

To construct a study guide, the teacher first targets an important section of text and determines whether or not it is particularly difficult to understand. If it is, the teacher then analyzes the passage, identifies the content to be emphasized, and develops a series of questions about that content. Alongside these questions, the teacher lists the page numbers on which answers can be located. This is done to focus students' attention on the most important passages or sections of the text. Once the study guide has been prepared, it is distributed to students. Students then read the passage and answer the study guide's questions. Once finished, they self-check their answers using an answer key.

Graphic Organizers

Graphic organizers can also be used to adapt text passages to help academically diverse groups of learners better comprehend a reading selection (Horton, Lovitt, & Bergerud, 1990). Graphic organizers are simply visual illustrations that depict relationships between two or more pieces of information; they are commonly arranged in a sequential, compare/contrast, or hierarchical format (Hudson, Lignugaris-Kraft, & Miller, 1993). Various terms are used for different formats of graphic organizers, including *tree diagrams, semantic maps,* and *flow charts.* Organizing information into these formats helps students to understand how individual pieces of content information combine to form a more meaningful whole.

As with study guides, before using a graphic organizer, the teacher identifies a passage of important text and determines whether that passage is particularly difficult to understand or poorly organized. If so, the teacher constructs an outline of the passage, highlighting its main ideas. Next, he or she selects a graphic organizer format appropriate for organizing these ideas, and constructs a version of the graphic organizer that contains all the important information from the passage. This version will be used as the answer key. A second version, with several of the main ideas omitted, is distributed to students. While reading the passage, students fill in the missing information. Then, using the answer key, they self-check their responses.

Vocabulary Drill Sheets

Another device that helps improve comprehension of textbook passages is the vocabulary drill sheet (Lovitt & Horton, 1994). Vocabulary drill sheets are used in advance of reading to develop students' understanding of key words in a passage. Once students have command of these words, they are better able to read and comprehend the passage.

To construct a vocabulary drill sheet, a teacher identifies the important vocabulary words in a passage of text and records them in the top left corner of a sheet of paper. Below these words, the teacher draws a table with five rows and five columns, forming 25 squares. In each of these squares, the teacher records a blank line and the definition for one vocabulary word, chosen at random. On the back of the sheet, the teacher writes the vocabulary words together with their definitions.

Once the vocabulary sheet has been constructed, copies are distributed to students. Then, without skipping any items, students fill in the correct vocabulary words on as many blank lines as they can in one minute. If they need assistance, they can look at the definitions listed on the back of the sheet. After the minute expires, students self-check their performance using an answer key. Additional copies of the vocabulary drill sheet are completed until students master the vocabulary words. Once they have achieved mastery, the students read the textbook passage.

The Effectiveness of Textbook Adaptation

Using study guides, graphic organizers, and vocabulary drill sheets has been shown to help mediate the learning of academically diverse groups of students. In one research study, students recalled significantly more main ideas from the text when they used teacher-prepared study guides while reading, compared to when they did not use study guides (Horton & Lovitt, 1989). In a second study, students understood significantly more information from the text when they used graphic organizers while reading, compared to when they did not use organizers (Horton et al., 1990). Results from a study on the vocabulary skill sheet reported similar findings (Lovitt, Rudsit, Jenkins, Pious, & Benedetti, 1986).

Because students use study guides, graphic organizers, and vocabulary drill sheets independently, teachers can use these adaptations with relative ease. Once students are familiar with important content-area information, the teacher can then help them to process this information at deeper levels, by using content-enhancement routines or by connecting the new information to "big ideas."

ENGAGING STUDENTS IN PEER TUTORING

In addition to learning from teachers, students in academically diverse classes can mediate one another's learning using peer tutoring.

Peer tutoring takes advantage of students' natural proclivity to interact with one another (Tharp & Gallimore, 1988). During tutoring sessions, the tutor helps the tutee learn content-area information by engaging him or her in instructional activities that increase opportunities for practice, clarification, and feedback (Delquadri, Greenwood, Whorton, Carta, & Hall, 1986). Two methods that can help students in secondary content-area classes to mediate one another's learning are Classwide Peer Tutoring and Classwide Tutoring Teams.

Classwide Peer Tutoring

In Classwide Peer Tutoring (Meheady, Sacca, & Harper, 1988), a secondary teacher divides a class into two teams that will engage in a contest for a one- to two-week period. Students then work in pairs for 15- to 30-minute tutoring sessions, following a structured, teacher-developed lesson written on a study sheet. The study sheet is comprised of factual questions, answers, and correction statements (see Figure 2-13). To begin instruction, the tutor asks the tutee the first question on the study sheet. If the tutee's response is correct, two points are recorded. If the tutee's response is incorrect, the tutor reads the correction statement, and the tutee writes the correct answer three times. The tutor then awards one point and proceeds to the next question. Once all questions have been completed, the tutor and tutee switch roles, and the process is repeated. At the end of the contest period, all students take a test on the information studied, and additional points are awarded for correct responses on the test. Finally, each team's points are totaled, and the winning team is announced.

Classwide Tutoring Teams

As in Classwide Peer Tutoring, students in Classwide Tutoring Teams (Meheady, Sacca, & Harper, 1987) work together to support one another's mastery of content-area information by completing a

Figure 2-13.
Study Sheet (from Pomerantz, Windell, & Smith, 1994, p. 31).

Study Sheet

Question	Answer	Corrections
1. What are the strongest storms on earth?	Hurricanes	Hurricanes are the strongest storms on earth.
2. Between what months do hurricanes occur?	June through November	Hurricanes occur between June and November.
3. Do hurricanes form over warm oceans or land?	Warm oceans	Hurricanes form over warm oceans.
4. Do hurricanes form near the poles or over the equator?	Equator	Hurricanes form over the equator.
5. What do we call a storm that forms over warm oceans neat the Equator?	Hurricane	Hurricanes are storms which form over warm oceans near the equator.
6. True or False: Hurricanes bring little rain and low winds.	False	Hurricanes do not bring little rain and low winds.
7. True or False: A violent storm forms when warm, moist air rises quickly then condenses.	True	Violent storms form when warm, moist air rises quickly then condenses.
8. What do we call storms with thunder and lightening, heavy rain, and strong winds?	Thunderstorms	Thunderstorms are storms with thunder, lightening, heavy rain, and strong winds.

structured, teacher-developed lesson. In this approach, however, students work in teams, not pairs. When using this approach, a secondary teacher breaks the class into ability-heterogeneous groups of four or five students each. Each team is provided with a study sheet and a deck of cards. One student on each team begins the tutoring session by selecting the top card from the shuffled deck. The number on the card designates the question on the study sheet to be presented. The student sitting directly across from the card selector serves as the tutor for that round and reads the question to the team. All members of the team, except for the tutor, answer the question in writing. Each student who writes a correct answer receives two points. If a student's answer is incorrect, he or she writes the correct answer three times and receives one point. The practice sheet is then passed to the next student, and the process is repeated.

The Effectiveness of Peer Tutoring

Research studies have indicated that students in academically diverse classes can successfully mediate one another's learning by engaging in peer tutoring. In several studies, students recalled substantially more content-area information when they engaged in Classwide Peer Tutoring and Classwide Tutoring Teams than when they did not receive tutoring (Meheady et al., 1987; Meheady et al., 1988). Moreover, teachers and students alike indicated that they enjoyed peer tutoring.

TEACHING STUDENTS HOW TO LEARN

Students in academically diverse classes can also learn to mediate their *own* learning, using learning strategies (Palincsar, David, Winn, & Stevens, 1991). A strategy is simply an approach to a task. Strategies include the ways people think and act when planning, executing, and evaluating their performance on a task (Deshler & Lenz, 1989). When students use learning strategies, they become active problem

solvers who learn information efficiently and effectively. Many
students perform poorly on academic tasks because they lack the
strategies for efficiently and effectively processing content-area information. Fortunately, students can be taught these needed strategies in
their content-area classes, using the Strategic Instruction Model, the
Strategies Integration Approach, and the Integrated Strategies Instruction Model.

The Strategic Instruction Model

One approach that has been widely used to teach learning strategies
to academically diverse groups of students is the Strategic Instruction
Model (Deshler & Schumaker, 1988). Originally designed to be used
by special education teachers, this model has also been applied by
secondary teachers in content-area classes. Through this model,
students are taught learning strategies over two phases of instruction.
In the first, called the *acquisition* phase, the teacher describes the
strategy, models how the strategy is used, provides students opportunities to practice talking about and using the strategy, and gives
students feedback on how to improve their use of the strategy. Once
students have mastered a learning strategy, they are taught how to
apply, modify, and use it in new classroom settings; this second phase
of instruction is called *generalization*.

The LINCS Strategy. The Strategic Instruction Model has been used
to teach a learning strategy called LINCS (Ellis, 1992). This learning
strategy was designed to improve students' understanding and recall
of content-area vocabulary words. Using the strategy, students independently construct a LINCS Card for each vocabulary word they are
studying. An example of a LINCS Card is presented in Figure 2-14
on the facing page.

   During the acquisition phase of strategic instruction, the teacher
describes for students the rationale behind the five steps of the LINCS
Strategy:

1. *List* the parts (the new word being learned and its definition are written on a flashcard);
2. *Imagine* a picture (a mental image of the definition is made);
3. *Note* a reminding word (a word that sounds like the new vocabulary word is written on the card);
4. *Construct* a story (the reminding word and the mental image of the definition are combined and written in a short phrase); and
5. *Self*-test (the student checks her/his recall and understanding of the information on the flashcard).

After describing the strategy to students, the teacher models how it is applied. Students then begin practicing the strategy with a set of simple vocabulary words. As students' ability to use the strategy improves, they practice with increasingly difficult words. Once the steps are mastered, the teacher initiates the generalization phase of instruction: students learn to apply the strategy to vocabulary words from their content-area classes, and then modify the strategy to approach related tasks.

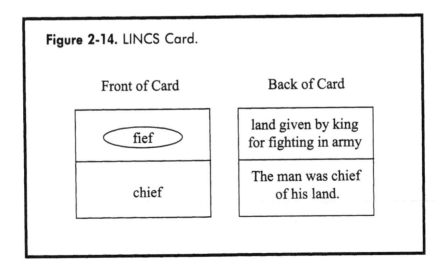

Figure 2-14. LINCS Card.

Front of Card / Back of Card

fief — land given by king for fighting in army

chief — The man was chief of his land.

The Strategies Integration Approach

In the Strategic Instruction Model, students are taught learning strategies separately from content-area information. As a result, teaching learning strategies using this model requires additional instructional time. Unfortunately, this additional time requirement prevents many teachers from implementing strategy instruction as often as they would like. In an effort to increase students' opportunities to learn and use strategies, the Strategies Integration Approach (Scanlon, Deshler, & Schumaker, 1996) was developed. This approach integrates instruction in learning strategies with instruction in content-area information. It is comprised of three instructional phases. In phase 1, the teacher introduces students to the concept of strategic learning. During phase 2, the teacher describes and models the learning strategy using classroom content. During phase 3, students practice using the strategy to learn classroom content.

The ORDER Strategy. The Strategies Integration Approach has been used to teach an academically diverse groups of students in secondary content-area classroom a strategy called ORDER (Scanlon et al., 1996). The ORDER Strategy enables students to identify key information presented in class and depict how that information is related using one of four major expository structures: *sequence, descriptive, compare/contrast,* or *problem/solution.*

To teach this strategy, the teacher begins by introducing students to the concept of strategic learning. Next, the teacher describes the five steps of the ORDER Strategy:

1. *Open* your mind and take good notes (the student takes notes about the content being studied);
2. *Recognize* the structure (student selects expository structure that best fits the organization of the content is selected);
3. *Design* an organizer (the student constructs an organizer using the selected expository structure as a guide);
4. *Explain* it (each student describes his or her organizer to

another person); and
5. *Recycle* it (the student uses the organizer to study for a test).

After describing the strategy, the teacher models the strategy as often as possible using course content. With each successive model, the teacher involves students in the identification and design of organizers. Finally, the students are required to use the strategy independently, and the teacher provides them with support and feedback on their performance.

PASS and the Integrated Strategies Instruction Model

Another approach for teaching learning strategies in conjunction with content is the Integrated Strategies Instruction Model (Ellis, 1993). This model is comprised of four instructional phases. In the first phase, the teacher orients students to understand that learning strategies can help them learn information. In the second phase, the teacher frames how a particular strategy is used during a learning task. In the third phase, students apply this strategy independently. Finally, in the fourth phase, students are taught how to extend this strategy to other areas.

Unlike other models in which students learn a strategy that can be applied to a particular task, this model teaches students a "master" strategy—called the PASS Metacognitive Strategy—that can be adapted and applied to a variety of academic tasks. The PASS Metacognitive Strategy (Ellis, 1993) is comprised of four basic steps:

- *Preview*, review, and predict;
- *Ask* and answer questions;
- *Summarize* information; and
- *Synthesize* information.

In the Integrated Strategies Instructional Model, students learn how to adapt these basic steps to approach tasks such as surveying textbook material, analyzing visual aids, and memorizing information.

For example, a teacher could teach students to adapt these steps into a strategy for writing themes. First, the teacher would write a theme with students, guiding them to understand the ways a theme might be organized. Next, the teacher and students could frame this information into a writing strategy. The steps of this writing strategy might be as follows:

- Preview, review, and predict:
  Preview your knowledge, your audience, and your goals.
  Review the main ideas and details you plan to tell.
  Predict the best order for information.
- Ask and answer the following sets of questions:
  How can I activate the readers' knowledge in the first sentence?
  Does this make sense? Should I rephrase this to make it more clear?
  Have I left anything out?
  Should I explain this idea more? What else should I say?
  Should I give an example of what I mean?
- Summarize the message in the last sentence.
- Search for errors and correct.

After framing the strategy, students would then apply it to complete class assignments (e.g., term papers, essay questions, etc.). Finally, students would learn how to extend the four basic steps of the PASS Metacognitive Strategy to other tasks.

The Effectiveness of Learning Strategies

A small number of research studies have measured the effects of teaching students in academically diverse classes how to mediate their own learning of content-area information. Results from two of these studies indicated that teachers could successfully teach students learning strategies in their content-area classes through both the Strategic Instruction Model (Wedel, Deshler, & Schumaker, 1988) and the Strategies Integration Approach (Scanlon et al., 1996).

CONCLUSIONS

Teaching content-area information to an academically diverse group of students is not an easy task for any secondary content-area teacher. However, teachers can respond to this challenge using the methods described in this chapter—revising the curriculum they teach and the ways they teach it, redirecting their planning, enhancing their instruction, adapting textbooks, engaging students in peer tutoring, and teaching students how to learn. These six methods give teachers a wide array of options for providing balanced instruction to students. For example, teachers can choose to:

- help students recall specific facts (the Recall Enhancement Routine) and understand unifying ideas (the Big Ideas Curriculum);
- engage students in text-based (the study guides) and activity-based learning (the Concept Mastery Routine);
- determine what information should be taught (the Planning Pyramid) and how it should be taught (Semantic Feature Analysis); and
- determine whether instruction should be teacher-directed (the Survey Routine), peer-directed (Classwide Peer Tutoring), or student-directed (the LINCS Strategy).

Much has been learned about how to facilitate the learning of academically diverse students in content-area classrooms. As a result, teachers like Ms. Nichols can more effectively meet the educational needs of all their students. Still, more work remains to be done. As our nation moves toward the next century, the levels of academic diversity among students is only expected to grow. If all of these students are to be prepared to participate in society and attain personal hopes and dreams, new and improved ways of teaching them will certainly be required.

REFERENCES

Armbruster, B.B. (1984). The problem of "inconsiderate text." In G.G. Duffy, L.R. Roehler, & J. Masson (Eds.), *Comprehensive instruction* (pp. 202-217). New York: Longman.

Bos, C.S., & Anders, P.L. (1992). A theory-driven interactive instructional model for text comprehension and content learning. In B.Y.L. Wong (Ed.), *Contemporary intervention research in learning disabilities: An international perspective* (p. 81-95). New York: Spinger-Verlag.

Brown, J.S., Collins, A., & Duguid, P. (1989). Situated cognition and the culture of learning. *Educational Researcher, 18,* 32-42.

Bulgren, J.A., Deshler, D.D., & Schumaker, J.B. (1993). *The Concept Mastery Routine.* Lawrence, KS: Edge Enterprises.

Bulgren, J.A., Deshler, D.D., & Schumaker, J.B. (1995). *The Concept Comparison Routine.* Lawrence, KS: Edge Enterprises.

Bulgren, J.A., & Lenz, B.K. (1996). Strategic instruction in the content areas. In D.D. Deshler, E.S. Ellis, & B.K. Lenz (Eds.), *Teaching adolescents with learning disabilities: Strategies and methods* (pp. 409-473). Denver, CO: Love Publishing.

Bulgren, J.A., Lenz, B.K., Deshler, D.D., & Schumaker, J.B. (1995). *The Concept Comparison Routine.* Lawrence, KS: Edge Enterprise.

Bulgren, J.A., Schumaker, J.B., & Deshler, D.D. (1988). Effectiveness of a concept teaching routine in enhancing the performance of LD students in secondary-level mainstream classes. *Learning Disability Quarterly, 11,* 3-17.

Bulgren, J.A., Schumaker, J.B., & Deshler, D.D. (1994a). *The Concept Anchoring Routine.* Lawrence, KS: Edge Enterprises.

Bulgren, J.A., Schumaker, J.B., & Deshler, D.D. (1994b). The effects of a recall enhancement routine on the test performance of secondary students with and without learning disabilities. *Learning Disabilities Research & Practice, 9*(1), 2-11.

Carnine, D. (1991). Curricular interventions for teaching higher-order thinking to all students: Introduction to the special series. *Journal of Learning Disabilities, 24*(5), 261-269.

Carnine, D. (1994). The BIG Accommodations Program. *Educational Leadership, 51,* 87-88.

Cawley, J.F. (1994). Science for students with disabilities. *Remedial & Special Education, 15*(2), 67-71.

Cognition and Technology Group at Vanderbilt. (1993a). Anchored instruction and situated cognition revisited. *Educational Technology, 33*(3), 52-70.

Cognition and Technology Group at Vanderbilt. (1993b). The Jasper experiment: Using video to provide real-world problem-solving contexts. *Arithmetic Teacher, 40,* 474-478.

Cognition and Technology Group at Vanderbilt.(1995). Problem based macro contexts in science instruction: Theoretical basis, design, issues, and the development of applications. In D. Lavoie (Ed.), *Toward a cognitive science perspective for scientific problem solving* (pp. 191-214). Manhattan, KS: National Association for Research in Science Teaching.

Delquadri, J.C., Greenwood, C.R., Whorton, D., Carta, J.J., & Hall, R.V. (1986). Classwide peer tutoring. *Exceptional Children, 52*(6), 535-542.

Deshler, D.D., & Lenz, B.K. (1989). The strategies instructional approach. *International Journal of Disability, Development, & Education, 36*(3), 203-224.

Deshler, D.D., & Schumaker, J.B. (1988). An instructional model for teaching students how to learn. In J.E. Zins & M.J. Curtis (Eds.), *Alternative educational delivery system: Enhancing instructional options for all students* (pp. 391-411). Washington, DC: National Association of School Psychologists.

Deshler, D.D., Schumaker, J.B., Alley, G.R., Warner, M.M., & Clark, F.L. (1982). Learning disabilities in adolescent and young adult populations: Research implications. *Focus on Exceptional Children, 15*(1), 1-12.

Ellis, E.S. (1992). *LINCS: A starter strategy for vocabulary learning.* Lawrence, KS: Edge Enterprises.

Ellis, E.S. (1993). Integrative strategy instruction: A potential model for teaching content area subjects to adolescents with learning disabilities. *Journal of Learning Disabilities, 26*(6), 358-383.

Engelmann, S., Carnine, D., & Steely, D.G. (1991). Making connections in mathematics. *Journal of Learning Disabilities, 24*(5), 292-303.

Fisher, J.B., Schumaker, J.B., & Deshler, D.D. (1995). Searching for validated inclusive practices: A review of the literature. *Focus on Exceptional Children, 28*(4), 1-20.

Hodgkinson, H. (1991). Reform versus reality. *Phi Delta Kappan, 73*(1), 8-16.

Hofmeister, A.M., Engelmann, S., & Carnine, D. (1989). Developing and validating science education videodiscs. *Journal of Research in Science Teaching, 26*(8), 665-667.

Horton, S.V., & Lovitt, T.C. (1989). Using study guides with three classifications of secondary students. *Journal of Special Education, 22*(4), 447-462.

Horton, S.V., Lovitt, T.C., & Bergerud, D. (1990). The effectiveness of graphic organizers for three classifications of secondary students in content area classes. *Journal of Learning Disabilities, 23*(1), 12-22.

Hudson, P., Lignugaris-Kraft, B., & Miller, T. (1993). Using content enhancements to improve the performance of adolescents with learning disabilities in content classes. *Learning Disabilities Research & Practice, 8*(2), 106-126.

Joint Committee on Teacher Planning for Students with Disabilities. (1995). *Planning for academic diversity in America's classrooms: Windows on reality, research, change, and practice.* Lawrence: The University of Kansas Center for Research on Learning.

Kantor, R.N., Anderson, T.H., & Armbruster, B.B. (1983). How considerate are children's textbooks? *Journal of Curriculum Studies, 15*(1), 61-72.

Kelly, B., Gersten, R., & Carnine, D. (1990). Student error patterns as a function of curriculum design: Teaching fractions to remedial high school students and high school students with learning disabilities. *Journal of Learning Disabilities, 23*(1), 23-29.

Kinder, D., & Bursuck, W. (1991). The search for a unified social studies curriculum: Does history really repeat itself? *Journal of Learning Disabilities, 24*(5), 270-284.

Lenz, B.K., Alley, G.R., & Schumaker, J.B. (1987). Activating the inactive learner: Advanced organizers in the secondary content classroom. *Learning Disability Quarterly, 10,* 53-66.

Lenz, B.K., & Bulgren, J.A. (1994). *ReflActive Planning: Planning for diversity in secondary schools* (Research Report). Lawrence: University of Kansas Center for Research on Learning.

Lenz, B.K., Bulgren, J.A., Schumaker, J.B., Deshler, D.D., & Boudah, D.A. (1994). *The Unit Organizer Routine.* Lawrence, KS: Edge Enterprise.

Lenz, B.K., Deshler, D.D., Schumaker, J.B., Bulgren, J.A., Kissam, B., Vance, M., Roth, J., & McKnight, M. (1994). *The Course Planning Routine: A guide for inclusive course planning* (Research Report). Lawrence: University of Kansas Center for Research on Learning.

Lenz, B.K., Marrs, R.W., Schumaker, J.B., & Deshler, D.D. (1993). *The Lesson Organizer Routine.* Lawrence, KS: Edge Enterprise.

Lovitt, T.C., & Horton, S.V. (1988). How to develop study guides. *Journal of Reading, Writing, and Learning Disabilities, 2,* 213-221.

Lovitt, T.C., & Horton, S.V. (1994). Strategies for adapting science textbooks for youth with learning disabilities. *Remedial & Special Education, 15*(2), 105-106.

Lovitt, T.C., Rudsit, J., Jenkins, J., Pious, C., & Benedetti, D. (1986). Adapting science materials for general and learning disabled seventh graders. *Remedial & Special Education, 7*(1), 31-39.

McIntosh, R., Vaughn, S., Schumm, J.S., Haager, D., & Lee, O. (1993). Observations of students with learning disabilities in general education classrooms. *Exceptional Children, 60*(3), 249-261.

Meheady, L., Sacca, M.K., & Harper, G.F. (1987). Classwide tutoring teams: The effects of peer-mediated instruction on the academic performance of secondary mainstreamed students. *Journal of Special Education, 21*(3), 107-121.

Meheady, L., Sacca, M.K., & Harper, G.F. (1988). Classwide peer tutoring with mildly handicapped high school students. *Exceptional Children, 55*(1), 52-59.

Palincsar, A.S., David, Y.M., Winn, J.A., & Stevens, D. (1991). Examining the contexts of strategy instruction. *Remedial & Special Education, 12*(3), 43-53.

Scanlon, D., Deshler, D.D., & Schumaker, J.B. (1996). Can a strategy be taught and learned in secondary inclusive classrooms? *Learning Disabilities Research & Practice, 11*(1), 41-57.

Scanlon, D., Schumaker, J.B., & Deshler, D.D. (1994). Collaborative dialogues between teachers and researchers to create educational interventions: A case study. *Journal of Educational & Psychological Consultation, 5*(1), 69-76.

Schumaker, J.B., Deshler, D.D., & McKnight, P.C. (1991). Teaching routines for content areas at the secondary level. In G. Stoner, M.R. Shinn, & H.M. Walker (Eds.), *Interventions for achievement and behavior problems* (pp. 473-494). Washington, DC: National Association of School Psychologists.

Schumm, J.S., Vaughn, S., & Leavell, A. (1994). Planning Pyramid: A framework for planning for diverse student needs during content area instruction. *The Reading Teacher, 47*(8), 608-615.

Scruggs, T.E., & Mastropieri, M.A. (1992). Effective mainstreaming strategies for mildly handicapped students. *Elementary School Journal, 92*, 389-409.

Scruggs, T.E., Mastropieri, M.A., & Sullivan, G.S. (1994). Promoting relational thinking: Elaborative Interrogation for students with mild disabilities. *Exceptional Children, 60*(5), 450-457.

Tharp, R.G., & Gallimore, R. (1988). *Rousing minds to life.* New York: Cambridge University Press.

Vaughn, S., Bos, C.S., & Schumm, J.S. (1997). *Teaching mainstreamed, diverse, and at-risk students in the general education classroom.* Needham Heights, MA: Allyn & Bacon.

Wedel, M., Deshler, D.D., & Schumaker, J.B. (1988). *Effects of instruction of a vocabulary strategy in a mainstream class.* Unpublished master's thesis, University of Kansas, Lawrence.

Woodward, J. (1994). The role of models in secondary science instruction. *Remedial & Special Education, 15*(2), 94-104.

Woodward, J., & Noell, J. (1991). Science instruction at the secondary level: Implications for students with learning disabilities. *Journal of Learning Disabilities, 24*(5), 277-284.

CHAPTER THREE

Developing Social Competence in Diverse Secondary Schools and Classrooms

ANTHONY K. VAN REUSEN, Ph.D.,
The University of Texas at San Antonio

"Leticia doesn't like to work with other students. She's often late to class, she's rude to me, and she rarely has her materials. Her attitude and behavior suggest that she's not ready to learn."

"Enrique is too aggressive in class; he makes derogatory comments to other students, and he dresses and acts like a gangster."

"Bing is moody most of the time and doesn't say too much."

When teachers talk about their students' social behaviors and actions, they often describe problems like these. Most teachers can easily identify students who have difficulty working with others or engaging in socially appropriate behavior and interactions with peers and adults. Often, however, we overlook the complexity, variety, and number of social skills and behaviors secondary students need in order to effectively communicate, learn and work with others. Moreover, we sometimes overlook the differences found among today's diverse secondary students in their attempts to deal with factors such as physical growth and puberty, language and cognitive development, identity development, political and social values, race and ethnicity, idealism, religion, rebellion, and sexuality—all within the context of social development.

What are "social skills," and why are they important for students' success in school and beyond school? Who determines social demands and expectations, and how do students perceive and respond to them? In order to understand how students' social skills and behaviors can be developed or enhanced, we must look beyond those students who exhibit inappropriate, negative, or antisocial behavior. A more profitable approach is to identify and teach students the specific skills and behaviors used by people who are judged as competent, effective and successful in working and interacting with others on a day-to-day basis.

In this chapter, I examine the nature and complexity of social skills and the concept of social competence, and I address the demands and expectations secondary students must meet in order to attain social competence. The chapter culminates with a discussion of ways to provide social skill instruction to diverse groups of students in the secondary classroom, as well as approaches and specific strategies to help individual students enhance their social skills and behavior.

THE NATURE AND COMPLEXITY OF SOCIAL SKILLS AND SOCIAL COMPETENCE

One of the most important factors contributing to students' achievement in school is their ability to use a variety of social behaviors to successfully relate, communicate, and work with teachers and peers. These behaviors are commonly called *social skills*; this term generally refers to a variety of verbal and nonverbal behaviors that people use for effective interpersonal functioning, and that involve thoughts and actions taken in specific social situations or contexts (Combs & Slaby, 1977; Eisler, Hersen, Miller, & Blanchard, 1975; Kavale & Forness, 1996). People use social skills when they interact with others and attempt to influence or manipulate environments (Rinn & Markle, 1979). Students with good social skills know how and when to modify or redirect their interactions and behavior as situations and contexts evolve and change. These students are thought to monitor and regulate their use of social skills to promote effective interactions and elicit positive reinforcement from their peers, teachers, and parents (Campbell & Siperstein, 1994; Hoy & Gregg, 1994; Scanlon, 1996).

The degree to which students demonstrate appropriate social behavior and skills in specific situations represents their *social competence.* According to Bender (1995), social competence involves the interaction of personality development variables and social interaction factors. Campbell and Siperstein (1994) suggest that social competence represents a broad range of perceptions, judgments, and behaviors that enable students to act appropriately in various settings and to be successful in their social interactions. Similarly, McFall (1982) argues that social competence represents an evaluation based on the judgments and perceptions of others about whether or not a social task, event, or activity has been performed competently.

In short, whether or not a student is viewed as socially competent is usually determined by that student's awareness and use of appropriate social skills in a given context or situation. Specifically, most secondary students are viewed as socially competent in school and in their communities when they:

- Exchange greetings and converse with adults and peers
- Dress appropriately for school, work, and social events
- Share ideas, information, and opinions in an appropriate manner
- Compliment others
- Offer help or assistance
- Respect the beliefs, rights, and property of others
- Exercise self-control and resist peer pressure
- Display courtesy and manners
- Recognize positive and negative reactions to behavior
- Accept positive and negative feedback

As basic as these 10 behavioral descriptions seem, in actuality, they require students to use a broad range of complex and interrelated verbal and nonverbal behaviors. They also require students to monitor and regulate their verbal and nonverbal behavior across and within various contexts and situations. These behaviors range from using effective *interpersonal and communication skills* in class discussions (e.g., conversational turn-taking, listening and responding, asking questions, providing information or explanations, comparing ideas, and negotiating) to using and interpreting *paralinguistic codes* (e.g., intonation, emphasis, and hesitations superimposed on speech to signal attitude or emotion). They also include using and interpreting *nonlinguistic cues* (e.g., gestures, posture, facial expressions, eye communication, head and body movement, and physical distance) when interacting with other people.

Another way students demonstrate social competence is by using different styles of verbal and nonverbal behaviors (called *pragmatic social registers*) based on the conditions and the characteristics of the individuals within a social and/or communicative context (e.g., age, gender, culture, native language use, functions, and roles). One common example of how adolescent students display a change of register is when they clown around or joke with their friends before class starts, but as soon as the bell rings—and without prompting—they skillfully and naturally modify this behavior and direct their attention to the teacher.

Similarly, peers can have a profound impact on students' use of informal mode of communication or dialect in classroom settings. For example, in response to receiving a paper with notations indicating a need for corrections, a teacher may hear a student utter, "Why you be dissin' my paper?" This type of casual register is called *vernacular variation*. In most instances, this shifting of style is used only with a peer group. However, some secondary students may not recognize the classroom as a setting where more formal modes of communication are expected. In contrast, socially competent students differentiate their use of registers and style shifting; they recognize that if they fail to do so in certain settings or situations, their behavior can have profound consequences.

Another important aspect of register is *politeness* (Lakoff, 1977), which is achieved by using polite words and phrases ("Please," "Thank you," "You're welcome"), a pleasant tone of voice, and indirect requests ("May I borrow a sheet of paper please?" instead of "Gimme some paper").

People who are skilled in changing their registers often use this ability to their benefit. For example, when students regulate the content and tone of their discussions with teachers over a difference of opinion regarding class rules, they often find teachers more willing to modify the nature or scope of those rules. Similarly, the manner in which a person adapts to being stopped by a police officer for a minor traffic violation might mean the difference between a written citation and a warning.

One important aspect of competent register use by adolescents is the ability to perceive situations accurately and to recognize when to use a different style or manner of speaking to manipulate outcomes. This requirement alone challenges secondary students to display a large repertoire of skilled behaviors; the ability to demonstrate competent social behavior requires adolescents to predict the outcomes of their verbal and nonverbal behaviors, evaluate their effectiveness, and change their behaviors as events dictate (Dodge, 1986; Fagan, Long, & Stevens, 1975; Kasen, Johnson, & Cohen, 1990). Anderson (1992) argues that competence in knowing when to switch one's register varies with age and experience.

Knowing when and how to regulate one's register is also important for *self-advocacy*. Van Reusen, Bos, Schumaker, and Deshler (1994) define self-advocacy as "an individual's ability to effectively communicate, convey, negotiate or assert his or her own interests, desires, needs and rights. It involves making informed decisions and taking responsibility for those decisions" (p. 1). Socially competent adolescents identify and prioritize their needs, set and monitor their learning and development goals, and work toward the attainment of those goals. These students take responsibility for their decisions and actions. Further, socially and academically competent adolescents understand that regardless of the learning situation, *they* ultimately control what, how, how well, and why it is important to learn. These students recognize situations in which they must assertively but calmly state their needs, wants, or desires. Likewise, they determine and pursue the supports they need to attain their goals and assume responsibility for obtaining those supports. Both in and out of school, they identify and respond to situations in which they need to advocate for themselves.

People are also viewed as socially competent when, without prompting, they recognize and respond to the expectations or demands of a particular context by using and regulating a large repertoire of *personal management, problem-solving, learning, or work skills and knowledge* (e.g., when people make effective decisions about which skills, behaviors, or tools to use in a situation, or draw upon their available knowledge and skills repertoire to devise, carry out, evaluate, and revise a plan of action). Secondary students are viewed as socially competent when they respond to situations and take personal responsibility in preparing for and participating in learning activities (e.g., organizing a notebook and/or assignment calendar, gathering and bringing needed materials to a class or job site, dressing appropriately, focusing their attention, working independently, working cooperatively in groups, managing time, solving problems, and consciously using specific study skills or strategies to achieve academic and employment success). These students are also persistent and resourceful in completing tasks or assignments; they are volitional (i.e., they resist distractions and control their thoughts) in their efforts to attain successful outcomes (Zimmerman, 1994).

In sum, secondary students must use a considerable number of interrelated and complex social skills to achieve even a marginal level of social competence. Interestingly, in most schools today, the social skills and behaviors of secondary-level students do not have to be extraordinary to be viewed as even marginally competent. They must simply be sufficient and appropriate to meet the demands and expectations of persons they interact with on a daily basis.

Factors Contributing to Perceptions
of Students' Social Competence

Cultural and linguistic factors, along with mistaken beliefs about human differences, can contribute to positive and negative perceptions of secondary students' social competence. For example, McLaren (1989) argued that in some schools, teachers, administrators and students often value and reward the "cultural capital" of the majority students, while devaluing or overlooking the cultural capital of minority and disadvantaged students. The term *cultural capital* refers to the general cultural background of a group and includes "ways of talking, acting, modes of style, moving, socializing, forms of knowledge, language practices and values" (McLaren, 1989, p. 190). Some teachers, majority students, and others may view linguistic, cultural, and ethnic differences as deficits and treat those who exhibit them unequally. In the same way, some secondary students may be valued less and treated differently by others in the school community because of their physical, mental, or behavioral differences, compared to students considered to be "normal." Bogdan and Biklen (1977) coined the term *handicapism*, currently referred to as *disablism*, which represents "a set of assumptions and practices that promote differential and unequal treatment of people because of apparent or assumed physical, mental, or behavioral differences" (p. 59). In secondary schools and classrooms, disablism can be displayed in many different ways. Socially, it is displayed consciously or unconsciously through bias, prejudice, stereotyping, and avoidance behavior by teachers and peers who do not directly interact with students with disabilities or engage them in learning and social activities. The more the social skills of students with disabilities vary from those judged to be socially competent, the greater the probability that these students will be viewed as socially deficient or socially incompetent.

Thus, in some school settings, perceptions of adolescents' social competence may have more to do with appreciation or depreciation of their cultural capital or unalterable differences than with an objective evaluation of their social behaviors. However, more and more teachers and administrators are recognizing that the development of social skills and social competence is critical for all students regardless of their cultural, linguistic, physical, or mental differences. These professionals recognize that teaching students with diverse backgrounds to learn, work, and interact together in an effective manner requires specific skills that cannot be left to chance. Further, they recognize the importance of social skills and social competence as they attempt to prepare all secondary students for the responsibilities of adult life, including employment, meaningful participation in communities, as well as successful personal and professional relationships.

Differentiating Social Competence and Social Skills

Conceptually, our level of social competence is determined by our ability to adequately and appropriately use a wide variety of social behaviors in various settings. However, the complexity of the verbal and nonverbal behaviors and actions subsumed under the concept of social competence sometimes makes it difficult to differentiate between social competence and social skills. Dodge (1986), and Dodge, Pettit, McClaskey, and Brown (1986), suggested that social competence consists of three major components: (a) perceiving, decoding, and interpreting social cues; (b) selecting an appropriate response; and (c) appropriately enacting a social response. Similarly, Vaughn and Hogan (1990) found that social competence includes four components: (a) positive relations with others; (b) accurate and age-appropriate social cognition; (c) absence of maladaptive behaviors; and (d) effective social behaviors. Thus, on a conceptual level, we find considerable agreement among researchers on what constitutes social competence on the part of students.

Vernon, Schumaker, and Deshler (1993) suggested that social competence is a broad term that includes socially accepted performance of a variety of social skills in an effective, efficient manner. They defined a social skill as an appropriate behavior related to meeting a social demand. They contended that a social skill can be a general nonverbal behavior, a specific verbal behavior, or a specific nonverbal behavior.

In summary, for learning purposes in today's diverse and inclusive classrooms, the social behaviors that secondary students need to acquire and use to demonstrate social competence are those verbal and nonverbal behaviors and actions that enable them to become proficient when they initiate, maintain, adapt, and discontinue verbal and nonverbal situational communications. Acquisition and mastery of these behaviors permit adolescents to form and maintain appropriate interactions and relationships that are socially acceptable and mutually satisfying to all involved. Secondary students with an appropriate social skills repertoire can attain positive outcomes in school, develop positive personal and work relationships, and be socially active participants in their communities.

THE DEVELOPMENT OF SOCIAL COMPETENCE

Typically, secondary students' social skill repertoires are learned vicariously through observations of and interactions with parents or guardians, other adults, and peers in their environments. Such repertoires are commonly based on cultural norms (Kammeyer, Ritzer, & Yetman, 1990), and they are often modeled and reinforced in varying degrees.

Many secondary students can profit from examining the importance of skilled, competent social behaviors. Some may need to reexamine or refine their ability to use these behaviors and skills in school, the work force, adult life, and their personal relationships. Others may need to first explore the verbal and nonverbal social behaviors of their native cultures in order to compare and promote their conceptualizations of the social skills needed for access and success in American society (Cummins, 1986). Still others may need direct experiences with peers and others whose social skill repertoires are sufficiently large, flexible, and representative of prevailing cultural norms (Wong-Fillmore, 1991).

Rather than contrived or forced social contact with those who use good social skills, most adolescents require real contacts that provide both the motivation and the opportunity to learn or improve social skills. Observing social skill exchanges in *natural* settings (e.g., classrooms, offices, restaurants, stores, dances, etc.) provides adolescents with social contexts and models that enable them to interpret how social skills are structured and used.

Secondary students who are learning English as a second language but also need to improve their social skill repertoires may need instruction that uses both their native language and English to facilitate their use and understanding of social skills used in American society. This approach can accelerate the acquisition process of some components of social skill development for bilingual students (Whitaker & Prieto, 1989). It also allows teachers to give students more accurate and timely feedback regarding their social skill performance (Baca & Cervantes, 1984; Omark & Erickson, 1983).

For some adolescents, instruction in the use of social skills may need to be combined with other interventions (e.g., behavior therapy, cognitive behavior modification, psychotherapy, counseling, etc.) in order to have a significant impact on social behavior. Secondary students who manifest chronic, serious, or pervasive antisocial behaviors and conduct disorders often require continuous, comprehensive services. Such adolescents frequently demonstrate hostility and aggression toward others, break rules, defy authority, destroy property and, in some cases, openly violate the social norms and mores of their communities. Unfortunately, these students may be highly resistant to intervention as well as unresponsive to social influence (Coie & Jacobs, 1993; Kazdin, 1985, 1987). These students usually require an intensive, extensive regimen of instruction conducted in specifically designed settings outside the general education classroom.

Social Expectations in Various Types of Situations

The various situations where secondary students are expected to effectively use social behaviors to interact, learn, work, and socialize with others (inside and outside school) may be categorized as "structured" or "unstructured." Campbell and Siperstein (1994) described *structured* situations as those in which students are closely supervised or receive specific directions and behavioral controls from adults, as in a classroom. In these settings, expectations for students' social interactions and behavior are often defined by the nature of the activity, and their opportunities for interaction and behavior decisions are usually limited. For example, during most classroom lessons, student interactions consist of asking questions, providing answers, or contributing to discussion; the content and behavior related to any student-to-adult or student-to-student interactions are generally directed to the topic of the lesson. Classroom behavior expectations may be explicit or implicit—either class rules are posted, or students are expected to follow rules outlined in student handbooks.

In *unstructured* situations, students have less adult supervision and fewer behavior controls. No formal tasks or directed activities guide or control students' interactions and behavior. These situations include waiting for a classroom to be opened, passing in the hallways between classes, engaging in extracurricular after-school activities, hanging out at McDonald's during lunch period, going to the movies with friends, and so on. In these types of situations, adolescents have more opportunities to informally interact with one another, and they have more behavioral decisions and choices to make.

Regardless of the situation or setting, adolescents demonstrate social competence when they are perceived as willing and able to assume personal responsibility for their verbal and nonverbal behavior. Situational social demands are complicated by the persons who impact the nature and type of interactions that take place within a given context; in most secondary schools, the social demands that students are expected to meet are constructed or affected by their teachers, administrators, and other school personnel, by their peers, and by their own thoughts, values, beliefs and perceptions.

Expectations set by school personnel. Most of the social demands adolescents face in school are established by teachers, administrators, and others who formally and informally interact with students and supervise their behavior. Student behavior is usually influenced by such factors as instructional methods or techniques, class activities, schedules, pacing of instruction, grouping arrangements, and various teachers' interpersonal skills (Campbell & Siperstein, 1994). Student behavior can also be influenced by teachers' instructional knowledge, organizational and presentation skills, and attitudes toward the teaching-learning process and about individual students (Bos & Vaughn, 1994).

It is important to recognize that the amount of control and structure used by school personnel in providing instruction and managing student behavior can have positive or negative influences on students' willingness and efforts to respond to the social demands of school. For example, some teachers and administrators may be overly authoritarian in establishing and maintaining their expectations for students' academic and social behavior. In many instances, this approach results in a lack of open communication and trust with students. Others may take a more laid-back or laissez-faire approach, setting few guidelines for students to follow. While too much structure may be overwhelming or restrictive for some students, little or no structure can lead other students to demonstrate apathy toward learning and toward using appropriate social behavior. Some students may use verbal and nonverbal defiance, aggression, or antisocial behavior in either situation. The challenge for teachers and administrators is to establish and maintain a continuum of structure and support for developing the social skills and competence of all students.

In addition to teachers, a variety of other school personnel also set and influence social expectations for secondary students. These persons may include:

- Administrators, who set and maintain behavior guidelines;
- Secretaries, who interact with and provide information to students and parents;
- Staff or security personnel, who supervise students in the

hallways and during lunch and after-school activities (e.g.,
sports, dances, pep rallies, etc.);

- Paraprofessionals and teaching assistants, who work with
  students;
- Cafeteria personnel, who oversee lunch arrangements and
  food services; and
- Maintenance personnel, who set and model cleanliness standards for a campus.

Socially competent secondary students demonstrate flexibility as
they adapt and respond to the multiple rules and expectations set by
school personnel. As they move from one setting to the next, these
students recognize and respond with little difficulty to the explicit and
implicit demands placed by others on their behavior. For less-skilled
students, differing situational demands can be a significant source of
difficulty; in some instances, these can cause confrontations between
adolescents and the adults in their environments.

Expectations set by peers. In addition to teachers and other school
personnel, peers and classmates also set expectations for social behavior. Often, peer-set expectations are less flexible and more critical than
those of adults (Bendtro, Brokenleg, & Van Brocken, 1990; Dodge,
Coie, & Brakke, 1982; Downs & Rose, 1991). Interestingly, although peer expectations are usually implicit—unstated or under-
stated—they are clearly established; secondary students who frequently display incompetence in meeting peer-set expectations are
often subjected to peer rejection (Patterson, Reid, & Dishion, 1992).

Students with pervasive problems in social and communicative
competence can become subjects of rejection and avoidance by their
more socially competent peers. For example, in a meta-analysis of 152
studies that focused on the social skills deficits of students with
learning disabilities (LD), Kavale and Forness (1996) found that 75%
of such students manifested social skills deficits that distinguished
them from comparison groups. The primary dimensions of their
negative evaluations by peers were found to be "associated with less

interaction and lower social status for the students with LD which resulted in their being less popular, less often selected as friends, and viewed as less cooperative" (p. 234). Kavale and Forness surmised that the negative social evaluations often received by students with LD may reflect these students' lack of social and communicative competence, both verbal and nonverbal, as well as their reduced ability to exhibit empathetic behavior.

In a study on aggressive, socially rejected students, Coie, Dodge, Ladd, and their colleagues found that many of these students make numerous errors in decoding and interpreting the social cues and behavioral feedback they get from peers (see Coie, Belding, & Underwood, 1988; Dodge, 1980, 1986; Dodge & Fame, 1982; Ladd & Oden, 1979). Thus, some secondary students may respond inappropriately to the well-intentioned social demands of peers because they misinterpret the implicit social cues.

Peer-established expectations for social behavior are most visible in unstructured settings—during lunch, in the hallways between classes, in the library, and so on. In these settings, peers establish expectations for both the quantity and the quality of interactions—including content, form, and location. For instance, when passing in the hallways between classes, students usually talk about a variety of school-related and non-school-related topics, using informal language patterns; they recognize and greet friends, and gather at their lockers. In these situations, they have opportunities to interact informally and make choices about how to behave. Moreover, they determine for themselves whom to contact and whom to avoid.

Naturally, the expectations for social interactions in these contexts are very different from those in structured settings, but socially competent adolescents recognize intuitively that certain social demands are operational in *all* settings. These include extending greetings, responding politely, using a pleasant tone of voice, engaging in eye communication, and avoiding physical conflict. In contrast, adolescents who do not recognize the subtle changes in social demands as they proceed from one situation to the next, or who have trouble adapting their behavior, often stand out by demonstrating inappropriate behavior. Consequently, for some secondary students, efforts to improve their social interactions among peers may need to include identification of environmental conditions or cues to prompt the use or adaptation of specific social behaviors.

Self-imposed expectations. Individual students also impose demands and expectations for their own social behavior (Bauer & Sapona, 1991). Most secondary students encounter few problems with their self-imposed social behavior when it is appropriate for the context and meets the expectations of their teachers and peers. However, some students may impose standards on, or hold beliefs about, their own social behaviors that are age-, gender-, or situationally inappropriate. Others may establish social demands for themselves that are unrealistic, unacceptable, or beyond their current ability. Difficulty in social behavior can occur when students develop behavior expectations for themselves that are do not match what is expected by teachers and peers. For example, Tomas may believe that getting a laugh from his peers in biology class is more important than contributing to discussions or focusing on his work. On the surface, it may appear that Tomas simply does not care. However, he may simply lack the background knowledge or the conversational skills to make positive contributions to the topic of discussion. Further, he may not recognize the social expectations of the classroom; he may be unable to subtly adjust his use of humor to make it more appropriate for class discussions while still obtaining peer approval. Consequently, he may feel less than adequate during discussions and use humor as a coping device to avoid participating.

Another student with inappropriate self-imposed social expectations is Sharon. Sharon sees herself as an intelligent person because she earns good grades. However, she often engages in confrontational behavior with her teachers, and her peers find her condescending. She tends to argue with teachers over minor issues, and she dominates her classmates when making group decisions, resulting in poor interpersonal communications and relationships. For both Sharon and Tomas, their beliefs, expectations, and demands for their own social behaviors undermine their social competence in the classroom.

Although self-imposed expectations are some of the most critical factors affecting students' social behavior, they are usually left unidentified. Furthermore, some teachers and administrators may view the classroom social behavior of adolescents like Tomas and Sharon as representative of personality traits, such as temperament and self-concept; they may conclude that these students need behavioral intervention or disciplinary action, rather than social skills instruction.

One way to identify students' self-imposed expectations for their own social behavior is to engage them in conversations (as individuals or groups) to better understand their sense of the social expectations operating in the classroom and in society at large. Another way is to closely examine their responses and reaction patterns to classroom demands, and determine how they monitor and evaluate their own performance on tasks and activities. Used in combination, these two approaches can shed a great deal of light on adolescents' misperceptions and on discrepancies between their self-imposed social expectations and the expectations of the classroom. Secondary students who misunderstand or become discouraged about their social behavior often self-impose demands they cannot attain. Helping students establish realistic expectations for their social behavior is an important factor in enhancing their social competence.

Explicit and Implicit Classroom Expectations

The manner in which classroom social expectations are established and communicated to students is another factor that contributes to their understanding and use of competent classroom behavior. In many school systems, students receive a handbook that contains a variety of information about the school, the district, and the curriculum. These handbooks typically outline a code of conduct, discipline policies, or school rules. In most instances, students are expected to share these handbooks with their parents, who are expected to read them and sign a statement indicating that they and their children understand the policies.

In addition, many classroom teachers explicitly list their expectations for students' social behavior. Many teachers post rules that students are expected to follow. However, posted rules are of little value if they are vague or unclear, or if a student has difficulty reading or understanding them. For example, in one ninth-grade classroom, the following rules were posted on the bulletin board: "1. Obey all class rules; 2. No arguing during group activities/work; 3. Participate in class discussions." Although these rules are explicitly posted, and do indicate some expectations for student behavior, as presented they are subjective and unclear. Furthermore, many teacher expectations for student social behavior are implicit in nature—based on the day-to-day social interactions people have, rather than on explicit rules. For example, the ways in which students and teachers greet each other, cooperate, communicate, and offer assistance are usually regulated by implicit expectations.

To be effective, classroom rules need to provide secondary students with clear, specific information about the behavioral and academic responses required of them. Furthermore, classroom rules are only effective to the degree to which the teacher describes, models, maintains, and reinforces them. Thus, it is important to teach adolescents that appropriate behavior results in positive consequences and that inappropriate or negative behavior results in punishment or the withdrawal of positive consequences. The following steps, partially adapted from Walker, Colvin, and Ramsy (1995, p. 157), are recommended for establishing this important principle.

- *State rules explicitly* so that it is clear to everyone (students, teachers, observers) when a rule or rules have been followed or broken. Rules need to be precise, practical, and clearly worded.
- *Develop functional rules* that focus on student behaviors and responses that facilitate instruction and learning. If rules are to be posted, post no more than four to five rules. The following are examples of functional rules: (a) be on time for class; (b) enter the classroom quietly; (c) organize your

materials and bring them to class; (d) go to your assigned area promptly; (e) listen to the teacher's directions or explanations; (f) raise your hand if you wish to speak; (g) do not take or use other people's property without permission; (h) participate in class discussions; (i) use a proper heading on all work turned in for grading; (j) start and finish assigned work on time; (k) ask for help only after you have tried by yourself; (l) clean up your area before leaving.

- *Establish classroom rules immediately* on the first day of the new school year or semester; it is more difficult to establish rules at a later time. Remember to explain class rules to students who enroll in the class after the first day.
- *Reward rule compliance* through positive reinforcement, including social reinforcers (e.g., smiles, praise, attention), privileges (e.g., free time, tutoring, listening to music, playing a game), and activities.
- *Cue or prompt* students to follow the classroom rules before an activity or lesson begins.
- *Review the rules regularly* so that students are constantly reminded of them. This practice allows teachers and students to identify any rules that are not working or that require further clarification.
- *Practice frequently broken rules* by modeling appropriate behaviors and simulating situations in which the behaviors are required, followed by a debriefing or feedback session.

Class rules for social and academic responses can be developed and refined with student involvement. Such involvement does not mean allowing students complete freedom to establish, refine, or rewrite the classroom rules whenever they please. Rather, it means teaching how to identify and make decisions regarding appropriate social or academic responses. This type of involvement is directed toward increasing students' understanding that regardless of the context, they ultimately control what, how, how well, and why they behave, communicate, learn, or work with others. The idea of involving secondary students in establishing classroom social expectations is based on research showing that students who have a perception of choice and control over their behavior, learning activities, and abilities are more willing to work successfully with adults in their environments (Schunk, 1989, 1990).

This type of involvement may also be critical for secondary students with low social competence. Thorson (1996) used ethnographic methods to examine the beliefs of a group of students who had histories of social and behavioral problems in school that resulted in disciplinary actions. The group included students with culturally and linguistically different backgrounds. Thorson reported that as a group, these students did generally recognize the need for classroom rules and believe that school and classroom rules should be followed. The majority believed they got in trouble because they did not understand the rules, because a teacher or administrator was unfair in applying the rules, or because the rules were unfair. In reflecting upon their situations, these students all complained about a lack of honest and ongoing communication between themselves and their teachers.

Thus, it appears essential to have secondary students—particularly those with social skill and behavioral deficits—play a key role in determining the behavioral expectations in the classroom. Consequently, efforts to enhance students' classroom social behavior may need to include routines that allow students to take an active role in establishing and reviewing the social and academic demands of their classrooms. This type of communication and involvement could avert many adverse situations and solve problems for many secondary students, thereby reducing disciplinary action while concurrently addressing their inappropriate social behavior.

As discussed earlier, peers also set implicit demands and expectations for social behavior inside and outside the classroom. These implicit demands and expectations—never written down or expressed in a formal sense—impact the way adolescents communicate verbally and nonverbally with one another; they can direct the topics students choose for conversations, and they can impact the language patterns students use. The ability to recognize and respond to these implicit demands can impact secondary students' social acceptance, working relationships with peers, and success in initiating and maintaining friendships. In short, in order to meet the social and academic demands and expectations in a classroom, secondary students must not only comply with posted rules and follow teachers' directions, but also recognize and adjust to requirements and expectations from teachers and peers that may never be explicitly stated.

The social behavior problems of many adolescents can be attributed to their failure to recognize and respond to many of these demands. As a result, when thinking about the social demands of their classrooms, secondary teachers should carefully identify those basic social skills students must have in order to respond appropriately to both explicit and implicit demands.

Developing and Teaching a Social Competence Curriculum

Developing and teaching social competence as a curriculum for today's diverse secondary student population requires a reconceptualization of the way we plan and provide social skills instruction in inclusive classrooms and schools.

Interestingly, in most secondary settings today, the social skills curriculum is *unwritten*. At best, it is usually embodied in a short list of school and or classroom rules and an implied sense of what it means to behave appropriately in a secondary school setting. Further, attempts to address social skills are usually carried out in a reactive or indirect manner. In many instances, the expectation for demonstration of good social skills becomes more of a compliance issue than an instructional emphasis. For example, adolescents who do not meet our expectations for social behavior are often provided with after-class discussions with teachers and others about their inappropriate social behavior and reminded of the class or school rules. Those with more challenging social behaviors may be subjected to reprimands or disciplinary actions; students with chronic social skill problems may be referred for behavior improvement programs, or placed in alternative secondary schools where they may or may not receive direct social skills instruction.

In contrast, by conceptualizing social competence as a repertoire of behaviors that secondary students can acquire and use inside and outside school, we can teach social skills as a curriculum by: (a) identifying the social skills that successful people use; (b) determining, with students, their priorities for the skills they want to learn or improve; (c) attending to the critical elements for personalizing social skills instruction to meet group and individual needs; (d) teaching social skills using procedures that are based on sound instructional principles and are powerful enough to enable students to acquire specific skills as quickly and efficiently as possible; and (e) using validated approaches to delivering social skills instruction.

A well-defined social skills curriculum and a sound instructional model are central to this effort, essential for planning and providing effective group and individual social skills instruction. The following sections offer suggestions for how to design and present social skill instructional lessons.

Identifying social skills used by successful people. As reflected in the beginning sections of this chapter, socially competent people use a broad array of complex, interrelated skills (verbal and nonverbal) in specific situations. One way to begin planning a social skills curriculum for secondary students who demonstrate difficulties with social behavior is to conduct a functional analysis of the students' classroom social behavior, to determine the specific social skills that need to be addressed. Prior to designing a social skills instructional program, it is also essential to identify the purpose or goal(s) of the program. For example, a functional analysis could be conducted to compare a student's classroom social behaviors to a list of age- or grade-appropriate skills that socially competent people use. In this way, a teacher can identify the priorities for social skills instruction that will meet a specific need. This also prevents unnecessary instruction, because teaching secondary students social skills they already have serves little purpose.

In order to perform an accurate functional analysis, teachers need specific instruction in how to conduct it. O'Neill et al. (1997) provide an excellent and comprehensive treatment of this procedure. First, skills that are commonly demanded in inclusive secondary schools and classrooms should be identified (e.g., interpersonal and communication skills, nonlinguistic skills, social registers, politeness, cooperative learning, etc.). One useful source is *A Resource Guide for Social Skills Instruction by Alberg, Petry, and Eller* (1994), one of the most complete guides for selecting and targeting social skills curricula across the grade levels (from preschool to postsecondary). A list should be developed, based on a careful consideration of the full range of social behaviors that successful people and students demonstrate, that will serve as a touchstone for identifying the goals or desired outcomes for instruction. This list should contain the skills that are expected for the situation or setting, as well as those behaviors you wish to address based on student needs. It is also helpful to prioritize the skills the students need to acquire.

Van Reusen, Bos, Schumaker, and Deshler (1994) suggested teaching secondary students how to make a *personal inventory* as a way to identify the social skills they use and the skills they want to learn or improve, and to prioritize their social skills goals. This information is then used to establish instructional priorities based on individual and group needs, as well as to plan and carry out specific instruction and activities for students trying to improve their social skills. By providing a format and process by which students can identify and prioritize their own needs, choose their own goals, and monitor their own progress, we increase their efforts and interest toward learning and using appropriate social skills.

Even when students possess the necessary verbal and nonverbal behaviors to learn new social skills, some do not succeed. A commonly cited reason is lack of motivation. Some students who have experienced social behavior problems are reluctant even to attempt to learn new social skills. Others begin, but set unrealistic goals or give up before they reach their goals. To this end, Van Reusen et al. (1994) recommended providing students a variety of skills lists to assist in for making learning and development decisions. Table 3-1 presents one example of such a list.

The objective of such lists is to provide students with choices regarding their social competence needs, particularly when selecting specific skills to acquire, and to involve them actively in making choices during instruction. Be sure to include skills related to empathy and socially responsible decision making, as research shows that secondary students with social skill problems tend to be weak in these areas (Walker, Schwarz, Nippold, Irvin, & Noell, 1994). The skills the students select become the goals for instruction, so that the instructional process is driven by student goals rather than teacher-imposed goals. Once the social skills lists have been developed, its important to turn your attention to the critical elements for providing social skills instruction that will meet group and individual needs.

Critical elements for personalizing social skills instruction. For social skills instruction to have a significant impact on secondary students' behavior and performance, particularly for diverse groups of students in inclusive schools and classrooms, a number of critical instructional elements need to be addressed. The following elements provide a framework for delivering an effective social skills program within a secondary classroom:

1. Identify the students' perceptions, feelings and beliefs in relation to all aspects of the social skills program.
2. Build positive, trusting relationships with students as an initial step toward influencing their social behavior and development.
3. Provide a wide variety of materials and options so that instruction can be tailored to students' perceptions, motivation, developmental levels, and cultural and linguistic characteristics as well as their social skill needs.
4. Provide a continuum of structured activities to ensure communication, direction, and support for the students in the acquisition of social skills. Include activities that require the

Table 3-1. Social Skills List (from Van Reusen, Bos, Schumaker, & Deshler, 1994).

CAN YOU:

1. Actively listen to others?
2. Introduce yourself to strangers?
3. Start a conversation with someone?
4. Correctly interrupt someone while they are doing something else?
5. Have a long conversation with someone?
6. Easily make friends?
7. Accept and give compliments?
8. Accept and give criticism?
9. Apologize to someone when you've made a mistake?
10. Resist peer pressure?
11. Respect the beliefs and values of others?
12. Understand and respond to the feelings of others?
13. Accept a "no" from someone?
14. Ask others for help?
15. Give good rationales to others for explaining your position?
16. Effectively work with others to solve a problem?
17. Persuade others to your point of view?
18. Negotiate with someone so both parties win?
19. Plan a social activity or date?
20. Dress appropriately for school, work or a social event?
21. Participate effectively as a member of a team/group?
22. Take the lead in starting an activity with someone else?
23. Use good table manners?
24. Provide help when needed?
25. Teach others something new?

© 1994 by Van Reusen, Bos, Schumaker, & Deshler.
Reprinted by permission.

students to work both cooperatively in small groups and independently, with and without adult supervision.

5. Provide students with ongoing response opportunities, feedback, and incentive systems in the classroom to facilitate their demonstration and mastery of appropriate social skills.

6. Actively involve the students in making instructional decisions to increase their perception of commitment, responsibility, and control in learning and using good social skills.

7. Hold individual formal and informal conferences with the students to communicate a review of progress, instructional decisions, options, and goal setting related to their social performance.

8. Involve parents or primary caregivers in the social skills program. (Recognize that in some cases, there may be little to no cooperation or interest, and you may need to work at parent/caregiver involvement.)

9. Use contracts or other written agreements to increase the students' motivation and commitment by clarifying their perceptions of need, personal choice, description of desired behavior(s), and evaluative criteria.

10. Provide ongoing formal and informal evaluation of students' social skills as a means of monitoring their daily social behavior and progress, and modify instructional activities to improve the match between the students' perceived needs and the social skill curriculum.

Contemporary approaches to teaching social skills to groups. Currently, the professional literature offers two major approaches to teaching or improving social skills, particularly for group instruction: *social skills training,* and *interpersonal cognitive problem solving* or *social problem solving* (Hollinger, 1987). Social skills training, as the term implies, is skills-based, whereas social problem solving is strategy-based.

Skills-based approaches assume that social competence is based on key skills that can be identified and taught systematically. This type of approach is usually presented through direct instruction using coaching, modeling, behavioral rehearsal, verbal elaboration, feedback, and reinforcement to teach specific social skills. Sometimes skills-based approaches involve videotaped depictions, workbooks, role-playing, and discussion (Zaragoza, Vaughn, & McIntosh, 1991).

On the other hand, social problem-solving approaches focus on teaching generic or core social strategies (combinations or series of social skills) that can be used and adjusted for various social situations in and out of school. These strategies are designed to be adaptive, and their use is intended to promote social competence. Social problem-solving approaches emphasize covert processing, self-instruction, and learner mediation. These approaches may be used in conjunction with skills-based approaches.

Unlike their younger counterparts, most adolescents possess relatively advanced cognitive and language abilities and are able to monitor and regulate these processes. Thus, intellectual analysis is a major theme in these approaches—teaching secondary students to recognize critical features of both typical and problematic social situations, to identify and use appropriate social responses, and to think through alternative solutions to situations before acting. For example, Vernon et al. (1993) developed a cooperative strategies series called *The SCORE Skills: Social Skills for Cooperative Groups.* This work provides a plan for teaching a set of five *cooperative strategies* that students need to cooperate successfully with others. Each strategy consists of a series of steps students can use to effectively meet the demands of a teaming or cooperative learning situation. The series defines a social skill strategy as a sequence of social skills plus guidelines and rules related to selecting a strategy and making decisions about its use. Accordingly, the authors constructed social skill strategies to involve: (a) perceiving situations accurately; (b) selecting the best strategy to use; (c) translating skill steps into appropriate words and actions; (d) performing social skill steps when needed; (e) monitoring and adjusting performances; (f) creating a "flowing interaction;" and (g) motivating oneself to perform the skill.

The five social skills are:

- *Share* Ideas,
- *Compliment* Others,
- *Offer* Help or Encouragement,
- *Recommend* Changes Nicely, and
- *Exercise* self-control.

These skills are sufficiently complex and numerous that learning them may be difficult for some adolescents with learning problems, but they are very appropriate for secondary level students.

Another sound social problem-solving approach that can be used to enhance student participation in class with appropriate and productive behaviors can be found in the "SLANT" Strategy (Ellis, 1991). The five steps of this strategy are:

- *Sit* up,
- *Lean* forward,
- *Activate* your thinking,
- *Name* key information, and
- *Track* the talker.

A further example of combining a set of social skills and behaviors into a social-problem solving strategy is found in the "SHARE" behaviors (Van Reusen, Bos, Schumaker, & Deshler, 1987, 1994). This acronym is used to cue students to combine and use the verbal, cognitive, and nonverbal behaviors needed for self-advocacy. The steps and substeps of this problem-solving approach are:

- *Sit* up straight,
- *Have* a pleasant tone of voice,
- *Activate* your thinking (tell yourself to pay attention, participate, and compare ideas),
- *Relax* (don't look uptight, tell yourself to stay calm), and
- *Engage* in eye communication.

Interestingly, reviews of skill-based approaches and problem solving approaches reveal no clear advantages of one over the other; both appear to present promising outcomes for groups of diverse secondary students (Ager & Cole, 1991; Zaragoza et al., 1991). The two approaches also work well in combination.

Basic Instructional Principles and Practices for Teaching Social Skills

At this point we have discussed identifying the social skills used by successful people and students, targeting the specific social skills to be taught, personalizing social skills instruction in a group setting, and determining the approaches to be used. We now turn to the basic instructional principles and practices for teaching social skills. The following six principles have been adapted from instructional models developed by Ellis, Deshler, Lenz, Schumaker, and Clark (1991) and Walker et al. (1994).

1. Develop prerequisite verbal and nonverbal behaviors before social skills instruction begins. Mastery of the behaviors required for positive social interactions should be in place before social skills instruction begins. For example, teaching adolescents how to compliment others (telling others something nice about them or what they have done) may depend on instruction in related prerequisite verbal and nonverbal behaviors, such as using a pleasant expression and using eye communication. Similarly, instruction in self-control (Vernon et al., 1993) will be more effective if students first learn what it means to "remain calm" and "think about what you want to say and how you want to say it." Some verbal and nonverbal behaviors may need only a brief review; others may require more support or intensive instruction.

As a general guideline, secondary students should be able to use or demonstrate prerequisite verbal and nonverbal behaviors before instruction in a more complex skill is initiated. Because of the range of abilities found in today's inclusive secondary schools and classrooms, students' verbal and nonverbal behaviors must be assessed to determine whether they demonstrate the component behaviors necessary for successful application of a general or specific social skill.

Establishing a minimum level of competence in prerequisite behaviors prior to social skills instruction has two primary benefits. First, any instruction will be better matched to the developmental needs of the students, reducing the probability of student failure or poor performance. Second, this process makes social skills instructional efforts more efficient and effective, because it reduces the time needed to review or prompt the necessary prerequisite behaviors. It also affords secondary teachers and students a more direct approach in the acquisition and application of social skills targeted to the classroom setting.

2. *Teach social skills regularly, intensively, and with variations in their appropriate application.* In order to enhance secondary students' social skills repertoires, targeted social behaviors need to be taught and addressed consistently. Ideally, this requires daily opportunities with skills-based and/or social problem solving approaches in the classroom setting. Keep in mind that simple explanation of or exposure to social skills or strategies may not be enough for many students.

One way to ensure intensive instruction is for teachers and students to set daily, weekly, and semester goals for social skill/ strategy acquisition and generalization. Without clearly defined goals, both teachers and students tend to get off track, resulting in very little progress. By sharing goals, teachers can provide diverse groups of secondary students with effective models for setting goals, express and demonstrate the value of setting goals, and collectively evaluate student attainment of goals. It is crucial, too, to elicit student input on application of social skill variations based on culture, ethnicity, gender, age, and situations.

3. *Emphasize personal effort and responsibility.* Adolescents need to understand that social competence in its simplest form means selecting and using, to the best of their abilities, social skills and behaviors

that can effectively address social demands. Thus, teachers should remind students regularly that social success results when they make sound social behavior decisions, use appropriate words and actions, put forth significant personal effort, and take responsibility for their actions in any social situation.

One way to reinforce this concept is teach students a *formula* for social success, such as: "Perceive situations accurately + Use appropriate words and actions + Personal effort and responsibility = SOCIAL SUCCESS." Such a formula can be developed collaboratively with students. Posting the formula in the classroom and referring to it over a sustained time period can increase students' comprehension of their role in the learning process. Further, reference to the formula can be used in discussing progress and providing feedback.

4. *Focus on mastery.* Secondary students are more likely to acquire, use, and generalize social skills when they can perform them at specified levels of mastery. Ellis et al. (1991) identified two dimensions that make up mastery performance: correct performance and fluent use, sometimes called "automaticity." The initial stages of most social skills instruction emphasize learning and correctly performing individual verbal and nonverbal behaviors or actions. Once these behaviors are learned, instructional focus should shift to the fluency of social skills. It is important here to keep in mind that older students often can handle and demonstrate more complex social behavior repertoires. Some secondary students will take longer than others to master sound social skill routines and repertoires. It is often difficult to establish a single mastery criterion for all students.

5. *Incorporate sound teaching behaviors and routines.* Providing social skills instruction for diverse groups of secondary students requires teachers to draw upon what they already know about effective teaching. In other words, social skills instruction can use the instructional procedures and routines that are effective for teaching academics—e.g., using lesson plans and organizers, pretesting, describing, modeling, requiring verbal elaboration, charting or graph-

ing performance, role-play, use of video depictions, discussions, questioning, checking for mastery, providing feedback, group practice and feedback, individual practice and mastery, and required application in and outside the classroom.

Further, teachers need to make decisions about which social skills to teach, how to organize and translate those social skills into easy-to-understand formats, and how to present the skills in memorable ways. Based on Lenz, Marrs, Schumaker, and Deshler's (1993) research and work, it can be argued that secondary students learn more (a) when they are actively involved in the learning process, (b) when abstract social concepts or complex social skills requiring multiple behaviors are presented in concrete forms, (c) when social skills are organized in an understandable and useful manner, (d) when relationships among social behaviors are made explicit, and (e) when they are involved in an apprenticeship where they are shown how, where, and why to learn general and specific social skills. Lenz et al. (1993) specifically recommend the use of lesson organizers for teaching social skills.

6. *Socially validate targeted social skills with students.* In order to match instructional efforts to students' social skill needs and beliefs, it is crucial to help them develop rationales for learning general and special social skills. This "big picture" details not only the nature of the skills to be taught, but also the advantages students can expect after learning, improving, and using appropriate social skills. In many secondary classrooms today, students are like critical consumers; they need to understand the relevance of what, why, and how they are supposed to learn something before they are willing to put forth effort. More specifically, when most secondary students are offered solutions to address or overcome their difficulties, they are like consumers trying to decide whether to give up some of their resources (time and effort) in order to learn some new skills. To make a sound choice, they need to know the costs (i.e., amount of time and effort to reach mastery) and the benefits they can expect (i.e., how they can influence and manage their social experiences and environments). In short, to be actively involved in acquiring or improving social abilities, secondary students must value and believe in the importance of using appropriate social skills that reflect sensitivity to human and situational differences.

APPROACHES TO ASSISTING INDIVIDUAL STUDENTS

It is generally recognized that acquisition of social skills in instructional settings does not guarantee their application in natural settings (Walker et al., 1994). This is particularly true for secondary students encountering social problems or difficulties that interfere with learning and disrupt the classroom. For some of these students, teachers are faced with the challenge of assuming a counseling role. Yet many teachers are unprepared—or do not want—to take on this role. Most often, secondary teachers work with over 150 students per day, and their non-instructional time is limited. However, many secondary students are more likely to seek assistance from their teachers than from other school personnel (e.g., school counselors, principal, school psychologist, nurse, etc.). Consequently, many teachers find themselves in situations where they need to teach social problem solving skills while they apply counseling skills.

In addressing this need, Crank, Schumaker, and Deshler (1995) developed *Surface Counseling,* a problem-solving and decision-making process that can be used to help an awkward student. Embedded in this process is a problem-solving strategy which teachers can share with individual students and teach them to use independently. While the goal is to help students resolve problems through a systematic process, a cooperative, trusting relationship between student and teacher must be established before starting the process, and maintained during the process, to yield successful outcomes.

The surface counseling approach consists of two independent components: *relationship-building skills* and *problem-solving steps.* Relationship-building skills include:

- Creating an appropriate surface counseling environment

- Listening actively
- Asking clarifying questions
- Making reflective statements
- Making summary statements
- Making statements that express concern and empathy

These skills allow the teacher to establish better rapport, gain the students' confidence, and build trust. They are designed to help the teacher develop an atmosphere in which the secondary student can openly and honestly communicate problems, discuss difficult or personal issues, and work in a partnership with the teacher to develop or create viable solutions. The problem-solving steps and their associated skills provide a structured format for the counseling. The sequenced steps are used by the teacher and student in an interactive format that facilitates student learning and later independent use of the steps.

The problem-solving steps, which can be used to address a variety of social behavior issues or problems, include the following:

- Specify the problem
- Plan solutions
- Summarize solutions
- Specify consequences for solutions
- Rate solutions and select the best one
- Specify and role play the solution steps
- Set a time to discuss the outcome
- Enact the solution
- Review the outcome

A self-instruction manual is available that allows teachers to learn the skills and steps of the surface counseling procedures (see Crank et al., 1995).

Intensive Social Skills Instruction for Individual Students

For secondary students with severe and pervasive social skills deficits or behavior problems, group-oriented approaches to social skills instruction and individual surface counseling procedures may not be enough. If a secondary student brings to school an inappropriate social behavior pattern, characterized by (a) a high frequency of occurrence, (b) occurrence across multiple settings and under various contexts, and (c) expression in multiple forms, that student is at risk for rejection by peers and teachers (Patterson et al., 1992). Peer and teacher rejection is commonly associated with poor academic performance, especially at the secondary level. Many of these students seek out others with similar social behavior; if left unchecked, many of them develop more aggressive and antisocial behavior patterns, including gang involvement.

Unfortunately, many of these students are placed in isolated programs away from their appropriately-behaving peers—who could be a very good source of social models and peer mentors. While alternative placements for these students should be considered and utilized when appropriate, it is important to recognize that social skills instruction for these students is generally more effective when it is: (a) individually tailored and planned; (b) designed to addresses specific social skills deficits or social competence problems (e.g., accurately perceiving potentially problematic situations); (c) conducted in a variety of contexts; (d) actively planned and organized by teachers and others who have daily contact with the students; (e) initiated using validated techniques and adequate time and resources for promoting the acquisition, generalization, and maintenance of newly learned social skills and strategies; and (f) used in conjunction with behavioral management interventions (Bain & Farris, 1991; Walker et al., 1995).

In short, social skills instruction for some secondary students may need to address not only general and specific social skills and strategies, but also anger management and control, resolution of social conflicts, social problem solving, resisting peer pressure, and responsible decision-making. The following social skills curricula and instructional programs are designed for students with social and behavior deficits including aggressive and antisocial behavior patterns.

- *The Walker Social Skills Curriculum: The ACCEPTS Program (A Curriculum for Children's Effective Peer and Teacher Skills)*, by H. M. Walker, S. McConnell, D. Holmes, B. Todis, J. Walker, and N. Golden. Published by Pro-Ed, Austin, TX.
- *ASSET: A Social Skills Program for Adolescents*, by J. S. Hazel, J. B. Schumaker, J. A. Sherman, and J. Sheldon-Wildgen. Published by Norman Baxley & Associates, Inc. Distributed by Research Press, 2612 N. Mattis Ave, Champaign, IL 61820
- *Managing Anger Skills Training (MAST)*, by L. Eggert. Available from National Education Service, 1610 West 3rd Street, P.O. Box 8, Bloomington, IN 47402.
- *Second Step: A Violence Prevention Curriculum Committee for Children.* 172 20th Ave., Seattle, WA 98122.
- *Aggression Replacement Training: A Comprehensive Intervention for Aggressive Youth*, by A. Goldstein and B. Glick. Distributed by Research Press, Inc., 2612 North Mattis Ave., Champaign, IL 61821.
- *Peer Mediation: Conflict Resolution in Schools*, by F. Schrumpf, D. Crawford, and H. Chu Usadel. Available from Research Press, Inc., 2612 North Mattis Ave., Champaign, IL 61821.
- *Helping Kids Handle Anger: Teaching Self-Control*, by P. Huggins. Available from Sopris West, Inc., 1140 Boston Ave., Longmont, CO 80501.
- *The Tough Kid Book: Practical Management Strategies*, by G. Rhode, W. Jensen, and H. K. Reavis. Available from Sopris West, Inc., 1140 Boston Ave., Longmont, CO 80501.

RECOMMENDATIONS FOR SUCCESSFUL SOCIAL SKILLS INSTRUCTION

In providing social skills instruction, secondary teachers must use the same carefully planned and organized instructional procedures they apply to teaching academic skills and content in inclusive classrooms. Teachers and others concerned about the social competence of their students need to carefully identify and socially validate the skills or strategies to be developed. To clarify the expected outcomes, functional analysis approaches and curriculum organization procedures similar to those used in the teaching of academic skills and content at the secondary level should be applied. Further, to increase involvement in and ownership of the development of their social competence, adolescents should be actively involved in selecting and monitoring the social skills and behaviors they want to learn or improve. Given the diversity of today's secondary student population, particular attention must be paid to identification and instruction of social skills and behaviors that are both sensitive to and reflective of cultural norms and human differences. Secondary students should be given ample opportunities to apply each new skill inside and outside the classroom; teachers and others need to specifically establish opportunities for secondary students to practice their newly learned social skills in a variety of natural settings in addition to the classroom. Finally, parents, other primary caregivers, and representatives from the community must be included in the social skills program to ensure that such instruction will be valued, reinforced and maintained.

The importance of social competence for interpersonal, working, and community relationships makes the teaching of social skills and appropriate social behavior vitally necessary. The development of social competence among our diverse secondary student population cannot be left to chance, for the future civility of our nation depends upon it.

REFERENCES

Ager, C., & Cole, C. (1991). *A review of cognitive-behavioral interventions for children and adolescents with behavioral disorders.* Behavioral Disorders, 16(4), 276-287.

Alberg, J., Petry, C., & Eller, A. (1994). *A resource guide for social skills instruction.* Longmont, CO: Sopris West.

Anderson, E. (1992). *Speaking with style: The sociolinguistics skills of children.* London: Routledge.

Baca, L., & Cervantes, H. (Eds.). (1984). *The bilingual special education interface.* St. Louis: Times Mirror/Mosby College Publishing.

Bain, A., & Farris, H. (1991). Teacher attitudes toward social skills training. *Teacher Education and Special Education, 14,* 49-56.

Bauer, A.M., & Sapona, R. (1991). *Managing classrooms to facilitate learning.* Boston: Allyn & Bacon.

Bender, W.N. (1995). *Learning disabilities: Characteristics, identification, and teaching strategies* (2nd ed.). Boston: Allyn & Bacon.

Bendtro, L.K., Brokenleg, M., & Van Brocken, S. (1990). *Reclaiming youth at risk: Our hope for the future.* Bloomington, IN: National Education Service.

Bogdan, R., & Biklen, D. (1977). Handicapism. *Social Policy, 7*(5), 59-63.

Bos, C.S., & Vaughn, S. (1994). *Strategies for teaching students with learning and behavior problems.* Boston: Allyn & Bacon.

Campbell, P., & Siperstein, G. (1994). *Improving social competence.* Boston: Allyn & Bacon.

Coie, J., Belding, M., & Underwood, M. (1988). Aggression and peer rejection in childhood. In B.B. Lahey & A. Kazdin (Eds.), *Advances in clinical child psychology.* New York: Plenum Press.

Coie, J., & Jacobs, M. (1993). The role of social context in the prevention of conduct disorder [Special Issue]. *Development and Pyschopathology, 5*(1/2), 263-276.

Combs, M.L., & Slaby, D. (1977). Social-skills training with children. In B.B. Lahey & A.E. Kazdin (Eds.), *Advances in clinical child psychology* (Vol. 1). New York: Plenum Press.

Crank, J.N., Deshler, D.D., & Schumaker, J.B. (1995). *Surface counseling.* Lawrence, KS: Edge Enterprises.

Cummins, J. (1986). Empowering minority students: A framework for intervention. *Harvard Educational Review, 56*(1), 18-36.

Dodge, K. (1980). Social cognition and children's aggressive behavior. *Child Development, 51,* 1162-1170.

Dodge, K. (1986). A social information processing model of social competence in children. In M. Perlmutter (Ed.), *Cognitive perspectives on children's social and behavioral development* (pp. 77-125). Hillsdale, NJ: Erlbaum.

Dodge, K., Coie, J., & Brakke, N. (1982). Behavior patterns of socially rejected and neglected adolescents. The roles of social approach and aggression. *Journal of Abnormal Child Psychology, 10,* 389-410.

Dodge, K., & Frame, C.L. (1982). Social cognitive biases and deficits in aggressive boys. *Child Development, 53*(3), 620-635.

Dodge, K., Pettit, G. S., McClaskey, C.L., & Brown, M. (1986). Social competence in children. *Monographs of the Society for Research in Child Development, 51*(I, Serial No. 213).

Downs, W.R., & Rose, S. (1991). The relationship of adolescent peer groups to the incidence of psychosocial problems. *Adolescence, 26,* 473-492.

Eisler, R.M., Hersen, M., Miller, P.M., & Blanchard, E.B. (1975). Situational determinants of assertive behaviors. *Journal of Consulting and Clinical Psychology, 43,* 330-340.

Ellis, E.S. (1991). *SLANT: A starter strategy for class participation.* Lawrence, KS: Edge Enterprises.

Ellis, E.S., Deshler, D.D., Lenz, B.K., Schumaker, J.B., & Clark, F.L. (1991). An instructional model for teaching learning strategies. *Focus on Exceptional Children, 23*(6), 1-23.

Fagan, S.A., Long, N.J., & Stevens, D. (1975). *Teaching children self-control.* Columbus, OH: Merrill.

Hoy, C., & Gregg, N. (1994). *Assessment: The special educator's role.* Pacific Grove, CA: Brooks/Cole.

Hollinger, J. (1987). Social skills for behaviorally disordered children as preparation for mainstreaming: Theory, practice, and new directions. *Remedial and Special Education, 8*(4), 17-27.

Kammeyer, K.C.W., Ritzer, G., & Yetman, N.T. (1990). *Sociology: Experiencing changing societies.* Boston: Allyn and Bacon.

Kasen, S., Johnson, J., & Cohen, P. (1990). The impact of school emotional climate on student psychopathology. *Journal of Abnormal Child Psychology, 18,* 165-177.

Kavale, K.A., & Forness, S.R. (1996). Social skill deficits and learning disabilities: A meta-analysis. *Journal of Learning Disabilities, 29,* 226-237.

Kazdin, A. (Ed.). (1985). *Treatment of antisocial behavior in children and adolescents.* Pacific Grove, CA: Brooks/Cole.

Kazdin, A. (1987). *Conduct disorders in childhood and adolescence.* London: Sage.

Ladd, G., & Oden, S. (1979). The relationship between peer acceptance and children's ideas about helpfulness. *Child Development, 50,* 402-408.

Lakoff, R. (1977). What can you do with words: Politeness, pragmatics, and performatives. In A. Rogers, B. Wall, & J. Murphy (Eds.), *Proceedings of the Texas conference on performatives presupposition, and implications.* Arlington, VA: Center for Applied Linguistics.

Lenz, B.K., Marris, R.W., Schumaker, J.B., & Deshler, D.D. (1993). *The lesson organizer routine.* Lawrence, KS: Edge Enterprises.

McFall, R. (1982). A review and reformulation of the concept of social skills. *Behavioral Assessment, 4,* 1-33.

McLaren, P. (1989). *An introduction to critical pedagogy in the foundations of education.* New York: Longman.

Omark, P., & Erickson, J. (Eds.). (1983). *The bilingual exceptional child.* San Diego: College-Hill Press.

O'Neill, R.E., Horner, R.H., Albin, R.W., Sprague, J.R., Storey, K., & Newton, J.S. (1997). *Functional assessment and program development for problem behavior: A practical handbook.* Pacific Grove, CA: Brooks/Cole.

Patterson, G.R., Reid, J.B., & Dishion, T.J. (1992). *Antisocial boys: Vol. 4. A social interactional approach.* Eugene, OR: Castalia.

Rinn, R.C., & Markle, A. (1979). Modification of skill deficits in children. In A.S. Belleck & M. Hersen (Eds.), *Research and practice in social skills training.* New York: Plenum Press.

Scanlon, D. (1996). Social skills strategy Instruction. In D.D. Deshler, E.S. Ellis, & B.K. Lenz (Eds.), *Teaching adolescents with learning disabilities: Strategies and methods* (pp. 369-408). Denver, CO: Love Publishing Company.

Schunk, D.H. (1989). Social cognitive theory and self-regulated learning. In B.J. Zimmerman & D.H. Schunk (Eds.), *Self-regulated learning and academic achievement: Theory, research, and practice* (pp. 83-110). New York: Springer-Verlag.

Schunk, D.H. (1990). Goal setting and self-efficacy during self-regulated learning. *Educational Psychologist, 25,* 71-86.

Thorson, S. (1996). The missing link: Students discuss school discipline. *Focus on Exceptional Children, 29*(3), 1-2.

Van Reusen, A.K., Bos, C.S., Schumaker, J.B., & Deshler, D.D. (1987). *The education planning strategy.* Lawrence, KS: Edge Enterprises.

Van Reusen, A.K., Bos, C.S., Schumaker, J.B., & Deshler, D.D. (1994). *The self-advocacy strategy for education and transition planning.* Lawrence, KS: Edge Enterprises.

Vaughn, S., & Hogan, A. (1990). Social competence and learning disabilities: A prospective study. In H.L. Swanson & B.K. Keogh (Eds.), *Learning disabilities: Theoretical and research issues* (pp. 175-191). Hillsdale, NJ: Erlbaum.

Vernon, D.S., Schumaker, J.B., & Deshler, D.D. (1993). *The SCORE skills: Social skills for cooperative groups.* Lawrence, KS: Edge Enterprises.

Walker, H.M., Colvin, G., & Ramsey, E. (1995). *Antisocial behavior in school: Strategies and best practices* (p. 157). Pacific Grove, CA: Brooks/Cole.

Walker, H.M., Schwarz, I.E., Nippold, M., Irvin, L.K., & Noell, J. (1994). Social skills in school-aged children and youth: Issues and best practices in assessment and intervention. In M. Nippold (Ed.), *Topics in language disorders: Pragmatics and social skills in school age children and adolescents, 14*(3), 70-82.

Whitaker, J. H., & Prieto, A.G. (1989). The effects of cultural and linguistic variables on the academic achievement of minority children. *Focus on Exceptional Children, 21*(5), 1-10.

Wong-Fillmore, L. (1991). Second-language learning in children: A model of language learning in social context. In E. Bialystok (Ed.), *Language processing in bilingual children* (pp. 49-69). Cambridge, England: Cambridge University Press.

Zaragoza, N., Vaughn, S., & McIntosh, R. (1991). Social skills interventions and children with behavior problems: A review. *Behavioral Disorders, 16*(4), 260-275.

Zimmerman, B.J. (1994). Dimensions of academic self-regulation: A conceptual framework for education. In D.H. Schunk, & B.J. Zimmerman (Eds.), *Self-regulation of learning and performance: Issues and educational applications* (pp. 3-21). Hillsdale, NJ: Erlbaum.

CHAPTER FOUR

Enhancing Assignment Completion for Academically Diverse Learners

JOYCE A. RADEMACHER, University of North Texas

Many teachers are concerned over the growing number of students who fail to complete their assignments satisfactorily. Teachers often complain that assignment completion rates are low and that the quality of work that *is* turned in "on time" by their students is very poor. Failure to complete assignments is a major factor contributing to the poor academic performance and school failure of youth at risk and youth with disabilities (Davis, 1984; England & Flately, 1985; Gajria & Salend, 1995; Salend & Schliff, 1988). Poor assignment completion is also cited as being a criterion for student referral to special education programs (Bay & Bryan, 1992). The motivation and ability of students to complete assigned work are important because assignments represent a major vehicle for the mastery of content presented by their teachers.

As students move into secondary schools, they are increasingly expected to practice skills and content independently by completing a number of assignments outside of class. While during the elementary years, much time is spent in classrooms on practice activities to enhance the skills and knowledge being taught, the nature of secondary classrooms is such that teachers deliver instruction without allowing time for students to begin their work in class. These teachers may assume two things with regard to their pre-established assignment completion procedures. First, they may assume that the type of work they are giving will be acceptable to their students. Second they may assume that their students have the wherewithal to do it. Unfortunately, many students do not value the kind of work they are expected to do, and they attach little meaning to it (Glasser, 1991). Additionally, many students lack effective and efficient assignment completion strategies for completing the work.

Teacher concern over the lack of student interest in schoolwork prompted the U.S. Department of Education to identify student motivation as one of its top research priorities for the 1990s (Cross, 1990). Apathy is high among students who often complain that the schoolwork they are expected to do is boring and has little relevance to their lives. In classrooms where the work they are expected to do is acceptable, you see highly motivated students who are looking forward to the task, asking about it, and showing a willingness to participate in it (Adelman & Taylor, 1983). According to Griffin (1988), teachers can create conditions that stimulate a desire to learn and grow and that consistently invite students to be motivated. Planning motivating assignments that meet the needs and interests of students is possible and necessary in order to enhance learning for all students in the class.

Teachers are also concerned over the number of students who fail to finish their work because they lack the necessary skills and strategies to do an adequate job (Delquadri, Greenwood, Whorton, Carta, & Hall, 1986; Deshler, Schumaker, Alley, Warner, & Clark, 1983). For example, some adolescents with learning disabilities (LD), and those at risk for school failure, may read below grade level, have difficulty expressing their thoughts and ideas in writing, and/or lack important organizational skills for completing tasks (Putnam, Deshler, & Schumaker, 1992). However, the challenge of responding to the needs of a diverse group of students extends beyond special education students who are included for long periods of time in general education. Teachers must also differentiate assignments to meet the needs of students achieving in the average, above-average, and below-average range of academic performance as measured by teacher, school district, and state academic standards. This performance diversity may be attributed to individual differences among students in learning needs, culture, gender, life experiences, abilities, skills, language proficiency, beliefs, goals, personal characteristics or orientation, or values (Vance, 1995). Explaining assignments to academically diverse classes of students in a structured way is important and necessary so that students, who lack effective and efficient strategies for completing their work, will know what to do and how to do it in order to complete their assignments fully and correctly.

Throughout this chapter you will have an opportunity to visit Mr. Paxton, a 10th-grade social studies teacher, and meet some of his students. Mr. Paxton teaches in an economically, linguistically, and racially diverse urban school. He was once quite frustrated over the fact that his students failed to complete their assignments satisfactorily, thus they were falling farther and farther behind. However, Mr. Paxton learned routines for helping his students become more successful assignment completion strategists. Let's go back in time to see what you may have observed in three separate visits to Mr. Paxton's class *last year* (before he learned a better way to plan, present, and evaluate assignments with his students).

First Visit. The first time you visit Mr. Paxton's class, you note that he knows his content well and enjoys teaching. He tells you that his classes have grown in number from an average of 25 to 32 students since the beginning of the school year. He can depend on about one fourth of his students to pass with little or no difficulty. The remaining students in his classes vary in performance from average to low. Among the total group in this class, one student is gifted and talented, three students have specific learning disabilities, three have limited English proficiency, and two have serious emotional/behavioral problems that cause disruption for the class at times. Mr. Paxton states that he relies on various support teachers in the building to provide modified tests and assignments for these nine students.

As the students enter the classroom, they take their seats and wait for class to begin. Mr. Paxton lectures most of the period while the students take notes. As a traditional long-term assignment for each unit of study, Mr. Paxton passes out a packet of about 20 photocopied worksheets for students to complete before the exam. The worksheets consist of multiple-choice questions, and short essay and discussion questions that accompany chapters in the book. He tells the students to turn the packets in right before taking the test. Shortly before the bell rings, Mr. Paxton jots down a page number or two on the board to indicate pages from the packet that he wants the students to finish before class the next day. Some students copy the page numbers down in an assignment book, and others rely on their memory to remind them to complete the worksheets before papers are to be exchanged in class for grading the next day. Mr. Paxton tells you that on the following day, after the papers have been graded, he will have the students call out their grades as he records them in his grade book.

Second Visit. The second time you visit Mr. Paxton's class, he gives the students a list of assignments to choose from that relate to a topic of study. He passes around a sign-up sheet, and each student is told to select a different assignment. The assignment list is interesting, but the directions on how to complete the various assignments are not very clear. One student is dissatisfied because the assignment she wanted to do was already chosen by another student before the list came around to her. Mr. Paxton tells the students that once they finish their assignments, they will share them during class. One of the students invites you to visit on the day the students are to share their final products.

Third Visit. The third time you visit Mr. Paxton's class, it is to watch the students present their completed assignments. You and Mr. Paxton both notice that some of the students have performed high-quality work, while others appear to have exerted little effort. After their presentations, Mr. Paxton reflects on some of the students' apathetic attitudes toward assignment completion. He is quite bothered by the fact that over the past few semesters a high number of his students failed to turn their assignments in on time and/or complete them satisfactorily. He attributes this fact to the diversity among his students, yet he is unsure about what to do about it. While he cares deeply about his students and their success, he is uncertain about how to differentiate assignments for students in order to meet their individual needs.

As you can probably see, Mr. Paxton was in a quandary over how to best meet the needs of all of his students. Fortunately, much has been learned in recent years about student motivation and strategic instruction that can improve assignment completion procedures for teachers and students. As you proceed through the chapter, you will see that Mr. Paxton learned to rely on the integration of a number of approaches to teaching and learning that made a big difference in his life and in the lives of his students. Specifically, teachers can enhance learning for students through classroom assignments by: (1) planning assignments that all students can successfully complete and that are motivating; (2) presenting assignments to students in such a way that they know what to do and how to do it in order to complete an assignment to a high level of quality; (3) evaluating finished products in such a way that students understand how they performed and how they might improve in the future; and (4) integrating technology as a tool to enhance planning, presenting, and evaluating of assignment-completion experiences

PLANNING HIGH-QUALITY ASSIGNMENTS

The Current Nature of Secondary Assignments

Content-related assignments given in secondary classrooms consist of three types (Lenz, Ehren, & Smiley, 1991). The first type of assignment is a *study* assignment which requires students to prepare for a test or some type of class activity. These assignments focus on the process that students must go through to independently find, manipulate, and remember content information; they may not always end in a final product. An example of a study assignment would be to complete an outline of important information the teacher previously presented in class and then study for a test.

The second type of assignment, the *daily work* assignment, is characterized by routine follow-up activities designed to promote practice and understanding of the content. Examples of daily work assignments would be the completion of questions or worksheets.

The third type of assignment, a *project* assignment, usually spans multiple days and often requires that the student extend or apply the content. Examples of project assignments include reports, themes, visuals, product, and/or presentations. Although these three types of assignments fall into separate categories according to their distinct features, they are not mutually exclusive in that each sometimes accomplishes multiple purposes.

Each of these three types of assignments can be completed individually, with a partner, or in a group, depending upon teacher expectations. These assignments can be further categorized according to where students are expected to complete them. Specifically, assignments completed inside the classroom are considered *seatwork* assignments, whereas assignments completed outside of the classroom are classified as *homework* assignments (Paschal, 1988).

Characteristics of Seatwork Assignments. Gartland and Rosenberg (1987) described seatwork engagement as academic learning time. They argued that these instances of academic learning time can only be meaningful if students work on attaining new learning through assignments that are appropriately matched to their assessed strengths and weaknesses. However, Jorgenson (1977) reported that seatwork assignments are often too difficult for students. Similarly, Anderson (1984), noted that many low-performing students do not always understand the purpose of assignments, and therefore, often focus on finishing an assignment for the sake of getting it done rather than learning important content.

Doyle and Carter (1984), on the other hand, discovered that students are often expected to perform low-level, routine work. This type of work is presented through daily worksheets that require students to perform simple operations of word recognition through matching, reproduction of simple lists from chapter information, and practice on isolated skills not appropriately matched with important content; thus, little emphasis is placed on developing content understanding or meaningful applications through daily assignments. This research leads us to believe that the type of assignments given to many students in secondary classrooms may lack challenge and interest.

Dougherty and Barth (1997) maintain that poor and minority children, in particular, may be exposed to low-level assignments that are often boring. These researchers provide us with a snapshot of two typical assignments that were gathered from two separate secondary classrooms. In one city, eighth-graders were studying a social studies chapter on colonialism. The teacher wanted to give them an assignment that would build their reading comprehension and vocabulary based on new terms used in the chapter. She did not ask them to write their own definitions. Rather, students were asked to copy the definitions for the 12 words from the chapter's glossary. These 13- and 14-year-olds were then required to draw a picture for each word. The list included such words as "deism" and "smuggling."

The second assignment gathered by the researchers was from an eleventh-grade social studies class. The teacher assigned a "major project" about a famous person of their choice. Each student was supposed to spend an entire month studying a historical figure in depth. The culminating task, intended to show the results of the student's month long study, was to photocopy a picture of the person they had selected and glue it in the center of a poster board. They were then to write one or two sentences in each of the four corners summarizing what they had learned about the historical figure. The poster was the final grade for a five-week unit. Students who turned it in earned an A or B. Final products from the students consisted of a picture and five disconnected sentences.

When looking collectively at the kinds of assignments given to students in high-poverty schools, the researchers concluded that they shared four common characteristics. First, grades were based on process, not product. For example, if students turned in a neatly produced paper by using the computer, they would get an A or B with little consideration for how their work addressed the content. Second, assignments rarely required research and its accompanying documentation and citation. While bibliographies were seen, they were rarely embedded into the paper. It was also discovered that whole paragraphs were copied from outside resources without proper citations.

A third assignment characteristic noted by Dougherty and Barth (1997) was that high school students are routinely given easy assignments with little relevance. For example, they were asked to keep volumes of journals that had no explicit learning purpose, and consequently had nothing in them to show academic growth. Likewise, math assignments required students to do pages of computation and short story problems without real-world analysis or application.

The fourth observable characteristic had to do with assignment topics. For example, reading material was limited to textbooks or mediocre literary works. Writing topics required only reiteration, or description, with little opportunity for independent thinking. Additionally, science assignments consisted of multiple worksheets. While such accounts of school life are disheartening, there is hope that all students can learn to high levels when they are taught to high levels. If our goal is to close the achievement gap among diverse learners, taking a closer look at how to create better assignments that are linked to meaningful content seems a viable option.

Characteristics of Homework Assignments. Lee and Pruitt (1979) developed a conceptual model for classifying homework assignments. They set forth four major categories based on the purpose of the assignment in relation to learning the content: practice, preparation, extension, or creation. Practice assignments are designed to help students master specific skills and to reinforce material presented in class. Preparation assignments are intended to provide students with the necessary skills and/or knowledge for upcoming lessons. Extension assignments are those given to assist students in transferring new skills and ideas to new situations; extension assignments frequently require abstract thinking skills. Finally, creative assignments allow students to cleverly integrate many skills and ideas to produce a product. Creation assignments often take more time to complete, resulting in students working on the assignment over several days or weeks. In developing these categories, Lee and Pruitt (1979) determined that homework is most effective if it allows students to extend their knowledge and be creative in the way they manipulate the content.

In a national study on teachers' homework practices, Connors (1991) found that only a minority of classroom assignments met the criteria specified by Lee and Pruitt (1979). Specifically, she administered a questionnaire on homework practices to 1,079 middle school teachers, 80% of whom represented 22 different states. Survey results revealed that the majority of middle-level teachers assigned only practice and preparation assignments. She also concluded that practice homework is often boring, dull, repetitive, and unimaginative. Connors (1991) recommended that students have an opportunity to apply their learning in a personal way rather than go through a daily ritual of completing worksheets aimed at completing simple problems or memorizing facts. Likewise, the most common form of homework—requiring students to read a chapter and answer questions at the end—is generally not enticing for students. Instead, Connors recommended that teachers be innovative in their approach to homework by getting students excited about the content, using students' suggestions, providing options, and not relying heavily on the textbook. While this study revealed the poor quality of homework assignments, the majority of respondents polled believed that homework had the potential of increasing academic achievement.

Palardy (1995) reported that in addition to its academic benefits, teachers assign homework because it teaches self-discipline. Additionally, he reported that while homework can fulfill people's expectations and expand the curriculum, it also has its associated problems. Problems with homework include completion difficulties, uncoordinated assignments, interference with important out-of-school activities, fostering of undesirable student behaviors and attitudes toward the assignment completion process, uniform assignments for all students, and the lack of teacher feedback (Palardy, 1995).

Struyk, Epstein, Bursuck, Polloway, McConegy, and Cole (1995) conducted a study to examine the homework, grading, and testing practices used by teachers for students with and without disabilities. The study was prompted by teachers and researchers who were concerned about the integration of larger numbers of students with disabilities into general education classrooms at a time when reformers were calling for an increase in academic standards and accountability in those classrooms (Holcutt, Martin, & McKinney, 1990; Kauffman, 1989; Schumaker & Deshler, 1988). Given the fact that adolescents with disabilities receive about 60% of their academic credits in general education classrooms (Valdes, Williamson, & Wagner, 1990), it seemed appropriate to determine what secondary school teachers were doing in regard to homework practices.

Of the 352 teachers who returned the survey on homework practices, 76 were middle school teachers and 67 were high school teachers. Results indicated that homework is an integral component of general education curriculum and must be addressed if inclusion programs are to be beneficial to students with disabilities. It was learned that homework is typically assigned on a daily basis, and that the amount increases as students progress through the grades. Thus, one assumes that if each secondary teacher assigns homework daily, students who have four or five teachers may have from two to three hours of homework nightly (Struyk et al., 1995).

According to the teachers in this study, the predominant reasons for assigning homework to students were to practice skills already taught, to prepare for tests, and to complete unfinished classwork. Practice assignments appeared to be most helpful if assignments were designed to reinforce material learned in class so that students with disabilities could maintain newly learned skills. Enrichment activities and preparation for future class work were rated least helpful. Using a homework assignment sheet was also noted by the teachers to be very useful. While general education teachers indicated that they were responsible for adjusting homework assignments, only 25% of the teachers in the study had taken special education classes that focused on adapting materials, and only 30% had participated in inservice activities relating to adaptations.

Checkley (1997), in a review of homework practices, claims that research supports a correlation between homework and student achievement and the development of critical skills. She also reports that there is agreement among educators that homework can help instill in students a sense of responsibility, accountability, motivation, and self-confidence. She concludes that homework for the modern age must be an approach that respects the lives of students. Such an approach would include the following: (1) multiple ways to complete an assignment; (2) ensuring students have access to every resource necessary to complete assignments; (3) opportunities to relate assignments to real life situations; (4) ways for students to record their daily assignments and plan for assignment completion; and, (5) coordination with parents in the planning and execution of meaningful and interesting assignments. Homework can be a powerful way to extend learning beyond the classroom if each of these conditions are in place.

IMPROVING THE NATURE OF SECONDARY ASSIGNMENTS

Fortunately, much has been learned in recent years that can guide teacher efforts to plan highly motivating assignments that their students will accept as meaningful and enjoyable. While the curriculum defines general parameters for what is to be taught, only teachers can determine what skills and knowledge must be emphasized as the content of a particular assignment. Additionally, when students perceive assignment completion to be meaningful, personally relevant, interesting and fun, and if the context supports and encourages personal control, then motivation to learn and self-regulation of the learning process occurs naturally (McCombs & Whistler, 1989).

Considering the Content of Course Assignments. If each assignment is not linked to information to be learned in a particular unit of study, it is "busy work." Therefore, choosing the content of a particular assignment requires you to first examine the bigger chunk of learning to be completed and identify the most important pieces. Then, it is possible to identify the knowledge and skills that will be the target of the assignment. Rademacher, Deshler, Schumaker, and Lenz (1998) recommend the following steps to aid in the selection of assignments that will more likely engage students in meaningful ways.

1. Survey the content of the course and identify the big ideas and what is critical for all students to know. Create questions for a unit of study that reflect your decision. In other words, what do you want all students to be able to answer once the unit is complete?
2. Identify the structure of the information into a graphic representation, such as a content map that represents how you want students to think about the information. Place the big ideas at the top with the supporting categories that support the big ideas underneath.
3. Analyze your map and determine what knowledge (e.g. identifying the causes of the Revolutionary war, explaining the social conditions during the Depression) and what skills (e.g., writing a paragraph, multiplying decimals, locating resources in a library) need to be reinforced through extra practice in the form of an assignment.

Preparing Individual Assignments. Once you have decided what content you want to reinforce through the use of assignments, you are ready to create a plan for each assignment that is different than the traditional worksheet format. While worksheets are appropriate on many occasions, students can become bored and uninterested in schoolwork if that is the only way to express what they have learned. The following questions are recommended to guide your decisions. Ask yourself:

1. *What do I want students to accomplish as a result of finishing this assignment?* (For example, you may want them to *know* the phases of the digestive system, or you may want them to *apply* their knowledge of the digestive process.)

2. *How will students accomplish what I intend for them to do in an interesting way?* (For example, to show they know the steps of the digestive system, they may *label* the parts of the digestive system on a diagram and then *explain* the function of each part to the class. Or, you may have students *solve* a real-life problem related to which part of the digestive system is not working.)

3. *Why is it important for students to know what I am assigning them to do?* (For example, knowing and understanding the function of the digestive system is important for understanding how the whole body functions and grows. Understanding the digestive system is important for good health and promoting healthy eating habits. Identifying the benefits of the assignment to students' lives is a recommended component of motivating them to actually complete the assignment.)

Since its original development in the 1950s, Bloom's Taxonomy (Bloom, 1956) has been one of the most widely used systems for describing students' higher level thinking processes. There are six levels in the Taxonomy that are arranged in a hierarchy from simple to more complex. The thinking required within each broad category is as follows: *Knowledge* demands the recall of facts and information; *Comprehension* requires showing understanding through acquired knowledge; *Application* involves adapting and applying known information; *Analysis* includes breaking material down in component parts; *Synthesis* is concerned with putting information together in a new way; and, *Evaluation* has to do with judging the outcome of a particular event or situation. Understanding what students are required to do within each of the Bloom's thinking level categories can help you plan more challenging and interesting assignments.

Figure 1, the Assignment Idea Web, was created to help you plan

Figure 1: Assignment Idea Web

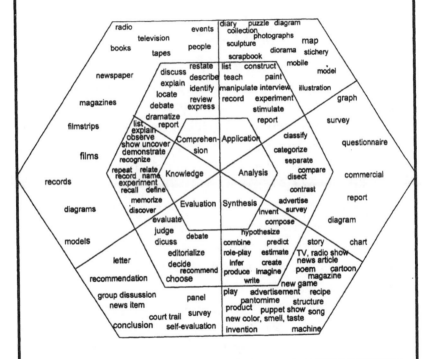

Information in the center and second section of this web was adapted from *Taxonomy of Educational Objective for the Cognitive Domain* (Bloom, 1956).

interesting assignments in each of the six thinking domains. The center part of the web depicts each of the six thinking domains according to Bloom (1956). The center part of the web lists thinking processes students may go through if they are expected to perform a particular task in one of the domains. The outside section of the web gives interesting assignment ideas that will match each domain and thinking requirement.

Adapting Assignments to Student Interests and Needs

Getting to Know Your Students. Implicit in the literature is the assumption that motivation plays a crucial role in academic success (Mehring & Colson, 1990). Many educators contend that motivation affects learning and learning affects motivation (Sprinthall & Sprinthall, 1987). Student motivation to learn is high in classes of diverse learners when students function as members of learning communities. Researchers at the University of Kansas Center for Research on Learning maintain that "learning communities" exist when students learn within a cooperative, diverse, interdependent group. There are three basic assumptions related to forming learning communities for the types of diverse learners we met in Mr. Paxton's class (Vance, 1995).

The first assumption is that teachers will make every effort to develop and use mechanisms to get to know and to form relationships with each member of the learning community. Clearly, the goal of getting to know students is something that most teachers value. Initial information can be gathered in a beginning-of-the-year questionnaire that students might complete for homework or as a seatwork assignment.

- Name, nicknames
- Parent or caregiver (s) names
- Siblings' names and birth order
- Towns and states in which the student has lived
- Places the student has visited

- Hobbies and interests
- Pets
- Most favorite activities outside of school
- Most favorite kinds of assignments
- Student's current job
- Involvement in school activities student would like to experience
- What the student expects to learn
- Concerns the student has about the course
- Things that help the student learn

For students who may have difficulty completing a written questionnaire due to limited English proficiency, an individual interview may be conducted. The following year after your earlier visits to Mr. Paxton's room, he decided that he would have his students work in pairs to complete an informational form. Each person then introduced his or her partner to the class and shared some of the personal information with the group.

The second assumption (Vance, 1995) in forming a learning community is that teachers will take time to know their students as individuals, which means to gain an appreciation of the commonalties and differences among students in terms of learning needs, culture, world view, life experiences, skills, language proficiency, beliefs, goals, personal characteristics, and values. In terms of cultural differences, this is especially important because, by the year 2000, the minority population will increase from 39% to 50% in the public schools (Quality Education for Minorities Project, 1990). By the year 2010, people of color will be a majority in Texas, New York, and Florida (U.S. Census Bureau, 1992). The more information we have about a student's cultural group, the easier it will be to personalize instruction.

In the ideal learning community, students and teachers will learn to accept and appreciate one another's differences, while also recognizing the commonalties we share. Dean, Salend, & Taylor (1993) recommends that teachers emphasize the following points in classrooms where cultural diversity prevails: (1) Every culture is important within the total group. (2) There are similarities, as well as differences, among cultures. (3) Cultures are better understood when they are an integral and ongoing part of the curriculum. (4) Cultural stereotyping is avoided because individual behavior varies within cultures. (5) Families and individuals experience their culture in personal ways.

The third assumption (Vance, 1995) for forming positive learning communities is that teachers will use their knowledge of students to plan and implement instruction and assignments that are inclusive and responsive to diverse learning needs within the community. If educational equity is to exist within the learning community, teachers must apply effective teaching strategies that capitalize on the unique learning and social characteristics of each individual.

Platt and Olson (1997) offer the following techniques to help meet the needs of adolescents from all cultures who may be at risk:

(1) Personalize instruction and assignments so that attention, support, and recognition is possible.
(2) Emphasize the importance and relevance of studying a particular topic and its link to the world of work.
(3) Give well-structured assignments that can be completed in cooperative groups.
(4) Offer a variety of ways to demonstrate learning so as to cater to numerous learning styles and ability levels.
(5) Evaluate student progress on assignments and give timely and frequent feedback.
(6) Base grades on other demonstrations of knowledge other than traditional paper and pencil examinations.
(7) Give concrete examples and/or models of new kinds of assignments students may be expected to complete.

Applying Multiple Intelligences. Some educators find Gardner's Theory of Multiple Intelligences (MI; Gardner, 1983) helpful in making their students more well-rounded, making school more engaging and motivating, and enabling more students to succeed.

Psychologist Howard Gardner, in his book, *Frames of Mind* (1983), argued that our traditional conception of intelligence—as primarily linguistic and logical abilities—is too narrow, and that all human beings actually have seven distinct intelligences. His definition of intelligence is "the ability to solve problems or to create products, that are valued within one or more cultural settings" (Gardner, 1993, p. 37). By cultivating a broad range of the seven distinct intelligences, teachers can uncover hidden strengths among students who may not excel at verbal or mathematical tasks. Thus, a multiple intelligences approach to teaching and learning recognizes and respects the different ways in which students learn and are assessed. Figure 2, Planning Assignments Based on Multiple Intelligence Theory, lists each of the seven intelligences, an explanation of each, and example assignments that may be constructed based on a particular type of intelligence.

Figure 2
Planning Assignments Based on Multiple Intelligence Theory

Course: *English*   Unit: *Prejudice*

Type of Intelligence	Definition	Example Assignments
Spatial	The ability to perceive the visual-spatial world accurately and to perform transformations upon one's perceptions	Work with artistic media (paints, clay, colored markers, pens, etc.) to express an idea or opinion; for example, what you think the 21st century will look like without prejudice. Visualize yourself in a different period of history and have an imaginary conversation on prejudice with someone from that time.
Bodily-Kinesthetic	Expertise in using one's whole body to express ideas and feelings, and facility in using one's hands to produce or transform things	Design and play a game of charades using common statements or comments surrounding prejudice. Play non-competitive games that involve physical activity and a lot of motion; for example, learn names of historical figures that have had an impact combating prejudice and use pantomime and/or physical gestures for others to identify them.

Figure 2 (Continued)

Type of Intelligence	Definition	Example Assignments
Musical	The capacity to perceive, discriminate, transform, and express musical forms	Use singing to express an idea; for example, rewrite the words of a popular tune to tell a story about a family that has experienced prejudice. Create a rap to practice a sequence of events to be remembered for a test on prejudice.
Linguistic	The capacity to use words effectively, either orally or in writing	Read a favorite story about prejudice and write a new ending. Make a speech on a topic surrounding prejudice about which you have a great deal of interest and excitement.
Logical-Mathematical	The capacity to use numbers effectively and to reason well	Create a convincing, rational explanation for something that is totally absurd; for example, the benefits of the square basketball in preventing prejudice during team games. Participate in an activity requiring use of the "scientific method"; for example, if you are not a cook, try making brownies from scratch following a recipe. Compare each ingredient and action to ingredients and actions that create human prejudice.
Interpersonal	The ability to perceive and make distinctions in the feelings, moods, intentions, and motivations of other people	Work with five members of a group to plan interesting assignments on prejudice for the class. Work with members of a class committee to design a mini workshop on sensitivity training to prevent prejudice.
Intrapersonal	Self-knowledge and the ability to act adaptively on the basis of that knowledge	Write a written reflection detailing your own prejudices and how they might be overcome. Identify your thinking strategies regarding ways to combat prejudice in the workplace.

Note: Intelligence types and definitions were adapted from *Multiple Intelligences in the Classroom* (Armstrong, 1994) and from *Seven Ways of Knowing* (Lazear, 1991)

It is important to note that the MI theory has broad implication for all children, including special education students, who participate in assignment completion activities in the general education setting. Because MI theory requires teachers to focus on what students *can* do in order to succeed in school, it is considered to be a growth paradigm. Thus, while acknowledging their learning difficulties, teachers who operate from this paradigm are more likely to regard students with special needs as basically healthy individuals who are able to achieve commensurately with their normally-achieving peers when given opportunities to do so (Armstrong, 1994). For example, while Jamie, a young man with autism, cannot communicate clearly, his teacher recognizes his gift of music. Billie, a student with LD, has great difficulty with reading and writing tasks, but his teacher gives him opportunities to exhibit his special drawing and designing gifts. Amy, a young adolescent with mental retardation, has great difficulty with abstract thinking tasks, but her teacher expounds upon her acting ability. And Juan, a student with cerebral palsy, has difficulty with motor tasks, but his teacher capitalizes on his exceptional linguistic and logical-mathematical aptitude.

Assessing the multiple intelligences of your students is possible through informal inventories, such as the "Checklist for Assessing Students' Multiple Intelligences" (Armstrong, 1994). Other ways to gather information about your students' multiple intelligences include keeping anecdotal records, looking at school records, talking with other teachers, talking with parents, setting up special activities and observing student participation, and asking the students themselves. Students are the ultimate experts on how they learn best. Many resources are available through the Internet to help teachers apply multiple intelligence theory in their classrooms.

Integrating Learning Styles with Multiple Intelligences. Another factor to consider when planning assignments is students' learning styles. Learning styles are students' individual approaches to learning. Over the years, you have probably developed at least one way of learning that seems to work best for you. This way of learning is your learning style. You may also have realized that you move from one learning style to another, depending on the task.

Most learning-style theory has its roots in the psychoanalytic community while multiple intelligence theory is the fruit of cognitive science. Whereas learning styles theory is primarily concerned with the personal *process* of learning, multiple intelligence theory centers on the *content* and *products* of learning (Silver, Strong, & Perini, 1997). Considering both styles and intelligences when planning assignments can help students learn in many ways.

Various informal tests may be administered to determine a students' learning style preference and make instructional recommendations. For example, if a student is considered to be a "visual learner," instruction that stresses visually oriented materials and techniques is recommended. Mercer and Mercer (1998) report that while this approach has been used in special education for many years, it is beginning to gain momentum in general education.

Silver, Strong, and Perini (1997) reviewed the work of a number of learning style researchers. They concluded that even though learning style theorists interpret the personality in different ways, they have two things in common. First, learning style models are concerned with how individuals absorb information, think about information, and evaluate the results. Second, learning is a personal, individualized act of thought and feeling. In addition to these two commonalties, most learning style advocates agree that all of us practice a mixture of styles as we live and learn, and that our styles flex and adapt to various contexts.

Research on the effectiveness of learning style theory is mixed. While it is recommended that educators not rely heavily on formal tests to determine learning style strengths and weaknesses, it is helpful to know your students' learning style preference and the conditions under which the preference exists (Mercer & Mercer, 1998). One way to classify learning styles is according to four modality preferences: visual, auditory, tactile, and kinesthetic. The major benefit in learning about your student's modality preferences is so that you can align assignments to the way(s) in which they prefer to learn, thus increasing motivation to complete a task.

For example, individuals who are *visual* learners recall what they see, follow written or drawn directions well, and learn by observing people, objects, and pictures. Visual learners may prefer assignments that allow them to use computer graphics, perform visual puzzles, look at or design maps, charts, graphs, diagrams, cartoons, posters, or bulletin boards. *Auditory* learners recall what they hear, follow spoken instructions, and learn by listening and speaking. Assignments for auditory learners may include talking, interviewing, debating, participating on a panel, asking and answering questions, or making oral reports. *Tactile* learners recall what they touch, follow instructions they write or touch, and learn by manipulating objects. Appealing assignments for tactile learners might be sketching, playing board games, building models, constructing dioramas and relief maps, setting up experiments, or tracing objects and information. *Kinesthetic* learners, on the other hand, recall what they experience, follow instructions that they perform or rehearse, and learn when engaged in physical activity. These types of learners may prefer playing floor games, assembling or disassembling objects, building models, participating in fairs, setting up experiments, acting, or role playing.

McCarthy (1996) studied the work of several researchers to develop the 4MAT System, a model of learning styles. The 4MAT System is a four-quadrant model of teaching to four different learning styles using right- and left-mode techniques. The incorporation of right- and left- mode techniques take into account how the two halves of the brain process information. For example, certain kinds of processing seems to favor the right mode: visuospatial, holistic, gestalt, subjective. Certain other kinds of processing favor the left mode: analytic, sequential, discrete, objective. McCarthy (1982) claims that educators need to develop teaching methodologies that will effectively teach to *both* modes. A theoretical underpinning of this model is that human beings perceive and process information experience and information in different ways, and that our learning styles are formed by our own perceiving and processing.

The four types of learners as described in the 4MAT System

model include imaginative, analytic, common sense, and dynamic (McCarthy, 1992). *Imaginative* learners perceive information concretely and process it reflectively. They prefer to learn by sensing, feeling, and watching. *Analytic* learners perceive information abstractly and process it reflectively. They learn best by thinking and watching. *Common sense* learners perceive information abstractly and process it actively. Their choices for learning are thinking and doing. *Dynamic* learners perceive information concretely and process it actively. They prefer to learn by sensing, feeling, and doing. Informational resources and training opportunities for the 4MAT model are available on the Internet.

It is significant to note that proponents of multiple intelligences and learning styles theory acknowledge the importance of good, solid teaching skills. For example, McCarthy (1982) claims that it is important for teachers to select key concepts to be learned across a particular course or grade level. As educators who believe in these theories teach those concepts they will focus on how students learn and the unique qualities of each learner (Guild, 1997). Far too many students are not succeeding in school for a variety of reasons. Thus, application of multiple intelligences and learning theories through assignment planning offers more students an opportunity to learn and be successful.

Incorporating Choice Theory. Choice theory teaches that we are all driven by four psychological needs that are embedded in our genes: the need to belong, the need for power the need for freedom, and the need for fun (Glasser, 1998). According to Glasser, we have specific pictures in our minds of how we want these needs met. Each person's pictures are different depending on his/her personal experience. Choice Theory, once called Control Theory (Glasser, 1986) is being taught by many educators throughout the country who have participated in Quality School training provided by the William Glasser Institute. Many of Glasser's concepts of how to create a quality school can be found in The Quality School (1990) and in The Quality School Teacher (1994).

Clearly, Glasser focuses on what quality is, how we teach it, and how we influence ourselves and others to self-evaluate and improve upon what we do. Glasser's reference to quality classrooms and quality schoolwork gives us some insight on what assignment completion procedures are necessary in order to create quality classrooms and motivate students to produce quality schoolwork.

According to Giasser (1990), the basic human needs of students must be met in order for students to engage themselves in academic learning. He offered the following suggestions on how to build quality instructional settings that foster nurturance of the four basic needs of belonging, power, freedom, and fun. First, to help students develop a sense of belonging, Glasser suggested that teachers build caring, cooperative environments where teachers and students work together to improve their work. Second, to foster a sense of power, he recommends that teachers recognize students in positive ways, provide them with opportunities to be noticed and looked up to by their peers, and help them experience the feeling of power that results in doing a high-quality job. Third, to develop a sense of freedom, he recommended that teachers provide students with choices on what to learn, how to learn, and how to demonstrate competency on what they have learned. Finally, to develop a sense of fun, he recommended that teachers make learning fun by interjecting humor and laughter, and also provide assignments that are enjoyable and satisfying.

In reference to motivating students to do quality work, Glasser (1998) claims that we must focus on life skills — speaking, reading, writing, calculation, and problem solving because all of these things satisfy needs. Additionally, we must involve all students in quality learning and eliminate coercion and criticism. For example, the practice of forcing students to acquire knowledge or memorize facts that have little or no value in the real world should be eliminated. Grading practices should also be closely examined because multiple failures and low grades may cause students to rebel to the point that they quit working altogether. Our goal should be to nurture a love of lifelong learning in all students, not destroy it.

Another important aspect of encouraging quality work by students is to make them part of the decision-making process (Glasser, 1990). Involving students in the planning and self-evaluation of their finished work can cause students to have more power and control over their own learning. One way to do this is to have the students set a rubric for each of their assignments. Before turning in their work, students can show and explain their work, self-evaluate it according to the established rubric, improve it based on recommendations from peers and/or the teacher, and redo it for a quality grade.

Using the Content Enhancement Approach. In order to adopt a new set of assignment completion procedures for his diverse learners, Mr. Paxton decided to adopt an instructional routine, *The Quality Assignment Routine*, from the Content Enhancement series (Rademacher, Deshler, Schumaker, & Lenz, 1998). Content Enhancement is an approach to teaching that involves making decisions about what content to teach, manipulating and translating that content into easy-to-understand and easy-to-practice formats, and presenting it in memorable ways (see Chapter Two of this volume). As we learned at the beginning of our chapter, assignments represented a major vehicle for Mr. Paxton's students to learn content, yet many students failed to take advantage of this learning opportunity. As a result of his frustration, Mr. Paxton was determined to create assignments that were meaningful and more motivational for students. In addition, he concluded that he needed to structure his assignment directions in such a way that his students knew what to do in order to complete their assignments fully and correctly. Thus, to help him design more meaningful and motivating assignments, Mr. Paxton learned to use the planning component of *The Quality Assignment Routine*. The key phases of this routine are described in the paragraph below.

The planning procedures in *The Quality Assignment Routine* are based on what researchers proclaim to be the characteristics of assignments that secondary students enjoy completing. Importantly, it is also includes what *students* perceive to be the characteristics of a high-quality assignment. Prior to the development of the routine, academically diverse groups of middle school students were asked to participate in focus group discussions to identify the factors that contribute to student completion of assignments at high rates and high levels of quality (Rademacher, Schumaker, & Deshler, 1996). Some of the characteristics they described were identical to those noted in the literature. Also, students with and without learning disabilities were in close agreement on the importance of each of the following characteristics.

First, the **purpose** of the assignment needs to be clear, and students need to understand the benefits that are related to completing the assignment. In other words, the work needs to be seen as **authentic** work that will yield positive outcomes for the student. Second, the assignment needs to appear to be **personally relevant** for students in today's world. It needs to relate to their interests and concerns. Third, it needs to be **optimally challenging** to students; it should not be too hard or too easy. Students should feel that they can complete the assignment given what they consider to be a reasonable amount of effort. Fourth, it needs to represent **variety**. Too much of the same thing is deemed "boring" by students.

A fifth characteristic identified by students and teachers is that a great assignment allows students to use their **creativity**. Students enjoy opportunities to make personal investment in their work. Sixth, a great assignment promotes **interaction** among learners. Last, but *most importantly* according to students, it allows students to make **choices**. Students want a feeling of autonomy as they do their school work.

Additional factors that promote student completion of the assignment at high levels of quality were also identified by students. While these factors become important during the time an assignment is presented to students, they must be considered ahead of time so that nothing is omitted that will hinder successful completion by students. For example, **directions are clear and well organized**. In order for directions to be complete, they must include the **action steps** to do the work, the **supplies/resources** needed, the **grading criteria**, the **due date**, and the **point value** of the assignment. Also, during the planning process it is important for teachers to consider any **pitfalls** students might encounter on the assignment, as well as determine a date for when the finished assignment can be discussed.

Returning to Mr. Paxton's class, we see that during the planning process he tried to create interesting assignments that all students in the class could complete. This was a challenge, considering the diversity of his class. Thus, during the planning process, Mr. Paxton had to think about the interests and skills of his students, consider the problems they faced when they had to complete an assignment independently, and make adjustments accordingly. For example, he knew that the reading range in his class was from the fourth to above the twelfth grade level, that some had difficulty writing simple sentences while others were capable of writing long papers. He also knew that the support they received at home varied from none to a great deal.

However, with careful planning, Mr. Paxton thought he could allow students to select an appropriate book at their reading level and to choose among a variety of options with regard to reporting on the content of the book (e.g., presenting an oral report, writing an advertisement, or creating a test over the book content). With a little creativity, he believed he could make the assignment interesting and fun. As a result, the majority of students would not only be able to complete the assignment, they probably would enjoy the assignment. He realized that as more book reports were completed, more reading would be done. As more reading was done, students would become better readers, their vocabulary would grow, and they would become better learners. Thus, the whole purpose in taking time to plan assignments was to ensure that more of his students would engage in authentic academic tasks that would help them become better learners, more skilled, and more knowledgeable about the world.

Mr. Paxton followed four steps to create meaningful and motivating assignments for his students. The mnemonic device, "PLAN," was created to help him and other teachers remember each step of the planning process. He used The Quality Assignment Planning Sheet to guide his thinking through each of the "PLAN" steps. An example of the worksheet Mr. Paxton completed as he created an assignment as part of a unit on Ancient Greece is depicted in Figure 3 on the next page.

As you can see from Figure 3, the "P" step on the worksheet prompts teachers to **Plan the purpose of the assignment.** In thinking about the overall purpose, teachers ask themselves what students will accomplish as a result of completing the assignment (the knowledge or skill to be gained), how they will do this (how to accomplish the purpose specified), and why it is important (benefits to future learning in students' lives). Note how Mr. Paxton completed the "P" step on the worksheet in Figure 3.

The "L" step on the worksheet prompts teachers to **Link the assignment to student needs and interests.** To help with this step, teachers think of the acronym "HALO." "HALO" stands for *H*igh, *A*verage, or *L*ow performing students, and *O*ther students whose unique needs must be kept in mind in teacher planning. The four questions in this section of the worksheet cause teachers to think about the motivational factors that can be built into the assignment so that students will want to do it. The first question is, "How can this assignment be made *personally relevant* for students?" In other words, what choices can be given to the students or what elements can be built into the assignment so the assignment becomes more meaningful to students as a group or to each individual? To answer this question, consider choices that relate to the students' physical, intellectual, social, emotional, cultural interests or characteristics.

The second question in the "L" section of the planning sheet to be answered is "What are some personal *options/choices* I can offer students for completing the assignment?" In other words, what options exist for how the assignment is to be completed. Options may fall into the following categories: (1) format, such as choosing whether the final product is completed as a written report, an oral report, a diagram, a picture, a poster, or a role-play; (2) content, such as allowing students to select the assignment topic based upon their interests, or certain questions to answer and not answer; (3) location, such as choosing whether they will complete the assignment in the library, at home, or in study hall; (4) resources, such as allowing

Figure 3: The Quality Assignment Planning Sheet

COURSE __World History__
UNIT __Ancient Greece__

The *Quality* Assignment
Planning Worksheet

P — Plan the purpose of the assignment

1. WHAT WILL STUDENTS ACCOMPLISH?
Analyze why the ancient Greek culture was destroyed.

2. HOW WILL THEY DO THIS?
By creating a journal from the perspective of someone who lived in ancient Greece.

3. WHY IS THIS IMPORTANT? (BENEFITS)
So we can understand why such a highly developed civilization fell apart, and prevent the same thing from happening to our own civilization.

L — Link assignment to student needs & interests (HALO)

1. HOW CAN THE ASSIGNMENT BE MADE PERSONALLY RELEVANT FOR STUDENTS?
Choose 1 aspect of Greek life that interests you (e.g., sports, art, politics, religion)

2. PERSONAL CHOICES FOR VARIATION AND CHALLENGE?
With partner or by self; Diary or audio tape; Athens/Sparta

3. PITFALLS TO SUCCESSFUL COMPLETION OF WORK?
1. Diary format
2. Find/use tape recorders

4. SOLUTIONS TO THESE PITFALLS?
1. Show sample diary
2. Tell where to get/how to use tape recorders

A — Arrange clear student directions

ACTION STEPS
1. Choose interest
2. Review resources
3. Outline events
4. Create diary or tape recording

RESOURCES
Class notes
Textbooks
Library books
Magazine articles
Movies
Imaginations

GRADING CRITERIA (PACE 1, 2...)
1. 7 entries--put date
2. 3 statements/entry
3. choose 1 good & 1 bad thing @ your interest; write @ in ea. entry

DUE DATE   POINTS
May 18   100

N — Note evaluation date & results

DATE TO REVIEW ASSIGNMENT OUTCOMES
May 22

RESULTS
Common error: volume control on tape recorders needed to be louder. Instructions on volume control.

RESULTS
Students had difficulty completing on time. Next year, set an intermediate deadline for handing in outline of 7 days.

From: Rademacher, J.A., Deshler, D.D., Schumaker, J.B., & Lenz, B.K. (1998). *The quality assignment routine.* Lawrence, KS. Edge Enterprises.

students to use computers, encyclopedias, textbooks, imaginations, or other people; (5) amount of social interaction, such as allowing students to choose whether they complete the assignment by themselves, with a partner, or in a small group; and (6) the due date, which means allowing students to choose from one or two announced dates by which all or part of the assignment must be turned in.

The third question is: "What are the *pitfalls* students might encounter as they try to complete the work?" In other words, considering a given assignment and the students' abilities, what obstacles might prevent students from completing the assignment successfully? For example, the presence of unknown vocabulary, an unfamiliarity with the type of assignment, and/or students' limited access to needed materials. Identifying these pitfalls is critical if you are to ensure that students do not get "hung up" while they are trying to complete an assignment independently.

The fourth question to ask yourself in the "L" section of the worksheet is "What are *solutions to these pitfalls*?" Here, you identify solutions to the identified pitfalls and jot them down. Note how Mr. Paxton completed the "L" section of the planning sheet in Figure 3.

The "A" step in planning assignments is to **Arrange clear directions**. As you will note on the planning sheet in Figure 3, there are three columns to complete: *Action Steps*, *Resources*, and *Grading Criteria* that includes (PACE 1,2,..), *Due Date*, and *Points*. In the Action Step column, teachers are to identify a few sequential steps to completing the assignment in a quality manner. In the Resources column, teachers list all potential resources that students might need to complete a quality assignment.

In the third column of the "A" section, teachers list the grading criteria that will be applied to the completed assignment, plus the assignment due date. The word "PACE" at the top of the third column refers to four standard requirements that will be applied to every assignment: the assignment must be Prompt (handed in on time), Arranged neatly, Complete, and Edited. The numbers "1,2,.." refer to any additional requirements associated with the assignment. (A full explanation of this self-checking process is found on page 190 of this chapter.) At the bottom of this column is a space for the assignment due date and the number of points the assignment is worth. This step in the planning process is important in order to structure assignment directions in such a way that students know everything that is required in order to produce quality work. Note how Mr. Paxton completed the "A" step in Figure 3.

The "N" step in PLAN is to **Note evaluation date and results**. This section on the planning sheet contains space for reviewing the appropriateness and outcomes of the assignment after the students' work on the assignment has been graded. To complete this step, teachers are prompted to complete the section by specifying a date for *reviewing* the assignment with students some time after the assignment is due and after it has been graded. The *Results* section of the worksheet is provided in order to record any common errors that were observed and to record any changes that might be recommended the next time such an assignment is given. Note this section that Mr. Paxton completed in Figure 3.

It is now early November in the following year of your earlier visits to Mr. Paxton's class. Mr. Paxton has used the Quality Assignment Planning Worksheet several times to plan assignments and is feeling rather comfortable with the basic procedures. He noted that when his students were given choices on how they could complete some of their assignments, that their motivation to complete those assignments increased. He also noted that the rate of assignment completion and quality of work on those particular assignments had improved. As a next step in his planning process, he has decided to invite a small group of students to help him plan assignments for an upcoming unit of study on Ancient Greece. Involving diverse learners in the planning of assignments for the whole class can result in positive outcomes in terms of assignment completion rate and improved grades (Rademacher, Cowart, Chism, & Sparks, 1997). Let's check with Mr. Paxton again to learn the results of his efforts.

Fourth Visit. As you walk down the hall, you see Mr. Paxton with a small group of five students. He is inviting them to attend a meeting to be conducted during his next planning period. As you approach them, they beckon to you. After greeting you, they invite you to attend their meeting and you accept.

As you enter the classroom, the students tell you to have a seat and take notes if you like. They inform you that they have been chosen to be "Assignment Expert Team" members, and that Mr. Paxton has selected them to help him plan assignments for the class during the next unit of study on Egypt. You immediately note the diversity in the five-member team seated around the small conference table. One student has a learning disability, one student has been referred to the office on numerous occasions for truancy, one student from Puerto Rico has limited English, and the other two are considered to be average to above-average performers in most of their classes. Mr. Paxton hands you a set of written guidelines he has prepared for you so that you can see the process he is following to engage the students in assignment construction. As he proceed with the lesson, you can see how he is adhering to the following Assignment Expert Team Guidelines:

1. Explain that the purpose of the meeting is for students to help plan a high-quality assignment.
2. State student expectations to participate and share ideas.
3. Briefly describe the upcoming unit of study on which the assignment will be based.
4. Share the Assignment Planning Sheet and the Assignment Idea Web with students.
5. Tell students the purpose of the assignment.
6. Engage students in constructing the assignment's directions, the options or choices that can be built in for completing it, the grading criteria, the supplies and resources to be used, and when the assignment will be due.
7. Determine whether the teacher or one of the students will explain the assignment to the class.

In summary, student motivation to complete assignments may

increase when teachers focus on planning meaningful and interesting assignments. Assignments are only meaningful when they are aligned with critical content that must be learned and mastered. Student motivation to complete assigned work may also increase when teachers offer reasonable choices to students on how to complete their work. In order to provide acceptable options to students, teachers can rely on information they gather from student interest surveys, learning style preferences, and multiple intelligence theory. Planning high quality assignments for and *with* students increases the probability that students will complete their assignments on time and at a high level of quality. As a result, learning for all students will improve.

PRESENTING ASSIGNMENTS TO STUDENTS

Simply improving the nature of secondary assignments may not solve the problem for many teachers who claim their students are not motivated to do the work and/or complete their work satisfactorily. While providing students with meaningful and satisfying assignments is the first factor to consider, the way in which teachers explain and give feedback on student performance is also important. Assignment explanations with active involvement by students is another critical variable in understanding the quality of schoolwork as it is performed by academically diverse learners. Thus, student behaviors and teacher behaviors during assignment presentations must be clearly delineated.

Critical Learner Behaviors

Winne and Marx (1989) claimed that three conditions must be met in order for students to perform a particular task. First, students must attend to the information as it is being presented by the teacher. Second, they must understand the intent and particular expectations of the assignment as it is explained by the teachers. That is, they must perceive the assignment in the same way the teacher does. Finally, students must be able to independently and successfully carry out the operations that will result in a satisfactory product. While giving clear directions for an assignment is the responsibility of teachers, making decisions about whether or not the directions are clearly understood becomes the personal responsibility of the student. To work independently, students must make sure they record important information for doing the assignment and devise a plan for satisfactory and timely completion of the work.

While clear directions for assigned tasks are important for all learners, they are especially critical for students with learning disabilities and other low achievers, as these students are known to possess ineffective/inefficient strategies for assignment completion (Hallahan, Gajar, Cohen, & Tarfer, 1978; Torgenson, 1977). A strategy is a guide to planning, execution and evaluation of performance on a task and its outcomes (Deshler, Schumaker, & Lenz, 1984). A good strategy is concerned with self-regulation, is a way to promote independent learning, and is often guided by a memory device to help students recall the strategy. All students can benefit from applying effective and efficient strategies for assignment completion to increase the likelihood that they will meet the demands of the assignment.

WATCH is a strategy developed by Glomb and West (1990) to help students with behavior disorders complete their assignments accurately and on time. The steps are:

W = Write down the assignment, the due date, and any special requirements in an assignment planner.

A = Ask yourself if you understand the assignment, and ask for clarification if necessary.

T = Task-analyze the assignment and schedule the task over the days available to complete the assignment.

Ch = Check each task as you can do it with CAN (substrategy):
  C = Completeness
  A = Accuracy
  N = Neatness

Archer and Gleason (1992) developed a similar four-step strategy to help students complete their assignments as part of their *Advanced Skills for School Success* series. The authors of this series have created a number of study skills and strategies to help students independently meet the demands of secondary settings. The steps for completing assignments include:

Step 1: *Plan it.*
- Read the directions carefully.
- Circle the words that tell you what to do.
- Get out the materials you need.
- Tell yourself what to do.

Step 2: *Complete it.*
- Do all the items.
- If you can't do an item, ask for help or go ahead to the next item.
- Use HOW:
  H = Heading
  O = Organized
  W = Written neatly

Step 3: *Check it.*
- Did you do everything?
- Did you get the right answers?
- Did you proofread?

Step 4: *Turn it in.*

Mr. Paxton expects his students to use the "REACT" Strategy to help them listen to and record the assignments they receive during his assignment explanations. "REACT" is part of *The Quality Assignment Routine* (Rademacher, Deshler, Schumaker, & Lenz, 1998) that can be taught to students in order to specify what they are to do during the time their teachers are presenting assignments. Another visit to Mr. Paxton's classroom is in order so that you can learn more about this strategy from one of his students.

Fifth Visit. As you enter the classroom, you notice that Mr. Paxton is in the middle of giving an assignment on Egypt that the Assignment Expert Team helped him develop by using the Quality Assignment Planning Sheet. The atmosphere this morning is a lot different from the one you experienced last year on your initial visits to observe Mr. Paxton giving assignments to his class. This time, each student has an assignment planning notebook open to record the assignment information.

As you circulate among the students, you also notice that a few of the students, including Juan, has a small bookmark on his desk that lists the REACT Strategy steps. Juan smiles at you and begins to softly explain what each of the step of the strategy cues him to do. The "R" step reminds him to **Review the directions** he has just written or been given. The "E" step cues him to **Examine whether the directions are complete**. To be complete, Juan tells you he must make sure he writes down a few action steps to get started, the resources or materials required for completing the assignment, any student choices or options offered by the teacher, the special requirements he must fulfill on the assignment to do a quality job, and the assignment due date.

The "A" step is one that Juan points out as being particularly helpful for him because it reminds him to **Ask questions to better understand** the directions. He states that sometimes he finds the directions confusing, or that some information may be missing from Mr. Paxton's directions that will prevent him from completing the assignment to Mr. Paxton's satisfaction. The "C" step, according to Juan, is also beneficial because it requires him to **Create a plan** for how he will get the assignment completed. For example, by using the strategy, he has learned to think ahead and plan time to complete his work promptly, to break the assignment into component parts and predict how long each part will take, and to schedule time to complete the work. The "T" step is to help him think of ways to improve his work. It is during this step that he must **Target some goals** to do better work, or else match his past performance that earned him a good grade. Later, you reflect on Juan's comments and realize that Mr. Paxton has taught his students some valuable lessons in how to approach a learning task that will be beneficial to them throughout their lives.

Critical Teacher Behaviors

As described in the educational literature, instructional time involves both teacher-directed instruction and directions for students to work independently, with seatwork and homework constituting the two major forms of independent practice (Gartland, 1990; Gartland & Rosenberg, 1987). The teachers' responsibility in directing assignment completion is to make sure that assignment explanations contain all the necessary information for their students to do an adequate job. Thus, teachers can benefit from devising a routine way to explain assignments that will incorporate the elements of an effective assignment presentation.

Lenz and Bulgren (1991) recommended that teachers induce learning and task completion for students who may possess poor strategies for completing assigned tasks by conceptualizing and presenting assignments as individual lessons. In doing so, they suggested that teachers use the following eight steps. First, teachers might provide an advance organizer by announcing the assignment and stating student expectations for the lesson. This is important for activating the students' attention to the assignment that is about to be given. Second, the teacher can give the assignment, state the evaluation criteria, and explain how the assignment is to be completed. Third, the teacher can model for the student and/or give examples of how each step of the assignment should be completed. Fourth, the teacher might check to see that students understand the directions as they have been explained. Fifth, the teacher can lead the students to do part of the assignment as a group to get the process started. Sixth, time in class might be allowed for working on the assignment. Seventh, the teacher should be prepared to re-explain or reconfigure the assignment if a student appears to be lost or confused after attempts to help have failed. Finally, the teacher can give a post-organizer to summarize the directions and remind students of assignment completion expectations.

Similar recommendations on how to better explain homework assignments have been offered to teachers by researchers. For example, the literature suggests that teachers (a) inform students of the assignment, its purpose, and how it is to be graded (Brophy & Alleman, 1991; Salend & Schliff, 1988); (b) involve students in the explanation process by having them make suggestions on how to accomplish the purpose of the assignment (Brophy & Alleman, 1991); (c) check for student understanding by asking students questions about the directions given (Salend & Schliff, 1988); (d) allow students to begin the work in class so it can be monitored by the teacher for accuracy (Connors, 1991; Cooper, 1989; Salend & Schliff, 1988); (e) conclude the assignment-completion process with some type of feedback on student performance after the work has been completed (Brophy & Alleman, 1991); and (f) interject strategies for motivating students to learn throughout the assignment completion process (Brophy, 1987; Brophy & Good, 1986).

Students who are acquiring English as a second language, such as Juan, will also benefit from structured assignment explanations in content classes. Northcutt and Watson (1986) suggest that when teaching lessons to students who may lack English proficiency they provide a clear focus, introduce the information in a concrete way, use modeling techniques, provide opportunities to practice the skill with students, and restate the purpose of the new information. Other ways to enhance assignment explanation routines for students who may be just acquiring English is to use gestures and visuals, simplify grammar and vocabulary, slow the pace of the presentation, use repetition, record assignments and/or make copies of the assignment directions for students (Richard-Amato, 1988).

Meece (1994) provides some suggestions to consider during assignment presentations for students with learning problems that might affect the learning outcomes. It seems these suggestions would also apply to all students who may have difficulty with assignment completion. According to Meece (1994), one or more of the following six ideas might be employed: (1) dividing the assignment into chunks and establishing timelines for each chunk; (2) extending the time to complete assignments; (3) allowing students to work in groups to complete parts of assignments; (4) requiring students to paraphrase important information that is needed to complete the assignment; and, (5) reducing the amount of copying required to record important assignment directions.

One way to decrease the amount of copying for students is to provide them with a handout of the assignment directions. Another way is to teach them a number of abbreviations to be used as they record information into an assignment notebook. Hughes, Ruhl, Rademacher, Schumaker, & Deshler (1995) developed an assignment planner for students that incorporates a table of common abbreviations students in secondary classrooms may use as they record their assignment information. Figure 4 on the next page depicts a list of those abbreviations.

Mr. Paxton decided to use the presentation component of *The Quality Assignment Routine* (Rademacher, Deshler, Schumaker, & Lenz, 1998) as his routine way to present assignments to his students. This part of the routine seemed a likely option for helping him guide each student in his class to think about the assignment as he gave them clear directions on how to complete it. Importantly, he thought the presentation procedures were a good way to engage the students during his presentations in a positive and constructive way.

Presentation Component Overview. The presentation component of *The Quality Assignment Routine* (Rademacher, Deshler, Schumaker, & Deshler, 1998) is based on what researchers claim to be highly important explanation factors by teachers. Importantly, like the planning component described in the previous section, it is also based on what *students* believe teachers should say and do in order to help them complete their assignments well. When diverse groups of learners met in focus group discussions prior to the development of the routine, they said that in order to do a good job on an assignment they needed **clear, well-organized directions, models or examples** of completed assignments, and a clear explanation of the **grading**

Figure 4: Assignment Notebook Abbreviations

Subject Area Abbreviations		Other Common Abbreviations	
Algebra	Alg.	Chapter	Chp.
English	Eng.	Definition	Def.
French	Fr.	Each	EA.
Geography	Geog.	Essay	Ess.
Geometry	Geom.	Even	Evn.
German	Ger.	Grading Criteria	GC
History	Hist.	Handout	HO
Language Arts	LA	Materials/Resources	M/R
Math	Mth.	Notebook	Nbk.
Reading	Rdg.	Numbers	Num. or #
Science	Sci.	Page(s)	Pg(s).
Social Studies	SS	Paragraphs	Para. or ¶
Spanish	Span.	Points	Pts.
Problems	Probs.		
Questions	Qs or ?		
Sentences	Sent.		
Textbook	Txt.		

From: Hughes, C.A., Ruhl, K.L., Deshler, D.D., & Schumaker, J.B. (1995). *The assignment completion: Instructor's manual.* Lawrence, KS: Edge Enterprises, Inc.

---

criteria. Students also said it was important for the teacher to give them **time to work** in class and give them timely **feedback.** All these factors are included in the presentation component of the routine.

Prior to using this part of the routine, Mr. Paxton conducted two lessons with his students. During the first lesson he and the students talked about the concept of "quality" and how they were expected to evaluate their own work before they handed it in to him. During the second lesson, he taught students how to participate in his assignment explanations and use the "REACT" Strategy—the strategy for thinking about and planning how to complete the assignment as described in the previous section. At the conclusion of his lessons, students knew how to state what quality work was, how to use a self-checking process for ensuring quality work, and how to use the REACT Strategy.

Initial Presentation Steps. The Cue-Do-Review sequence is the instructional sequence Mr. Paxton uses to explain a new assignment and get students to begin using it. During the Cue Phase, he draws students' attention to the new assignment and what they need to do by: stating that an assignment is about to be given, prompting them to record the assignment in their notebooks, and specifying what else they need to do, such as listen to the instructions, use the "REACT" Strategy and get started on the assignment.

During the Do Phase of his assignment explanation routine, Mr. Paxton implements the steps of REACT in an interactive way. That is, Mr. Paxton and his students co-construct the assignment directions as they go through each step.

Sixth Visit. As you visit Mr. Paxton's classroom again, you see him proceed through the Cue-Do part of the routine by using the following linking steps. As you observe, you are very impressed with the partnership-building that has developed between Mr. Paxton and his students since he has been more actively engaging them in his assignment presentations.

- Announce the assignment and its purpose.
- State clear instructions (as students write them in their assignment notebooks).
- Stop for students to use the REACT Strategy (add information to their notebooks, ask questions, set goals, etc.).
- Investigate student understanding.
- Give start-up time and offer help.
- Note expectations for students to evaluate their assignments for quality work.

Mr. Paxton explains that the Review Phase of his assignment explanation routine is done after he and the students have checked their work against a set of pre-established grading criteria. He states that during the Review Phase he gives the students feedback, and they conduct discussions on the finished assignment and its outcomes.

Knowing the importance of this aspect of assignment completion, you ask Mr. Paxton and his students if you may come back and visit on the day they are reviewing a particular assignment.

In summary, what teachers say and do as they present assignments to their students can make a significant difference in their students' knowledge of how to complete their work satisfactorily. During this phase of assignment completion, it is important to do everything possible to present clear instructions to students, give them time to ask questions and get answers to their questions, give them time to try out working on the assignment, and provide them with feedback about their initial attempts on the assignment. Students who traditionally have difficulty completing assignments need time to receive help so that they can get started doing the assignment successfully before they leave the classroom to complete the task independently. Teaching students how they are to attend to and record assignments in an assignment notebook is also recommended so that all students are better equipped to work on an assignment outside of the classroom. Once students finish an assignment, it is necessary to ensure that students understand how they performed on the assignment and how they might improve in the future. Thus, the assignment completion cycle is not complete until assignment evaluations are conducted.

EVALUATING ASSIGNMENTS WITH STUDENTS

Few topics in education are more controversial than grading, reporting, and communicating student learning. According to Guskey (1996), there are three premises on which to base our conversation surrounding the evaluation of student learning. First, the primary goal of grading and reporting is communication. The purpose of that communication should be to relate high-quality information to interested persons in a form they can understand and use effectively. Second, reporting is an integral part of the learning process only when it identifies where additional work is needed. Finally, the need for more detailed communication about student learning is critical as the goals of schooling become more complex.

Current education reform efforts, which advocate reporting how *all* students such as the ones in Mr. Paxton's class are doing against high, uniform standards brings the issue of grading practices to the forefront (Wiggins, 1994). Teachers are increasingly concerned over how and on what standards to measure the academic performance of students from varying cultures and backgrounds, as well as students with learning disabilities who are required by law to have unlimited access to the general education curriculum (Individuals with Disabilities Education Act Amendments of 1997).

As educators turn their attention to better ways of evaluating student performance, they are beginning to consider alternative forms for communicating student learning. Watts (1996) divides alternative forms of assessment for communicating student learning into four categories. Category one is visible evidence of student growth and achievement. This can be accomplished through methods such as portfolios, exhibitions, displays of work, presentations, and videos to send home. Category two is a ranking or rating of student achievement against clearly stated, predetermined standards. Methods that support this category include work sampling, rubrics, and report card checklists. Category three is evidence of learning through self-assessment or peer evaluation. Category four includes opportunities for two-way communication through conferences. During such conferences, what is known is not what something says to the other person, but reflects an understanding that is constructed between all parties in the conversation. One or more of these methods might be viable options for secondary teachers to consider in their quest for a better way to evaluate learning outcomes. In particular, the use of rubrics, self-assessment procedures, and two-way communication conferences are known to be effective throughout the assignment completion process.

Designing Rubrics. A rubric is a scoring guide used to evaluate the quality of student responses on assigned work. For example, rubrics can be used to check whether or not certain criteria were met on assignments such as written compositions, oral presentations, or science projects. Appropriately designed rubrics can contribute greatly to the development of quality work. When teacher and students develop rubrics together, the expectations of the task can be explored.

Popham (1997) describes rubrics as having three essential features; evaluative criteria, quality definitions, and a scoring strategy. Evaluative criteria are used to distinguish acceptable from unacceptable responses, can vary from rubric to rubric, and can be given equal weight or be weighted differently. Examples of evaluative criteria includes such elements as mechanics, word choice, supporting details, etc. Quality definitions describe the way in which student responses are to be judged. For instance, if mechanics is an evaluative criteria, it must be clearly explained to students. Thus, students must understand that to meet that criteria they must make sure their finished assignment shows evidence of handwriting that is dark enough to read, letters that are legible and well formed, and that spelling, punctuation, and grammar are correct. The scoring strategy used with a rubric can be either holistic or analytic. While holistic scoring takes all of the evaluative criteria into consideration for a quality score, an analytic approach requires the scorer to render a score for each criterion that may not be part of the overall score. Certainly, the use of rubrics requires teachers to be much more precise about the criteria for evaluating student work.

Because rubrics clarify expectations, they yield better feedback to students so that the quality of their work can be improved. Using rubrics with lower achieving students is beneficial because these students are able to see the concrete ways they can improve their work to meet a high standard. Thus, they are more likely to have the incentive to push themselves harder. Once students understand and internalize the criteria in a rubric, they can also help to develop rubric criteria, use the criteria to assist their peers in revising their work, and assess their own work (O'Neil, 1994). Teaching students how to evaluate their own work for quality is an important part of ensuring that the assignments they do turn in will earn them a better grade. Rubrics can become tools for encouraging the self-evaluation process.

Prompting Self-Evaluation of Assignments. A personal quality associated with job skills of the future includes self-management. For example, workers must be able to assess their own knowledge and skills accurately, set specific and realistic goals, and monitor their progress toward a goal. They must work hard to reach goals, even if the task is unpleasant, and they must produce quality work (Jones, 1995). Teachers can help students develop self-management skills through their established assignment completion procedures. Students who learn to manage their academic behaviors learn critical life skills that are important for future employment.

Self-management requires self-regulated learning. However, many students with learning problems have difficulty with self-regulation (Rooney & Hallahan, 1985). As a result, they have greater difficulty working independently. Self-regulation is an essential component of being able to function independently as a successful student and as an adult. Independent learning can be fostered when students are involved in goal setting, selection of assignments, and self-monitoring of progress (Wang, 1987).

Self-evaluation is the component of self-regulation that teaches students how well they are doing. Mercer and Mercer (1998) recommend three steps for teaching self-evaluation that can be incorporated into assignment completion procedures. The first step is to discuss the importance of evaluating one's own work and the benefits of doing so, such as determining whether or not satisfactory performance has been achieved. The second step is to model how to conduct a self-evaluation. During this step, the teacher demonstrates using a particular progress form designed to judge performance, and then has the students model the behavior to make sure they understand. The third step is to have the students practice and provide feedback. During this step the student practices to proficiency with comments from the teacher on how well they are doing.

In the lesson Mr. Paxton conducted prior to his implementation of the presentation component of *The Quality Assignment Routine*, he taught each of his students how to use a self-checking routine to evaluate their own work for quality. The rubric he and the students constructed together during his lesson regarding quality work was called "PACE 1,2..." This simple checklist system was designed to help him organize verbal feedback to be given on finished work. Group verbal feedback is provided to all individuals within the class. Individual feedback can be given to individual students as necessary.

The word "PACE" refers to four standard requirements that Mr. Paxton and his students agreed upon would be the *standard* requirements to be applied on all assignments. They agreed that the assignment must be **Prompt** (handed in on time), **Arranged Neatly** (no stray marks, even margins, well organized), **Complete** (all directions followed, all questions answered), and **Edited** (mechanics okay, ideas clear, content accurate). The "1, 2 ..." following "PACE" refers to any *additional* requirements associated with a particular assignment—for example, including a picture with a poem, creating a computer graphic to support an idea, etc.

Students were required to mark their finished assignments with "PACE 1, 2 ..." and make a check mark or a zero on one of the two lines below each letter and number. The second line was for Mr. Paxton to place a check mark if he was in agreement with how the student graded his finished work. Figure 5 on the next page gives options on how to use the "PACE 1, 2 ..." checklist system.

Conducting Two Way Communication Conferences. A valuable, but sometimes time-consuming form of communication is the two-way conference. A constructivist approach indicates that just as knowledge of subject matter content is constructed by the learner in interaction with people and the environment, so can knowledge about what students have learned as a result of a particular assigned activity (Watts, 1996). The process of learning about assignment completion should be considered as important as learning the content. Thus, discussions regarding the quality of assignments and the outcomes associated with assignment completion should be a regular part of classroom activities (Lenz & Bulgren, 1991).

Assignment discussions can be referred to as interactive instructional conversations (Saunders, Goldenberg, & Hamann, 1992).

Figure 5: Options for Formatting the "PACE" Requirements

Option 1

Option 2

```
P  ___  ___        P    A    C    E    1*    2*
A  ___  ___
C  ___  ___       ___  ___  ___  ___  ___  ___
E  ___  ___
1* ___  ___       ___  ___  ___  ___  ___  ___
2* ___  ___
                  *key words
```

From: Rademacher, J.A., Deshler, D.D., Schumaker, J.B., & Lenz, B.K. (1998). *The quality assignment routine.* Lawrence, KS. Edge Enterprises.

During such conversations, the following teacher behaviors and student behaviors are recommended (Goldenberg, 1992; Saunders, Goldenberg, & Hamann, 1992). First, although the teacher has an initial plan on what to focus the discussion on, the teacher is also responsive and helps the students explore their ideas. Second, the discourse is connected in that the teacher asks questions and students answer, but interactive turn-taking also occurs. Third, the discussion occurs in a non-threatening atmosphere with the teacher encouraging risk-taking and serving as collaborator more than evaluator.

Regardless of what evaluation process is used, giving feedback to students on completed work is important (Brophy & Alleman, 1991; Connors, 1991; Glasser, 1998; Palardy, 1995; Platt & Olson, 1997; and Rademacher, Deshler, & Schumaker, 1996) and can result in improved academic performance if properly applied (Fuchs, Fuchs, & Hamlett, 1994; Kline, Schumaker, & Deshler, 1991; Lloyd & Keller, 1989). Grades, coupled with verbal feedback, brings closure to the assignment completion process

Effective Feedback for Enhancing Assignment Completion Performance. Without effective feedback, students will be unable to improve their performance in a way that satisfies the requirements for a particular assignment. Clearly, all learners need feedback from appropriate sources in order to guide their future independent study and learning efforts (Serna, Schumaker, & Sheldon, 1992).

In order to be effective, assignment feedback must be closely aligned to established grading practices. Many teachers base grades for special education students on such behaviors as merely handing in an assignment regardless of its quality, attending a certain number of classes regardless of the students' level of participation, and consistently taking notes in class. These methods may not be effective for two reasons. First, grades based on effort are simply too vague to provide much valuable information. Second, students with disabilities quickly learn that all the teacher requires of them is to stay out of trouble and that the teacher really doesn't care whether they learn anything or not (Gersten, Vaughn, & Brengelman, 1996).

The goal of feedback should be to provide your students with information about their performance so that it leads to improved performance and increased independence (Lenz, Ellis, & Scanlon, 1996). Effective feedback is both positive and corrective. For example, in a review of research on effective feedback, Lenz, Scanlon, and Ellis (1996) concluded that feedback should include praise and information about what was done *right* during a particular task. Also, feedback should focus on correct behaviors and identify *specific errors*. Thus, teachers will focus the students' attention on the types of behaviors correctly performed, as well as types of errors made and how to avoid them (Howell, 1986; Kea, 1987; Kline, 1989).

In addition to timely feedback on assignments that is positive and corrective, it is also important to include a goal setting component. Goal setting places more responsibility on students to do what they need to do in order to improve their work based on the feedback they have been given. By having students set goals, you can also ensure they understand the desired behavior that is necessary to improve their work (Deshler, Schumaker, & Lenz, 1984; Ellis, 1985; Seabaugh & Schumaker, 1981) on particular assignments.

Learning to use feedback effectively can be of great benefit to students with learning problems in order to guide their performance on assignments. Kline, Schumaker, and Deshler (1991) developed and tested an elaborated feedback routine with students with learning problems and found it helped students achieve their learning goals in a timely and effective manner. They concluded that feedback procedures represent learning opportunities for students and teaching opportunities for teachers. Essential features of feedback are included in the following mnemonic:

- Find the score. (Explain the grade.)
- Enter the score. (Use a graph and goal setting to make it concrete and meaningful for students.)
- Evaluate the score in terms of the goal.
- Determine errors by examining the pattern.
- Begin error correction. (The teacher models a similar problem.)
- Ask the student to apply the correction procedure.
- Close out the session by giving positive feedback on the correction.
- Kick back and relax.

Mr. Paxton decided to use the evaluation component of *The Quality Assignment Routine* (Rademacher, Deshler, Schumaker, & Lenz, 1998) as his routine way to evaluate assignments with his students. This part of the routine seemed a likely option for helping him incorporate the use of rubrics, self-evaluation procedures, and two-way conferences that included the elements of effective feedback. The purpose of this phase of the routine is to ensure that students understood how they performed on the assignment and how they might improve in the future.

Evaluation Component Overview. The evaluation procedures in the *Quality Assignment Routine* are based upon what the literature claims to be effective evaluation and feedback guidelines. Importantly, it adopts the notion that students will unlikely improve the quality of their work unless given opportunities to do so (Glasser, 1990). The elements contained in this phase of the routine completes the assignment completion cycle for both teacher and students. It is during this time that the Review part of the Cue-Do-Review is conducted.

The Review Steps. The Review steps are conducted after an assignment has been scored by both teacher and students against the "PACE 1,2,.." set of uniform criteria. As you recall the last time you visited Mr. Paxton (during an assignment presentation), you asked to be invited back during the time he reviewed the finished assignments with the class. Let's go once more to Mr. Paxton's class to learn how he conducts assignment evaluations with his students.

Seventh Visit. As you enter the classroom, Mr. Paxton is handing out the assignments that were finished and then scored with "PACE 1,2,.." Mr. Paxton walks over to you and shows you one of the assignments that was rated by a particular student and himself using the "PACE 1,2.." checking routine. He said that in this particular case, he and the student had agreed on all but one of the quality criteria. He also said that as he checked all of the papers the day before, he analyzed student error patterns and correct responses so that he could give positive and corrective feedback. Mr. Paxton then goes to the front of the class and begins talking to his students about their finished work. In so doing, he first reviews the requirements for the assignment. Second, he explains which requirements were met well by the class and which ones were poorly met. Third, he engages the students in a conversation on how they can make appropriate corrections to improve their work. Finally, he extends two offers to the students. The first offer is to submit their corrected work to improve their grade by the following day. The second offer is to provide assistance to anyone who would like individual feedback on their assignments. Juan and Carla raise their hands and ask if they might meet with Mr. Paxton after school to clarify what must be done on each of their assignments in order to improve their grade.

After class, you talk to Mr. Paxton and tell him how impressed you are with the assignment completion procedures he is using and has taught his students to use. Mr. Paxton thanks you and says that as a result of his efforts, he has gotten to know his students very well. He is particularly pleased to see how the rate of assignment completion has gone up for the low performing and special needs students in his class, as well as their grades. However, he tells you that Carla, one of his gifted and talented students, and Stacy, a student with learning disabilities, were still not progressing as well as he thought they should have due to many problems with organizational planning. Therefore, he referred them to one of the teachers in the Academic Achievement Center (AAC) to provide those students with more intense instruction regarding assignment completion. As a result they were being taught *The Assignment Completion Strategy* (Hughes, Ruhl, Deshler, & Schumaker, 1995). Figure 6 shows the steps of *The Assignment Completion Strategy*.

TECHNOLOGY AS A TOOL FOR ENHANCING ASSIGNMENT COMPLETION

Teachers who use technology in the classroom have found it to be a powerful tool in guiding their students to become critical thinkers and independent learners. With access to computers, students can practice reading, writing, and math skills, as well as publish their own stories and create computer presentations. As we move rapidly toward an increased use of computer technologies, it becomes imperative to examine ways that technology can be integrated into assignment completion expectations so as to benefit *all* students in the learning community.

For students with limited English proficiency, the use of computers can promote literacy skills. The same features of computer technology that promote literacy are also helpful for students with learning disabilities, and those at-risk for academic failure (Fite, Ramos, Estrada, & Rivers, 1998). For example, students can write,

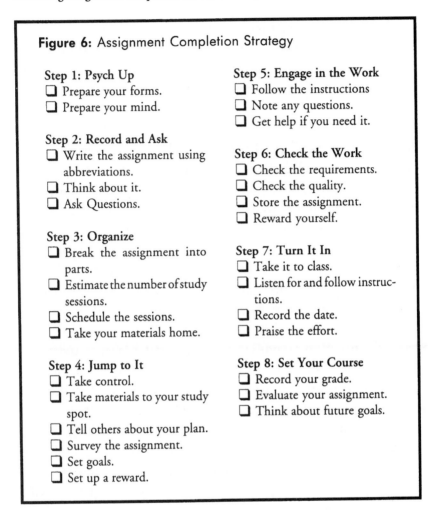

Figure 6: Assignment Completion Strategy

Step 1: Psych Up
- ❑ Prepare your forms.
- ❑ Prepare your mind.

Step 2: Record and Ask
- ❑ Write the assignment using abbreviations.
- ❑ Think about it.
- ❑ Ask Questions.

Step 3: Organize
- ❑ Break the assignment into parts.
- ❑ Estimate the number of study sessions.
- ❑ Schedule the sessions.
- ❑ Take your materials home.

Step 4: Jump to It
- ❑ Take control.
- ❑ Take materials to your study spot.
- ❑ Tell others about your plan.
- ❑ Survey the assignment.
- ❑ Set goals.
- ❑ Set up a reward.

Step 5: Engage in the Work
- ❑ Follow the instructions
- ❑ Note any questions.
- ❑ Get help if you need it.

Step 6: Check the Work
- ❑ Check the requirements.
- ❑ Check the quality.
- ❑ Store the assignment.
- ❑ Reward yourself.

Step 7: Turn It In
- ❑ Take it to class.
- ❑ Listen for and follow instructions.
- ❑ Record the date.
- ❑ Praise the effort.

Step 8: Set Your Course
- ❑ Record your grade.
- ❑ Evaluate your assignment.
- ❑ Think about future goals.

edit, and revise original works on the computer without the frustration encountered by completing these processes in a more traditional format. To add personal relevance to an assignment, students might utilize their computer skills to compose and illustrate their own storybooks. Carefully selected software can also ensure a task is not so hard that a student cannot complete it or so easy it is boring. Choosing software programs that provide students with specific knowledge of results can keep them motivated to remain on task. However, in addition to well-designed software programs, schools of the future will include two-way communication systems that will connect people across places and time. One tool that is becoming more readily available in the Internet. While the Internet may open the door for many students, it is the teacher that determines the best way to integrate it into curriculum and instruction so that all students reap its benefits.

Benefits to Internet Users. The Internet allows thousands of teachers and students to reach each other directly and gain access to quantities of information previously unimaginable. Using the Internet can make classrooms more student centered and collaborative. Assignments become more student centered when learners are allowed to research and connect with something that engages their curiosity and stimulates further exploration. Collaboration is stimulated when students of varying cultures, ages, and social classes are encouraged to build networks of understanding though e-mail. As more and more schools are connected through the Internet, teachers and students have a chance to communicate their work and ideas with the world.

Requiring students to learn and use the Internet when completing assignments will also help them acquire many of the skills they will need to prosper in the information age. These necessary skills include the ability to gather, analyze, and synthesize information from a variety of resources, and use technology as a tool for solving problems. These skills, in combination with the ability to communicate effectively with diverse colleagues, will empower students to be successful in the workforce of the future.

Becker (1995) completed a study of Internet usage among 21 of the United States and the District of Columbia. As a result, he reported the perceived benefits to students whose teachers incorporated Internet activities into the curriculum. First, students applied themselves for longer periods of time and took on more responsibility for their own learning. Second, "average" performing students communicated and produced products equivalent to "above average" performing students. Third, students worked more collaboratively among their peers with their expertise more equally distributed. Fourth, students took more interest in world events, foreign cultures, and societies, with a deeper understanding of the ideas they encountered. Finally, students had more interest in understanding the "adult" world, such as scientists and business people they had connected with, and were able to better communicate with them on a personal level.

Internet Assignment Ideas. As you have learned throughout this chapter, Mr. Paxton has incorporated many research-based procedures into the assignment routine he has chosen to implement with his students. As he learns more about how to use the Internet, he can use it wisely to plan, present, and evaluate assignments with his students. The following general ideas are offered as possible ways to integrate technology into Mr. Paxton's assignments in order to promote Internet usage by his students (Becker, 1995).

1. Search for specific information online.
2. Browse the network using Gopher or a World Wide Web browser.
3. Become an electronic penpal with someone.
4. Take an "electronic field trip" to a museum, science center, or to visit an adult conducting a scientific or creative activity.
5. Publish a group or individual assignment on the network.
6. Conduct a science investigation with a class in another location.
7. Conduct a writing project with a class in another location.
8. Participate in a "cultural exchange."

CONCLUSION

Although assignments represent a major vehicle that can be used to help students learn content, many students fail to take advantage of the learning opportunity. It can be difficult to plan assignments for student enrollments that are becoming increasingly diverse. For example, today's classes may include students judged as high-, average-, and low-achieving, as well as students who are considered to be gifted, students with disabilities, students with limited English proficiency, and those who are at risk for school failure. While the most commonly tried solution to these challenges involves tailoring instruction to the mythical mean of the class, research has shown that it misses more students than it hits. Teachers need instructional approaches that are not only effective, but acceptable to both teachers and students.

In adopting assignment completion procedures for academically diverse classes, it is recommended that teachers create a classroom learning community in which covering the curriculum is never as important as ensuring all students and teachers are working together in a supportive setting to learn what is considered critical about the curriculum and for life. Such a community will support students in becoming strategic learners, capable of creatively and effectively processing information. Inasmuch as the information age is resulting in rapidly changing knowledge bases, today's students must learn "how to learn" so that they can be independent learners and performers after they leave school and can deal with new knowledge as it emerges.

Teachers have opportunities to develop strategic learning in *all* students when they involve students in the learning community of the classroom by participating in the design of their own assignments that will motivate them to learn more about the topics at hand. While planning meaningful assignments is important, so is presenting assignments to students in such a way that they understand what they are asked to do, a prerequisite for learning. And, the assignment completion cycle is not complete unless students are involved in the evaluation of their own work, prerequisite for a community for learners. Powerful knowledge can be constructed when teachers and students work and learn together through high-quality assignments.

REFERENCES

Adelman, H.S., & Taylor, L. (1983. Enhancing motivation for overcoming learning and behavior problems. *Journal of Learning Disabilities, 16*, 384-392.

Anderson, L. (1984). The environment of instruction: The function of seatwork in a commercially developed curriculum. In G. Duffey, L. Roehler, & J. Mason (Eds.), *Comprehension instruction: Perspectives and suggestions* (pp. 93-103). New York: Longman.

Archer, A.I., & Gleason, M.M. (1992). *Advanced skills for school success.* North Billerica, MA: Curriculum Associates.

Armstrong, T. (1994). *Multiple Intelligences in the classroom.* Alexandria, VA: Association of Supervision and Curriculum Development.

Bay, M., & Bryan, T. (1992). Differentiating children who are at risk for referral from others on crucial classroom factors. *Remedial and Special Education, 12*(4), 27-33.

Becker, H.J. (1995). *The baseline survey of testbed schools.* University of California–Irvine.

Bloom, B.S. (1956). *Taxonomy of educational objectives. Handbook 1: Cognitive domain.* New York: David MacKay Publishing.

Brophy, J., & Alleman, J. (1991). Activities as instructional tools. A framework for analysis and evaluation. *Educational Researcher, 20*(4), 9-20.

Brophy, J. (1987). Synthesis of research on strategies for motivating students to learn. *Educational Leadership, 45*(2), 40-48.

Brophy, J., & Good, T. (1986). Teacher effects. In M.C. Wittrock (Ed.), *Handbook of research on teaching* (pp. 328-375). New York: Macmillan.

Checkley, K. (1997). Homework: A new look at an age-old practice. *Association for Supervision and Curriculum Development Education Update, 39*(7), 1-8.

Connors, N. (1991). *Homework: A new direction.* Columbus, OH: National Middle School Association.

Cooper, H.M. (1989). *Homework.* New York: Longman Publishing.

Cross (1990). National Goals: Four priorities for educational researchers. *Educational Researcher, 19*(10), 587-594.

Davis, F. (1984). Understanding underachievers. *American Education, 20* (10), 12-14.

Dean, A.V., Salend, S.J., & Taylor, L. (1993). Multicultural education: A challenge for special educators. *Teaching Exceptional Children, 26*(1), 40-43.

Delquadri, J., Greenwood, C.R., Whorton, D., Carta, J.J., & Hall, R.V. (1986). Classwide peer tutoring. *Exceptional Children, 52*(6), 535-542.

Deshler, D.D., Schumaker, J.B., & Lenz, B.K. (1984). Academic and cognitive interventions for LD adolescents: Part 1. *Journal of Learning Disabilities, 17,* 108-117.

Deshler, D.D., Schumaker, J.B., Alley, G.R., Warner, M.M., & Clark, F.L. (1983). Learning disabilities in adolescents and young adult populations: Research implications (Part 1). *Focus on Exceptional Children, 15*(1), 1-12.

Dougherty, E., & Barth, P. (1997). How to close the achievement gap: School-work that's worth doing. *Education Week,* April 2.

Doyle, W., & Carter, K. (1984). Academic work in classrooms. *Curriculum Inquiry, 14*(2), 129-149.

Ellis, E. (1985). *The effects of teaching learning disabled adolescents an executive strategy to facilitate self-generalization of task-specific strategies.* Unpublished doctoral dissertation, University of Kansas, Lawrence.

England, D.A., & Flately, J.K. (1985). Homework—and why. Bloomington, IN: Phi Delta Kappa Educational Foundation. (ERIC Document Reproduction Service No. ED 260 052).

Fite, K., Ramos, N, Estrada, D., & Rivers, G. (1998). Utilizing educational technology with students in at-risk situations. *The TECH Edge, 17*(4), 37-38.

Fuchs, L.D., Fuchs, D., & Hamlett, C.L. (1994). Strengthening the connection between assessment and instructional planning with expert systems. *Exceptional Children,*

Gajria, M., & Salend, S. (1995). Homework practices of students with and without learning disabilities: A comparison. *Journal of Learning Disabilities, 28,* 291-296.

Gardner, H. (1983). *Frames of mind: The theory of multiple intelligences.* New York: Harper & Row.

Gardner, H. (1993). Educating for understanding. *American School Board Journal, 180*(7), 20-24.

Gartland, D. (1990). Maximizing instructional time in the LD classroom. *LD Forum, 16*(1), 49-53.

Gartland, D., & Rosenberg, M.S. (1987). Managing time in the LD classroom. *LD Forum, 12*(2), 8-10.

Gersten, R., Vaughn, S., & Brengelman, S.U. (1996). Grading and academic feedback for special education students and students with learning difficulties. In Guskey, T.R. (Ed.), *Communicating student learning: 1996 ASCD yearbook.* Association of Supervision and Curriculum Development.

Glasser, W. (1998). *Choice theory.* New York: Harper & Row.

Glasser, W. (1991). *The quality school teacher.* New York: Harper & Row.

Glasser, W. (1991). *The quality school. Managing students without coercion.* New York: Harper & Row.

Glasser, W. (1998). *Control theory in the classroom.* New York: Harper & Row.

Glomb, N., & West, R.P. (1990). Teaching behaviorally disordered adolescents to use self-management skills for improving the completeness, accuracy, and neatness of creative writing homework assignments. *Behavioral Disorders, 15,* 233-242.

Goldenberg, C. (1992). Instructional conversations. Promoting comprehension through discussion. *The Reading Teacher, 46,* 316-326.

Griffin, R.S. (1988). *Underachievers in secondary schools: Education off the mark.* Hillsdale, NJ: Erlbaum.

Guild, P.B (1997). Where do the learning theories overlap? *Educational Leadership, 55*(1), 30-31

Guskey, T.R. (1996). *Communicating student learning.* Alexandria, VA. Association for Supervision and Curriculum Development. 1-6.

Hallahan, D.P., Gajar, A., Cohen, S., & Tarver, S. (1978). Selective attention and locus of control in learning disabled and normal children. *Journal of Learning Disabilities, 11,* (4), 47-52.

Holcutt, A., Martin, E., & McKinney, J.D. (1990). Historical and legal context of mainstreaming. In J.W. Lloyd & N.N. Singh (Eds.), *The regular education initiative: Alternative perspectives of concepts, issues, and models.*

Howell, S.B. (1986). *A study of the effectiveness of TOWER – a theme writing strategy.* Unpublished master's thesis, University of Kansas, Lawrence.

Hughes, C.A., Ruhl, K.L., Rademacher, J.A., Schumaker, J.B., & Deshler, D.D. (1995). *The quality quest planner.* Lawrence, KS: Edge Enterprises.

Individuals with Disabilities Act (IDEA) Amendments of 1997 (1997). Public Law 105-17. Washington, DC: U.S. Office of Education.

Jones, L.K. (1995). *Job skills for the 21st century: A guide for students.* Phoenix, AZ: Oryx Press.

Jorgenson, G. (1977). Relationship of classroom behavior to the accuracy of the match between material difficulty and student ability. *Journal of Educational Psychology, 69,* 24-32.

Kauffman, J.M. (1989). The regular education initiative as Reagan-Bush education policy: A trickle-down theory of education of the hard to teach. *Journal of Special Education, 23,* 256-278.

Kea, C.D. (1987). *An analysis of critical teaching behaviors employed by teachers of students with mild handicaps.* Unpublished doctoral dissertation. University of Kansas, Lawrence.

Kline, F. (1989). *The development and validation of feedback routines for use in special education settings.* Unpublished doctoral dissertation, University of Kansas.

Kline, F.M., Schumaker, J.B., & Deshler, D.D. (1991). Development and validation of feedback routines for instructing students with learning disabilities. *Learning Disability Quarterly, 14,* 191-207.

Lazear, D. (1991). *Seven ways of knowing: Teaching for multiple intelligences.* Palatine, IL: IRI/Skylight Publishing.

Lee, J.F., & Pruitt, K.W. (1979). Homework assignments: Classroom games or teaching tools? *The Clearing House, 53*, 31-37.

Lenz, B.K., & Bulgren, J.A. (1991). Promoting learning in the content areas. In P.T. Cegelka & W.H. Berdine (Eds.), *Effective instruction of students with learning difficulties: A text for general education and special education teachers.*

Lenz, B.K., Ehren, B.J., & Smiley, L.R. (1991). A goal attainment approach to improve completion of project-type assignments by adolescents with learning disabilities. *Learning Disabilities Research and Practice, 6*, 166-176.

Lenz, B.K., Ellis, E.S., & Scanlon, D. (1996). *Teaching learning strategies to adolescents and adults with learning disabilities.* Austin, TX: Pro-Ed.

Lloyd, J.W., & Keller, C.E. (1989). Effective mathematics instruction: Development, instruction, and programs. *Focus on Exceptional Children, 21*(7), 1-10.

McCarthy, B (1982). *The 4Mat System.* Arlington Heights, IL: Excel Publishing Co.

McCarthy, B. (1996). *About learning.* Barrington, IL: Excel, Inc.

McCombs, B.L., & Whistler, J.S. (1989). The role of affective variables in autonomous learning. *Educational Psychologist, 24*(3), 277-306.

Meece, R.L. (1994). *Teaching learners with mild disabilities: Integrating research and practice.* Pacific Grove, CA: Brooks/Cole.

Mehring, T.A., & Colson, S.E. (1990). Motivation and mildly handicapped learners. *Focus on Exceptional Children, 22*(5), 1-14.

Mercer, C.D., & Mercer, A.R. (1998). *Teaching students with learning problems* (pp. 95-135). New Jersey. Prentice-Hall, Inc.

Northcutt, L., & Watson, D. (1986). *Sheltered English handbook.* Carlsbad, CA: Northcutt, Watson, & Gonzales.

O'Neil, J. (1994). Making assessment meaningful. *Association for Supervision and Curriculum Development Update, 36*(6), 3-6.

Palardy, J.M. (1995). Another look at homework. *Principal, 74*(5), 32-33.

Paschal, R.A. (1988). Effects of homework on learning: A quantitative synthesis. *Journal of Educational Research, 78*(2), 97-104.

Platt, J.M., & Olson, J.L. (1997). *Teaching adolescents with mild disabilities* (pp. 115-145). Pacific Grove, California. Brooks/Cole Publishing.

Popham, W.J. (1997). What's wrong—and what's right—with rubrics. *Educational Leadership, 55* (2) 72-75.

Putnam, M.L., Deshler, D.D., & Schumaker, J.B. (1992). The investigation of setting demands: A missing link in learning strategies instruction. In L.J. Meltzer (Ed.), *Strategy assessment and instruction for students with learning disabilities: From theory to practice.* Austin, TX: Pro-Ed.

Quality Education for Minorities Project. (1990). *Education that works: An action plan for the education of minorities.* Cambridge, MA: Massachusetts Institute of Technology.

Rademacher, J.A., Cowart, M., Sparks, J., & Chism, V. (1997). Planning high quality assignments with diverse learners. *Preventing School Failure, 43*(1), 12-18.

Rademacher, J.A., Deshler, D.D., Schumaker, J.B., & Lenz, B.K. (1998). *The quality assignment routine.* Lawrence, KS: Edge Enterprises.

Rademacher, J.A., Schumaker, J.B., & Deshler, D.D. (1996). The development and validation of a classroom assignment routine for inclusive settings. *Learning Disability Quarterly, 19*(3), 163-177.

Richard-Amato, P. (1988). *Making it happen: Interaction in the second language classroom.* White Plains, NY: Longman.

Rooney, K.J., & Hallahan, D.P. (1985). Future directions for cognitive behavior modification research: The quest for cognitive change. *Remedial and Special Education, 6*(2), 46-51.

Salend, S.J., & Schliff, J. (1988). The many dimensions of homework. *Academic Therapy, 23*(4), 397-403.

Saunders, W., Goldenberg, C., & Hamann, J. (1992). Instructional conversation begets instructional conversation. *Teaching and Teacher Education, 8,* 199-218.

Schumaker, J.B., & Deshler, D.D. (1988). Implementing the regular education initiative in secondary schools: A different ball game. *Journal of Learning Disabilities, 21,* 21-42.

Seabaugh, G.O., & Schumaker, J.B. (1981). *The effects of self-regulation training on the academic productivity of LD and NLD Adolescents* (Research Report No. 37). Lawrence, KS: The University of Kansas Institute for Research in Learning Disabilities.

Serna, L.A., Schumaker, J.B., & Sheldon, J.B. (1992). A comparison of the effects of feedback procedures on college student performance on written essay papers. *Behavior Modification, 16*(1), 64-81.

Silver, H., Strong, R., & Perini, M. (1997). Integrating learning styles and multiple intelligences.

Sprinthall, N.A., & Sprinthall, R.C. (1987). *Educational psychology: A developmental approach* (4th ed.). New York: Random House.

Struyk, L.R., Epstein, M.H., Bursuck, W., Polloway, E.A., McConeghy, J., & Cole, K.B. (1995). Homework, grading, and testing practices used by teachers for students with and without disabilities. *The Clearing House, 69,* 50-56.

Torgeson, J.K. (1977). The role of non-specific factors in task performance of learning disabled children: A theoretical assessment. *Journal of Learning Disabilities, 10,* 27-34.

U.S. Census Bureau. (1992). *Current population survey.* Washington, DC: U.S. Department of Commerce.

Valdes, K.A., Williamson, C.L., & Wagner, M.M. (1990). *The national longitudinal transition study of special education students. Vol. 1.* Menlo Park, CA: SRI International

Vance, M. (1995). Getting to know you: Knowing myself and my students to guide learning. *Strategram, 7*(2),1-8.

Wang, M.C. (1987). Toward achieving educational excellence for all students: Program design and instructional outcomes. *Remedial and Special Education, 8*(3), 25-34.

Watts, K.H. (1996). Bridges freeze before roads. In T.R. Guskey (Ed.), *Association for Supervision and Curriculum Development 1996 Yearbook: Communicating student learning.* Association of Supervision and Curriculum Development.

Wiggins, G. (1994). Toward better report cards. *Educational Leadership, 50*(2), 28-37.

Winne, P.H., & Marx, R.W. (1989). A cognitive-processing analysis of motivation within classroom tasks. In C. Ames & R. Ames (Eds.), *Research on motivation in education: Goals and cognitions* (pp. 223-257). San Diego: Academic Press.

CHAPTER FIVE

Facilitating Transitions from Elementary Through High School

PAULA E. LANCASTER & PAT GILDROY

As Mrs. Morgan finished entering her last set of grades into her grade book, she paused for a moment to reflect on the past school year. This fifth-grade class had challenged her as a teacher. She had never dealt with such a wide range of abilities, interests, backgrounds, and personalities. She thought back to this very same time last year, when she and the other fifth-grade teachers had met with the fourth-grade teachers for several hours in an effort to prepare for the incoming fifth-graders. The fourth-grade teachers discussed each student's interests, abilities and family background. Because of this meeting, Mrs. Morgan had been able to spend the summer planning and preparing for them. Also, because the fourth-grade teachers had been available throughout the year to discuss students, brainstorm ideas on how to effectively reach particular students, and share ways to communicate with their families, the year had gone well. In just two more days, the fourth- and fifth-grade teachers would meet again to discuss next year's students.

Knowing how these meetings had helped her prepare for new students, Mrs. Morgan wondered how the various sixth-grade teachers at the junior high school would prepare for the students who were leaving her fifth-grade classroom. She worried about how well some of her students would adapt to the change of having multiple teachers and no longer having one specific teacher to monitor their overall progress. Would they have an adult to turn to if they were having problems? Would the teachers have the time to be able to guide the students through difficult material and assignments? How would her students react to having so many more classmates throughout the day instead of one close-knit group? Would her students get lost in the crowd? She was afraid that those students who had difficulty with this next phase in their education would begin charting a downhill course that might last a lifetime.

Meanwhile, Antonio, one of Mrs. Morgan's former students, was not looking forward to starting his freshman year at Central High School. While he was pleased that he would be seen as a high school student and that he was much closer to adulthood, junior high had been a real struggle for him. He clearly remembered the difficulty he had adjusting to junior high with the different schedules, the new teachers, and so many more students. Although organizing his assignments in junior high had always been difficult, the first couple of months were especially hard. He had really struggled to keep track of where he was supposed to be each period, as well as which rules and standards applied to which classroom. He felt like he needed more help than was available at the junior high school. In elementary school, getting help was easy. Usually the teachers knew when he needed more help or more time. Antonio missed having one teacher who really cared about him, who knew how he was doing in all his classes and who was interested about his life outside of school.

In junior high, the teachers seemed too busy with so many kids. How could any of them have much time for him? He felt like he was no longer Antonio, an individual who has many interests and skills, but had became Antonio, the kid that got a C– on the last paper or a D on his biology test. Because of his grades, Antonio was no longer in classes with some of his more academically focused friends. The worst part was that even though he had talent, he no longer qualified to play on the basketball team, his favorite part of junior high. Antonio had begun to hang out with some different kids after school. Some of their older brothers and uncles seemed to make pretty good money even though they did not finish high school. True, some of them got into trouble with the law, but that would never happen to Antonio. He began to wonder if getting a diploma was worth the daily struggle and constant feelings of failure.

At the same time, Kindra was thinking about her upcoming senior year. For most students, the senior year is a time of excitement, and although Kindra was excited, she was also concerned. She was determined to be the first member of her family to attend college. She had already decided that she wanted to use her tremendous math skills to major in engineering. She knew college was going to be very expensive even if she could get the scholarships and financial aid for which she had applied. Although her mother supported Kindra's dream, her father felt that college was unnecessary for girls. The little money the family had been able to save for college was earmarked for Kindra's two little brothers instead. Once Kindra graduated from high school, her father expected her either to stay at home and help support the family by working full-time, or to be out on her own. Her parents already worked three full-time jobs between them to support their five children, so Kindra had decided to continue working part-time at the bank where she had worked for the past two summers. She had hoped that between any financial aid she received and the extra money she earned, she would be able to go away to school. Unfortunately, the extra work hours would really put a strain on the time she had available to help with her siblings and to study. She knew she needed to maintain excellent grades in order to get into the college of her choice, and she also knew that her family needed her as well.

As stressful as this next year was going to be, Kindra was excited about meeting her new teachers. Last year, she really connected with Mr. Basta, her trigonometry teacher. He seemed to appreciate her talents and work ethic. He helped Kindra through some very stressful times by encouraging her to keep working toward her goals and by extending deadlines when he noticed that she was becoming overwhelmed. He also communicated well with her parents. This year she would have all new teachers; she wondered if any of them would be like Mr. Basta.

Each of these scenarios depicts the challenges related to successful transitions for students as they move from a set of familiar to unfamiliar circumstances. Mrs. Morgan has good reason to worry about some of her students as they enter junior high school, especially students like Antonio. While his perceptions that teachers were too busy to help him may have been inaccurate, his resulting feeling of helplessness certainly is an indicator that he is at risk for dropping out. Although Kindra is different from Antonio in that she would be considered a successful student, she has her own serious issues. The combination of her family situation and her drive to be successful could take a toll on her social-emotional health. For the thousands of adolescents like these two, the structures which are in place to support school transitions can potentially mean the difference between healthy productive lives and lives in which the individuals struggle against illness, poverty, crime, and early death. This chapter will explore some of the issues facing adolescents and describe areas that educators should attend to, in order to ensure smooth, successful transitions.

THE CHALLENGES OF TRANSITIONS INTO SECONDARY SCHOOLS

"Who am I? Where do I fit in? Where am I going? Does anyone care about me? *Should* anyone care about me? Am I a capable person? How can I cope with everything?" Questions like these often cause tremendous emotional upheaval as adolescents try to grapple with finding their own answers. Although most children emerge from high school poised to pursue successful adult lives, as many as one quarter of children ages 10 to 17 may be at-risk for long-range difficulties stemming from this turbulent period (Jackson, 1997). Children of this age not only become vulnerable to, but may engage in the high-risk behaviors associated with drug use, gang membership, crime, sexual promiscuity, eating disorders, and depression. These behaviors lead to unforeseen consequences that may remain with them for the rest of their lives.

Clearly, the number of changes and differing expectations that students encounter when moving from elementary school to the middle- and high-school settings can cause difficulties for *any* student. These transitions are especially difficult for diverse learners such as those who have cultural norms that are different than those which predominate in their schools, who have a disability, who are not proficient with standard English, and/or who come from low socio-economic backgrounds, or unstable home environments.

Though educators freely agree that frequent school transfers can disrupt and negatively affect the performance of students (Lacey & Blane, 1979), they may not realize that recent research has shown that transitions to different levels within the same school systems can also negatively affect student achievement (Kurita & Janzen, 1996). For all students, the transitions encountered from elementary through high school bring both environmental and social discontinuity (Rice, 1997). Additionally, the very structures inherent in secondary schools present roadblocks for students. A task force that studied the characteristics of young adolescents and the demands of the middle school setting, concluded that

> a volatile mismatch exists between the organization and curriculum of middle grade schools [junior high, intermediate, or middle schools] and the intellectual, emotional, and interpersonal needs of young adolescents (Carnegie Council on Adolescent Development, 1989).

In secondary schools, students must adjust to environmental changes such as increased school size, a decreased sense of school safety, increased pressure to achieve, greater autonomy related to choosing courses, and greater competition in academic as well as extracurricular activities. In a single day, middle-school and high-school students have to adjust to between six to nine classes with corresponding changes in subject matter, teachers, instructional methods and conditions, and classmates. The transition to a larger setting can disrupt the stability of students' social structures. For example, the loss of familiar teachers and peers may leave students feeling alone and disconnected.

Every year, up to a quarter of new middle-school-level students have difficulty coping with the stressors related to transitioning from elementary school (Leonard & Elias, 1993). In a series of studies on the transition from elementary to middle school, Simmons and colleagues found general declines in students' academic performances as well as socio-emotional well-being during this period (e.g., Simmons & Blythe, 1987; Simmons, Blythe, Van Cleave, & Bush, 1979), while Felner et al. (1993) found increases in problem behavior and higher rates of absenteeism, all of which have been found to be highly correlated with dropping out.

When asked the reasons for dropping out, former students responded in a national survey as follows: 43% did not like school; 39% cited their own school failure; 31% responded they could not keep up with schoolwork; 24% felt they did not belong; and 23% reported not being able to "get along with teachers" (National Center for Educational Statistics, 1996). Students from minority groups, from low socioeconomic backgrounds, and with disabilities represent the largest subgroups of the 3,000 students per day who drop out of school and the 3.4 million youths between the ages of 16-24 who have not completed high school (National Center for Educational Statistics, 1996).

A major contributor to students staying in or dropping out of school appears to be their ability to adapt to the changes brought about by school transitions from the elementary through the middle or junior high school to high school levels (Felner et al., 1993). Though the social and emotional issues experienced by many youths coupled with the tremendous upheaval they experience may seem daunting, teachers and schools can take positive actions to facilitate smooth transitions and support students as they face the often turbulent secondary school years. The quality of these transitions can be crucial in providing continuity and opportunities for immediate success or it can be disruptive and the source of discomfort and failure.

In fact, research has shown that well-developed transition program can positively affect student performance in school. For example, Smith (1997), in a study of the effectiveness of middle-school transition programs on high-school completion rates and student performance, found schools with transition programs that addressed and involved students, parents, and school staff, were able to increase student performance, and reduce dropout rates. Programs that targeted only one population — student, parent, or staff — showed no significant impact on student outcomes. According to Smith, when students from schools with fully developed transition programs were matched relative to demographics, family characteristics, and behavior with students in schools with limited transition programs, the students in schools without programs did not earn report card grades as high as those of students with fully developed transition programs and were 20% more likely to drop out of school.

Since transitions between school levels seem to be crucial to student success and since transition programs can be created to enhance that success, this chapter has been designed to review the elements that should be included in those programs. Four topics will be included: preparing students for upcoming transitions, supporting students in the new school settings, actively involving parents in the transition process, and developing comprehensive, school-wide transition programs.

PREPARING STUDENTS FOR TRANSITIONS

Before addressing how to best prepare students for transitions in their lives, educators might consider how adults prepare for transitions. Clearly, adults, often try to prepare as well as they can for expected major transitions in their lives. For example, when moving from one community to another, adults visit the new community, orient themselves to their new surroundings, locate essential services, and become acquainted with important individuals such as future co-workers, doctors, and educators. Unfortunately, students who face the major transitions of moving from elementary school to middle school/junior high or from middle school/junior high to high school often do not have an opportunity to become familiar with their new surroundings or acquainted with new people. Therefore, educators must arrange opportunities for students to have these experiences, in order to ease their arrival at the new setting. Educators can help prepare students for upcoming transitions by providing informational "Moving Up" packages, coordinating visits both to the new setting or from teachers and students currently in the new setting to the students' current classroom, and teaching students learning strategies that will insure success in the new setting.

Moving Up Packages

Realtors or community information centers often provide packets of helpful pamphlets, brochures, and maps to adult newcomers in an effort to help them become more familiar with their new surroundings and highlight local events. Teachers can help their students prepare for middle school or high school by creating *Moving Up Packages* (Howe, personal communication, 1998). One package can be prepared specifically for students, and another somewhat similar packet can be prepared for parents (this parent package will be discussed later). The *Moving Up Packages* for students can include any number of items such as maps of the new school, the school philosophy or motto, a calendar of events for the current as well as the next school year, academic and behavioral expectations, lists of clubs and activities and how to become involved, lists of the courses available, the names of the teachers and staff members, and a list of important phone numbers. By scheduling several class sessions in which different aspects of the *Moving Up Package* are introduced, teachers can help students begin to get a sense of what their new school experience will be like.

Visitations

When preparing for a major move, most adults visit the new city, neighborhood or job site to which they will be moving. Visitations can be useful for students, too, as they prepare to move to a new school. The more organized these visits are, the more successful they will be. A variety of organizational arrangements can be created. For example, Williamson and Johnston (1991) organized visiting elementary students into groups of four or five students each. Over the course of several weeks, the groups visited the middle school, and middle-school students known as "Buddies" led their tours. The visiting students attended several classes and had lunch before returning to their own school. Sometimes the Buddies also assumed the role of being a contact or mentor to the same students once they made the transition to the new school.

Incoming students can also be encouraged to attend public events at the new school. Using the current calendar of activities for the new school provided in the *Moving Up Package*, incoming students and/ or their parents can plan to attend any number of events (e.g., basketball games, band and choir concerts, art shows, etc.). Additionally, new students can be invited to a half-day orientation prior to the beginning of school in the fall where they will have the opportunity to meet the faculty and other students, walk through their upcoming schedule of classes, and become familiar with the various resources available at the new school.

For teachers, visits at the sending or receiving school can be quite helpful as well. These visits can help sending teachers decide what they should teach and what activities they should choose to prepare students for the transition. Visits also help receiving teachers learn much about preparing for the new students, including what they may need to review, reinforce, or teach at the beginning of the year.

Learning Strategies Instruction

Occasionally, when adults move into a new community, the new location may be remarkably different from the old one. For example, adults may move from a city into a rural environment or vice versa, to a different region, part of the country, or even different countries, or from an apartment into a house. When drastic changes such as these are about to take place, adults take special steps in order to prepare themselves for their new settings. They spend considerable time learning about the new location and how social interactions might be different there. If they are moving into their own home after living in a furnished apartment, they purchase any necessary household materials or appliances and learn how to operate them.

Students who move from elementary school to middle/junior high school or from middle /junior high school to high school are also making major setting changes. Because of the increased demands inherent in secondary schools, students are expected to behave differently than they did in elementary schools and to use different materials. They are expected to independently complete complex, multi-step assignments, acquire information from lectures and textbooks, remember complex information for tests and quizzes, and demonstrate their knowledge through lengthy writing assignments. They are expected to use organizational planners, multi-sectional notebooks, reference materials, and complex measurement instruments. Teachers in elementary schools, middle or junior-high schools can help their students be prepared for these new demands by teaching them critical learning strategies.

Several learning strategies have been developed to address the setting demands of secondary classes. For example, instruction in the Assignment Completion Strategy (Hughes, Ruhl, Schumaker, & Deshler, 1995) enables students to complete and turn in high quality assignments. As a supplement to the Assignment Completion Strategy, the Quality Quest Planner (Hughes, Ruhl, Rademacher, Schumaker, & Deshler, 1995) was developed to help students keep track of assignments on a monthly, weekly, and daily basis, plan weekly schedules to accomplish all their goals, and track their grades.

Other strategies such as the Word Identification Strategy (Lenz, Schumaker, Deshler, & Beals, 1984), the Visual Imagery Strategy (Schumaker, Deshler, Zemitzsch, & Warner, 1993), the Self-Questioning Strategy (Schumaker, Deshler, Nolan, & Alley, 1994), and the Paraphrasing Strategy (Schumaker, Denton, & Deshler, 1984) have been developed to help students acquire information from the complex reading materials used at the secondary levels. Research on these acquisition strategies described above has shown that students who had been reading below their grade levels and getting D's and F's on grade-level comprehension tests were able to apply the strategy in such a way as to raise their grades to B's on those tests.

Strategies have also been developed in an effort to help students organize and store information for future use. For example, instruction in the Listening and Notetaking Strategy (in prep.) enables students to identify, note, and study the important ideas and facts from lectures, while instruction in the First-Letter Mnemonic strategy (Nagel, Schumaker, & Deshler, 1994) teaches student how to create mnemonic devices such as words and sentences to remember facts (e.g., HOMES for the names of the Great Lakes) or steps in a process (e.g., FOIL for solving an algebraic equation). The Paired Associates Strategy (Bulgren & Schumaker, 1996) is designed to helps students create memory devices to remember information that is related (e.g., cities and states; products and countries; events, places and dates), and the LINCS Vocabulary Learning Strategy (Ellis, 1995) has been shown to help students learn how to remember the meaning of vocabulary.

Learning strategies related to the expression and demonstration of competence enable students to show teachers what they have learned. Strategies such as the Sentence-, Paragraph-, and Theme-Writing Strategies (Schumaker & Sheldon, 1985; Lyerla & Schumaker, 1990) build on one another and address teaching students how to write a variety of sentence forms, how to organize and write different types of paragraphs (i.e., sequential, descriptive, expository, and compare and contrast), and how to organize their thoughts and information in order to write well-composed themes. Use of a companion strategy such as the Error Monitoring Strategy (Schumaker, Nolan, & Deshler, 1985) enables students to edit their work. Finally, use of the Test Taking Strategy (Hughes, Schumaker, Deshler, & Mercer, 1984) helps students to allocate their time wisely when taking tests, attend to specific instructions on the test, make informed choices on multiple choice and true-false items, and complete fill-in-the-blank and short-answer items.*

---

* Information regarding Strategy Instruction may be obtained by contacting the University of Kansas Center for Research on Learning, 3061 Dole Building, Lawrence, KS 66045.

Strategy instruction, when done correctly, can be a powerful tool in helping students make successful transitions. Students who are adequately prepared for the complex demands of the secondary setting, and have an ample repertoire of strategies to draw upon are more likely to experience immediate success than those students who are underprepared and lacking useful strategies. In order to insure that students at-risk for school failure not only learn the steps involved in using strategies, but also generalize this use to other settings, elementary, middle and junior high school as well as high school teachers need to follow certain instructional procedures. For example, research has shown that teachers need to provide to students a description of the strategy and rationales for its use. Teachers must also model use of the strategy including the metacognitive processes undertaken. Further, students must commit to memory the steps of the strategy, practice using it on controlled materials (e.g., materials written at the student's current reading and functioning levels) followed by elaborated feedback from the teacher, and practice on grade-level assignments. Finally, teachers must instruct students on how to generalize the use of the strategy to other pertinent settings. Pre-tests prior to instruction and post-tests following instruction help to increase motivation and commitment to learn.

A Strategic Program

An example of a program designed to help students make successful transitions into high school that included strategy instruction as a key component is the Advancement Via Individual Determination Program (AVID). AVID has made a tremendous difference in the lives of thousands of students. Originating in San Diego over 15 years ago, AVID was developed by Mary Catherine Swanson as a college-preparatory program for primarily low-income and minority students. It has been adopted in over 500 schools in California and beyond. Of the 5,000 students who have been enrolled in AVID programs, 60% have gone on to four-year colleges, and of those students, 90% finish a four-year degree (Runzel, 1997).

The program began when Swanson, who was chairperson of the Language Department at her high school, found that her colleagues held very low expectations for the soon-to-be-bussed-in low-income and minority students from the inner-city. Swanson disagreed with her peers' prognosis for these students and developed a one-hour elective course that would provide the support these students would need to be successful in the standard college preparatory curriculum. She found that although most of these students wanted to go to college, they were naive about what that would require. The biggest hurdle seemed to be that these students had become passive learners who had not developed learning strategies to enable them to learn the content or earn the grades they would need in their high school coursework. Through the AVID Program, which involved the addition of a study strategy class to the students' schedule, these students not only made successful adjustments to high school, they also learned how to succeed in high school as well as prepare for college.

Initially Swanson taught students to take copious notes in class. The process of paraphrasing what the teachers had said, in addition to writing their own questions in the margins, became the cornerstone of the program. As a result of participating in the program, students began to pay more attention in class and used their notes to study for tests. Students also began to study together and reinforce each other's successes. Community volunteers, including undergraduates from the local colleges, were recruited to offer support to students during the AVID class. In addition, students learned what the requirements were for college, planned their coursework accordingly, visited college campuses, and learned how to access the appropriate resources to support themselves once they entered college. Although these students received no other accommodations in the college-prep courses, they proved to the other teachers, their parents, peers, and to themselves that they could make the grade.

PROVIDING SUPPORT TO STUDENTS IN THE NEW SCHOOL SETTING

Upon moving into a new community, adults are often greeted by the local "welcome wagon," an organization that welcomes newcomers with information about the community and opportunities to meet new people. Through the welcome wagon, adults have an opportunity to understand the culture of the community, make a personal connection in the community, learn about other members of the community, and become an active part of the community. These same opportunities should be afforded to students as they make the transition from elementary to middle/junior high school and middle/junior high to high school.

Understanding the Culture

A student's first impression of a school can be a lasting impression. Several studies have shown that not only are students' impressions of school usually based on accurate perceptions of specific aspects (e.g., expectations, teacher and student attitudes, safety) (Horwitz, 1979; Lundbenburg & Schmidt, 1989), but these impressions have been linked to student achievement, absenteeism rates, anxiety about school, and self-esteem (Epstein & McPartlannd, 1976; Moos & Moos, 1978; Nelson, 1984). If students interpret the school or classroom culture to be flexible and supportive, and the teachers hold high expectations for them, students will be more willing to strive to meet the higher standards. If, on the other hand, students perceive the culture to be rigid and unresponsive, and teachers hold low expectations, students will naturally be more apathetic. Special caution needs to be exercised so that students of racial and ethnic minority, low-socioeconomic class, and limited English proficiency, as well as students with disabilities, do not experience lower teacher expectations and less challenging educational programs than majority and middle-class students (Alvidrez & Weinstein, 1993). The type of welcome and orientation students receive upon arriving at the new setting will tell them much about the new school and will create their "first impression." Students need to get an immediate sense that the school culture is one of high expectations for *all* students and that the staff is committed to providing the necessary supports to make those expectations a reality.

A well-planned and coordinated orientation program is considered to be a valuable component in the transition program (Hirsch, DuBois, & Brownell, 1993). As a follow-up to visits taken prior to enrolling in the new setting, these orientation activities take place within the first day or two of school and give students additional opportunities to learn the layout of the campus, the overall school schedule, the academic and behavioral expectations, and to whom among the school staff they can turn with questions or problems. Students should be informed about the various roles of school personnel (e.g., the school nurse, the guidance counselor, the vice-principal, etc.) as they may differ from those at the elementary or middle-school levels. Opportunities for students to socialize with students from their former school as well as meet current classmates from other schools are also important for helping students develop a new social network.

Making a Personal Connection

Having a relationship with older students can be reassuring to new students. Often orientation activities are planned involving upper-classmen, leading school assemblies in which the school songs and traditions are shared, and having meetings during or after school to introduce new students to extracurricular activities. High schools in Crystal Lake, Illinois, for example, have a program in which student mentors meet with the same group of new students coming from different feeder schools once a week for the first nine weeks of school. In these 45-minute sessions the mentors answer any questions students might have, invite students to attend special events, and enable students to form relationships with others in the group. Mentors provide personalized follow-up with individual students who express needs that might not be met in a group setting. For example, mentors often provide tutoring or help students find tutors if they are encountering academic difficulties. Mentors also direct students to counselors and social workers as needed and facilitate meetings with coaches or sponsors of clubs and organizations in which students express an interest. Many new students have reported that the mentors have played a significant role in helping them create feelings of belonging and that the time spent with the group has helped them meet people and share experiences (Deppert, personal communication, 1998).

High school teachers in the Crystal Lake District have also become involved in mentoring students who are identified by junior high teachers as at-risk for failure. Interested teachers volunteer to meet with a small group of students for one class period a week over nine weeks in an effort to monitor students' academic work, offer study skills instruction, and provide any needed support. Guidance counselors match students and volunteer teachers based on a common free period and arrange for the meetings to take place. In most cases, teachers and students continue to meet on a regular basis after the original nine-week session has ended. With the combination of the student mentors and the teacher mentors, and the other students participating in the groups, students begin to encounter many familiar faces daily and forge relationships that can help make their transition a smooth one.

Becoming Part of the Community

When adults move to a new community, they often become a part of the community by getting to know their immediate neighbors and then members of their church and participants in other organizations. Adults often have a variety of resources to use in making themselves a part of a new community. They might have a well-honed set of social skills and a history of success in previous social situations and organizations. Unfortunately, students often do not. They may need a great deal of help from teachers and other school staff with regard to becoming truly integrated within a classroom or school community. Clearly, in today's schools, teachers face tremendous student diversity in their classrooms. Creating a classroom culture in which all students—regardless of their linguistic, ethnic, cultural, socioeconomic, experiential, educational, cognitive, social, and behavioral differences—feel they are valuable members of the classroom learning community can be a challenging task. Therefore, teachers must build in opportunities to get to know students individually, on both academic and personal levels. The following tools and methods can enable teachers to get to know their students quickly as well as provide a means for developing a strong classroom learning community.

One of the simplest yet most effective ways to get to know students is to ask well-formulated questions about students' interests and hobbies, perceived learning strengths and needs, and preferred methods for learning (e.g., What qualities do good teachers have? Should teenagers be given spending money or should they earn it? Should driving privileges be linked to staying in school? What kinds of music do you like and why?) (Stevenson, 1998). Open-ended questions about what students think and feel are particularly valuable. This types of inquiry enhances teachers' credibility with their students; young adolescents like to be asked what they think and believe (Stevenson, 1998). With this information, teachers can make learning more meaningful for students by developing content-based learning activities that also reflect students' interests and preferences.

Portfolios that are used to store students' work and teacher-student communication about that work can be very effective tools that help teachers get to know students individually and develop ongoing relationships with them. The use of portfolios in this way allows individualized feedback from the teacher and provides a mechanism through which the teacher can communicate with students about their academic progress and personal interests. Whatever the topic might be, if the communication from the teacher is sincere and meaningful, students will be more inclined to exhibit trust and responsibility within the classroom (Stevenson, 1998). Indeed, three outcomes can be achieved by maintaining portfolios:

1. Teachers can better understand what each student is thinking, doing, and learning.
2. Students can gain a better understanding about themselves as
   learners.
3. Schools can use student portfolios for formative and summative
   information about school programs.

Two portfolio-type tools that enable a wide range of communi-
cation between students and teachers are the Learning Express-Ways
Folder (Lenz, Adams, Vance, & Kissam, 1996) and the Destinations
Portfolio (Lenz, 1994).

The Learning Express-Ways Folder. The Learning Express-Ways
Folder (Lenz, Adams, Vance, & Kissam, 1996) is an effective and
efficient system that teachers can use in order to get to know their
students individually and to have ongoing personalized communications with them. By introducing the folder during the first week of
class, teachers can assure students that who they are individually and
how they are progressing during the course is important to the
teacher.

The Learning Express-Ways Folder is a flexible tool that can be
personalized by students as much as desired (see Figure 1 on the next
page). The outside, the public section of the folder, provides space for
an optional picture of the student and a brief autobiography or
statement about why the student is taking the class. Other information can be included such as the student's goals for the course,
important addresses, names, phone number, or other pertinent data
the student wishes to share.

The interior of the Learning Express-Ways Folder, the more
private section, helps students become more reflective about themselves and how they learn, and provides teachers with a more complete
understanding of their students as individuals. A mini-learning
inventory is provided for students to complete to help them think
about their learning strengths, potential areas of need, and learning
preferences. Another section of the folder's interior helps students

Figure 1
Information that can be Included in the
Learning Express-Ways Folder

- Student's schedule
- Student autobiographies
- Information on family
- Learning strengths
- Assessment preferences
- Student goals for the future

- Student's picture and address
- Rationale for taking the course
- Student interests and hobbies
- Learning preferences
- Student goals for the course
- Extracurricular obligations

identify their interests as well as educational and personal goals. To accommodate specific classroom needs, a section students and teachers can tailor for their own use is included. The information provided by students in these folders can be invaluable to teachers in making assignments and assessments more meaningful for their students.

Pages can be kept inside the folder which students and teachers can use for ongoing communications. One column on each page is for student comments; the other is for the teacher's responses. In their column, students can write comments, thoughts, or ideas regarding the content of the class or discuss more personal issues. They can ask questions about the content that they might not otherwise ask in public (due to shyness or not wanting to look "stupid" or too smart to their peers) as well as inform teachers of private matters which may affect their performance (e.g., an upcoming out-of-town trip, a relative's death, a divorce in the family). In their column, teachers are able to respond to all of these types of communications and provide the necessary supports or referrals while still enabling students to maintain their privacy. Other documents can be kept in the folders as well. For example, samples of the student's best work, the student's list of goals to be achieved in the class, and important reference materials can be stored in the folder.

The Learning Express-Ways Folder can be used in very creative ways and has proven to be an efficient means of enabling and maintaining regular student communication, even for teachers with over a hundred students per day. Used regularly, this folder gives students tangible evidence that they are valuable members of the classroom learning community. At the end of the course or school year, teachers and students can decide together which pieces of information should remain in the portfolio to be passed on to other teachers and which pieces will be taken out. This process allows the folders to become a transition tool that can be passed on to teachers whom the students will have in the coming year.

Teachers who have used these folders have found that the information they have received from students via this folder has enabled them to be more responsive to individual students as well as the class as a whole. Some teachers have found that their students' comments have even helped them make improvements in their courses (Berry, personal communication, 1998).

The Destinations Portfolio. The Destinations Portfolio (Lenz, 1994) is another tool that might be used to enhance transitions. Like the Learning Express-Ways Folder, the Destinations Portfolio is a folder that enables information to be shared between students and teachers. The Destinations Portfolio is designed to be course-specific in that sections of the portfolio contain information about the central concepts of the course as well as the relationships between the units of study and the overall course. The interior sections provide a means for an ongoing dialogue between the teacher and students but this one is specific to the students' progress toward the course goals.

The Destinations Portfolio includes a space to record the principles or values and standards that the teacher and students co-construct for the course. Teachers have found co-constructing classroom principles and standards with students to be extremely helpful in diffusing potential behavioral problems and reducing power struggles between themselves and their students. Rather than the teacher being the sole creator and enforcer of the rules or principles, students tend to take more responsibility for their own behavior when they are involved in developing them. Additionally, when specific principles and standards are developed for a course within the first couple of days of school, students understand the expectations immediately. This understanding makes the transition smooth since students do not waste time or energy trying to identify or test the behavioral and academic expectations of the teacher.

Used effectively, the information from the students' Destination Portfolios will help teachers make instructional decisions, document student growth over time, and keep students' attention on the big ideas of the course. For students, the Destinations Portfolio provides a source for understanding the demands and expectations of each course, a model for setting learning goals, a tool for self-monitoring, and a place to record and store assignments. Meaningful use of the Destinations Portfolio in conjunction with the Learning Express-Ways Folder can result in all students and the teacher working together in a supportive setting to learn what is considered critical about the curriculum and their lives. It will also save valuable time as students transition from course to course and try to adjust to different teachers.

Learning About Other Members of the Community

When adults become involved in neighborhood activities, church, and other community organizations, they not only share information about themselves, but they also learn about other people. Developing a classroom learning community involves students getting to know each other as well as the teacher getting to know each student. In order to ensure this happens, teachers can use a variety of activities at the beginning of a course. For example, a simple, quick, and non-threatening assignment that can help to build a sense of community is called the "Bag Speech." To complete this assignment, students are asked to fill a favorite bag (e.g., backpack, sports bag, or shopping bag) with various belongings that represent the many different facets of their lives (see Figure 2 on the next page). Students bring their bags to class, and to deliver their "Bag Speeches" they merely sit in front of the class pulling out each item and describing its significance. While each student is speaking, the rest of the class takes notes listing

Figure 2
Items to Include in the Bag Speech

- Photographs of people, pets, places
- Favorite books, stories
- Items that show a hobby (i.e., a bookmark for people who enjoy reading)
- Symbols of past experiences
- Favorite CDs, tapes
- Favorite articles of clothing
- Souvenirs, brochures
- Any sentimental belongings

the speaker's areas of interest or describing the items shown. To provide students with a model on how to present a "Bag Speech" as well as an opportunity to get to know them, teachers should give the first "Bag Speech." Student bag speeches can be followed with quizzes or journal writing in which students express unique insights they have gained about their fellow classmates. Bag Speeches are non-threatening in that students can choose what they bring, they have no lines to memorize, and they are extremely knowledgeable about the content of the speech.

Another similar activity involves students making a collage of pictures and phrases cut from magazines each of which represents some interest the student holds. Students can then explain their collages in a way similar to the way in which the "Bag Speech" is done.

Although the Bag Speech and collages may be helpful, teachers need to use caution when choosing "get acquainted" activities. In the first week or two of school, students may still be unsure of themselves and uncomfortable with other new students and teachers. Because adolescents are very conscious of the impressions their peers hold of them, placing students in group situations wherein the demands of the tasks are beyond their skill levels could be detrimental to students' self-esteem and drastically reduce the likelihood that they will take future risks in the class. If teachers are uncertain whether students have the prerequisite background knowledge, skills, or strategies to take part in get-acquainted activities, they should consider postponing them until the prerequisites are acquired. Group activities that may need to be postponed might include cooperative group work that requires students to read unfamiliar or different material, complete research work in a library, or solve complex math problems.

INVOLVING PARENTS/GUARDIANS IN THE TRANSITION PROCESS

In times of difficulty such as significant losses, illnesses, job changes, or moves, adults often turn to family for support and guidance. Family members, whether they are parents, grandparents, aunts and uncles, or siblings are often a comfortable, familiar source of support in times of great upheaval and change. Regardless of their age, students need to have their parents/guardians and family members' support and involvement in relation to school activities and especially during times of transition. While schools are responsible for providing an education for children, student learning is influenced by many factors including their non-school related activities and the amount of parental support they receive. As students make daily transitions from their home environment to school as well as the many other transitions that occur in school, educators and parents must work together as partners in supporting students' learning throughout the school years. Educators and parents need to keep in mind that although parental involvement is often high during the early grades when children are more dependent upon their parents, this involvement tends to decrease at the middle- and high-school levels. Although some adolescents and teenagers may discourage involvement, parents must insist on remaining involved in their children's education if their children are to succeed especially when students are making a transition from one level to the next.

Unfortunately, many schools do not include parent involvement as a formal component in the transition process (Smith, 1997). Parents and families can provide valuable information about their children that will never appear in a cumulative record. Having lived with their child from birth, parents have a unique perspective on their child's experiences, both in and outside of school. In addition, they often are willing and able to tell teachers about their child's interests, educational needs, and challenges, including what strategies do or do not work well with their child.

Although educators may view involving parents as a time-consuming project, the time spent is a worthy investment. Educators have many options for providing information and opportunities to engage parents in their children's education including (a) communicating with them via phone, mail, or newsletters, (b) inviting parents and family members to visit the new school and meet the staff, (c) explaining specific course content and expectations, and (d) engaging them as educational partners and active members of the school community.

Communicating with Parents

Communication between partners is the key to the success of the partnership. Before productive communication can occur between the home and school, educators need to address the values and perceptions they hold about the role of the family in relation to their students' education. Rivera and Smith (1997) point out that educators' "value system(s) and ways of perceiving information can, on occasion, impede or promote effective home-school communication and collaboration" (p. 36). Thus, educators need to be careful to not make false assumptions and judgments about students or families and instead should strive to come to an understanding about the families' strengths and needs.

One way to communicate with parents that will help the transition process go smoothly is to send them a parent version of the Moving Up Package in the spring before the transition in the fall. This package could contain any number of items including: an introductory letter, a description of the new school and its philosophy, the current semester's and the next year's calendar of events, courses available, course outlines, academic and social expectations, important phone numbers, a list of the characteristics of middle- or high school students, a parents' guide to homework, and parenting classes and resources. As students may need to choose their courses for the next level prior to beginning school, the Moving Up Package should also include information about the courses that are required for college admission or for other vocational opportunities. Without this information, their children may enroll in courses that will limit their educational or vocational opportunities.

Once students arrive at the new school, a Welcome Package can be sent home to the parents. This package can include: a school handbook for parents (see the sample table of contents in Figure 3), the school calendar of events, a staff directory including whom to contact regarding various issues, schedules for parenting support groups or classes, meeting schedules and contacts for parent associations, community resource phone numbers, and homework hotline numbers. In addition, individual teachers may want to send letters in the Welcome Package to explain about their specific courses. An example of a teacher letter is shown in Figure 4.

Inviting Parents to Visit

Another way to make parents and family members feel welcome is to invite them to visit the school or classroom prior to the start of the school year. This invitation can be extended in either the letter or packet described above. The visit can serve as an informal way for teachers to get to know families as well as for families to familiarize themselves with the school. When planned as a group activity for all parents, it provides a great opportunity for parents to meet one another. A visit might include a tour of the school, introductions to key personnel (principal, nurse, secretaries, librarians, etc.), and familiarization with materials or assignments students will be completing. Parents can walk though an abbreviated version of their son or daughter's schedule or just gather informally to talk about topics while enjoying refreshments.

Along with becoming familiar with the school and staff, parents should leave a visit feeling welcome in the school any time and recognized as important players in the educational process. In order

Figure 3
Sample Table of Contents for a School Handbook for Parents

I. **Welcome letter.** From the principal, School Governance Team, or entire staff, as an invitation to the parents to get to know the school

II. **Introduction.** A brief description of the school, (e.g., the address, important phone numbers, brief school history, numbers and characteristics of students and staff, motto, and mascot)

III. **Goals and Philosophy.** Mission statement and goals of the school

IV. **Characteristics of the Student.** Characteristics and how the school is responsive to needs of middle-school or high-school students

V. **Curriculum Organization.** A description of the programs, courses, types of skills, and social competencies to be learned, and a sample student schedule

VI. **Team Teaching and Inter-Disciplinary Instruction.** A short summary of the purposes of this type of teaming and a description of the team to which the student belongs

VII. **Meetings with Advisors.** The purposes of and types of topics to be covered

VIII. **Enrichment.** A list of activities in which students can participate to boost motivation and self-competencies

IX. **Parent/Community Programs.** A list of the types of programs and support services available for parents

X. **School Rules and Policies.** Rules, consequences, and how infractions are handled

XI. **Questions.** Common questions and answers

XII. **Concluding Comments.** A summary letter from the principal, governance team, or entire staff, aimed at reinforcing the integration of the philosophy and goals as described in the overall program and encouraging parents to become active members of the school community

Figure 4

Dear (Parents/Guardians):

My name is Susan Warner, and I am looking forward to having your son/daughter in English class this year. I like to think of my class as a year-long journey that I share with each one of my students. Throughout this journey we learn to appreciate literature and grow as writers, but we also learn to appreciate each other and grow as individuals. I will do everything I can to support your son/daughter's academic growth this year. In order for you to also lend support, I have some plans that I would like to share with you so that you know what your son/daughter will be required to do in English I.

First, we do a great deal of writing in this course. I try to make the assignments as interesting and useful as possible, so although I will choose some topics students will often write about areas of personal interest. Your son/daughter will be writing letters, short stories, lengthy explanations, and one research-based paper per semester. The due dates for these assignments will appear each Monday in your child's planner. Please ask to look at the planner on Mondays so you will know what is due.

We will also read several short stories and a few novels. Students will be asked to write journal entries that describe their thoughts on each reading assignment. I like to let students make some choices of their own, so twice a semester they will choose a book to read at home. They will also be required to write a report on the book. Dates on which these reports will be due will be recorded in your child's planner within the first week of class each quarter.

I will be asking your son/daughter to make a portfolio of all the assignments completed during the semester. I will allow students to continue to revise and improve their work throughout the semester. At the end of the semester, they will choose a variety of assignments to turn in for their final exam. They must also include a paper explaining how each assignment shows what they have learned. I have found this method to be not only fair, but also very motivating. You could support your child in this class by asking to see the portfolio occasionally and by reminding him/her that if he/she continues to revise work, grades will improve.

In return, if there is anything I can do to help make this year a smooth one, please don't hesitate to call. I am available to receive calls between 10:00–10:40 A.M. and 1:10–2:00 P.M. and before and after school and can be reached at extension 539. I am looking forward to meeting you at Parent's Night (at 7:00 P.M. on September 14) and your son/daughter at orientation.

Sincerely,
Mrs. Sue Warner

to do this, educators may dedicate a room in the school specifically for parents to use. This room should be equipped with comfortable furnishings and stocked with literature helpful to parents. This small investment of a couple of hours and a small space will pay huge dividends as the year progresses. Follow-ups to a visit can include newsletters with special information for parents of new students. Information might include hints for helping with homework and time management or more detailed descriptions of upcoming events.

Explaining Course Content and Expectations

Just as students need help and guidance adjusting to new courses and expectations that teachers hold for them, parents may need assistance in order to help them maintain involvement or begin taking a more active role in their child's education. Many parents have only their own experiences as students to rely upon as they help their children transition from one level of education to another. They may benefit from some fresh information on the courses their children will be taking, the behavioral and academic expectations of the new setting, and the many opportunities for their children's participation.

Again, this information could be included in a letter, an information packet, or discussed in a visit; however, some parents may require more explanation than can be shared in any of those options. When this is the case, a back-to-school night can be scheduled to inform parents about course content and expectations or personal meetings can be arranged. Sharing folders such as the Learning Express-Ways and Destination Portfolios with parents is one way of helping them to be clear about the expectations set for their children. Textbooks, sample assignments, grading scales, homework policies, and long-term assignments should also be shared. When strategy instruction is taking place, this should be explained to parents so that they can reinforce the use of strategies during homework time and encourage strategy use at school. Once again, an initial time investment could save many questions and frustrations later. Further, parents will feel more at ease about contacting teachers when they are unsure about assignments if the pattern for communicating about school work is established early.

Partnering with Parents

Building on early communication and visits can form partnerships. In a true partnership, teachers and parents work together to ensure that students have access to the best possible education. During transitions, success for many students will depend on this joint effort. For students who need systematic support from both the school and their parents, the Progress Program (Schumaker, Hovell, & Sherman, 1988) and the Check and Connect Program (Sinclair, Christenson, Hurley, & Evenlo, 1997) were developed.

The Progress Program is a system for parents and teachers to use for regular communication regarding a student's academic and/or behavioral progress. Although a daily progress check might be most appropriate at the middle or junior-high school level, a weekly progress check may be more appropriate at the secondary level and could be tied to the school planner. If the school does not disseminate a planner, the Quality Quest Planner, described earlier in this chapter, could be used. Ideally, the parents, student, and teachers can decide together which skills or behaviors the student needs to improve as well as a reward system for satisfactory progress. Once goals have been agreed upon and the reward system is in place, students become responsible for carrying progress reports between their parents and teachers. Students make sure teachers fill out the forms reporting the student's progress toward the goal. Students are also responsible for ensuring that the progress reports are seen by their parents and returned to school with the appropriate signatures. This extra measure of accountability for the student can help to prevent the development of more severe difficulties that would put students at an even greater risk of dropping out.

For those students with the highest risk of dropping out, those with emotional or learning disabilities, researchers have developed the Check and Connect Program (Sinclair et al., 1997). In this program, as soon as students show behaviors which put them at high-risk for dropping out (as early as upper elementary school) they are assigned a "monitor." Monitors are adults who have been trained to provide the necessary supports to these students by fulfilling a number of roles as needed (e.g., mentor, tutor, coach, friend, advocate, and case manager). The monitor follows the students' progress through each transition and subsequent school year within the feeder pattern until students are no longer at-risk for dropping out.

Monitors provide timely support for students through five essential elements: relationship building, monitoring, problem-solving, affiliation building, and persistence-plus. Monitors first build relationships with the students by being trustworthy and demonstrating persistence-plus, which means they don't give up because the students rebuke them. They "check" on students by "providing ongoing, consistent, and timely monitoring of student behavior for signs of early school withdrawal: tardies, absences, skipped classes, failing grades, and falling behind in credits" (Sinclair et al., 1997, p. 19). After seven years of research, findings show that students involved with this program have shown an increased rate of school engagement and graduation rates as compared to matched peers without this type of program.

This checking is important because researchers have found that students unknowingly underestimate the number of tardies and absences they have accrued. When shown their own records, students began to become more objective in looking at how their behavior contributes to their difficulties in school. Together, the monitor and student develop plans to resolve the most immediate problems and set long-term goals. The monitor also works with the student to create positive relationships with the people who can support the student in the students' home, school, and community environments (Sinclair et al., 1997).

Predictably, not all students are pleased initially with the monitor's role. This is where the persistence-plus term was coined. If the monitors are initially unsuccessful at connecting with students and their families, they persist to establish these relationships over an extended period of time. Home and community visits are common. Eventually, over time, most monitors have been able to establish strong relationships with students and their families. As valuable as programs like this can be, special funding may be required to pay monitors who may work with several schools at one time. Possible funding sources are those earmarked for dropout prevention.

SCHOOL-WIDE TRANSITION PLANS

When adults move to a new community, the way the community is organized to receive newcomers can make a big difference in the success of their transitions. For example, if a neighborhood has a formal neighborhood organization with a formal process of welcoming new neighbors, newcomers are likely to become integrated within the neighborhood. Such is the case for students as well. If a school has a comprehensive, school-wide transition program in place, students are likely to become fully integrated in the school. Successful comprehensive programs involve reorganizing the students' social system, restructuring the teachers' roles, instituting teacher teaming, coordinating the efforts of school staff members, and instituting articulated planning between sending and receiving schools. Gains in students' academic achievement, decreases in behavioral problems, and increases in the number of students completing high school have been linked to high implementation of comprehensive transition programs versus programs with few transition components (Felner et al., 1993).

One example of a successful, school-wide, comprehensive transition program that targets a combination of students, parents, and the school staff is the School Transitional Environment Project (STEP). The two main purposes of the STEP model were to reduce the contextual demands while increasing the coping mechanisms available to students (Felner et al., 1993). The STEP model was originally developed for and studied in the transition years only (i.e., the first year of middle/junior high school or high school). The STEP program focused on reorganizing the receiving school's social systems, increasing teacher support through teaming, and restructuring the homeroom teachers' roles (Felner et al., 1993). The original longitudinal implementation study and subsequent studies compared matched samples of primarily low-income students in STEP schools with students in schools without transition programs. Significant differences were found between the students. Students in STEP schools had higher attendance and graduation rates (23% higher in one study), fewer behavioral problems, and better self-reported adjustment (Felner et al., 1993). In addition, the STEP school teachers gave high satisfaction ratings to the program and voluntarily continued it.

The STEP model addresses the issues of connectedness and belonging through three components of the model. First, interdisciplinary teacher teams and student teams (4- 5 teachers with 100-125 students) are created for the transition year. All of the students within one team take their core courses with the same team of teachers. In addition, all STEP team classrooms are in close proximity so as to reduce the number and age range of other students with whom the STEP team students interact on a daily basis.

This type of teaming allows students and teachers to develop a sense of a learning community and belonging by choosing team names and mottos, establishing rules and consequences, and planning team projects and activities for both during-and-after school hours. As a result of this type of teaming, students report that they feel higher levels of accountability and connectedness to their schools, both of which are important for keeping students in school (Clark & Clark, 1994; Felner et al., 1993; George, Lawrence, & Bushnell, 1998).

Teachers who have worked in these types of teams reported a reduced sense of isolation because they have other teachers to help address student behavioral and academic problems. Teachers also reported increased efficacy and creativity as well as enhanced communications with families (Clark & Clark, 1994).

The second component of the comprehensive STEP model involves the provision of social-emotional supports to help students adjust to the new contextual demands. If any student has difficulty academically or socially, all of the teachers on the team are responsible for working together to develop a comprehensive plan to support the student in all of his or her classes and activities. The school counselors and special programs teachers are also available resources for the team. Teachers meet with their team on a daily basis to discuss student-related issues, brainstorm solutions, and to coordinate planning. Co-planning times also enable teachers to coordinate units of study, major homework assignments, testing days, as well as reinforcement and expansion upon what their students are learning in each other's classes.

The third component of the STEP model involves each of the STEP teachers serving as a homeroom or advisory teacher to 20 to 25 students within the team. While initially the role of the Advisory Teacher can seem overwhelming, by working together, teachers can develop a well-rounded program that can address a wide range of student needs. Keefe (1991) explained the rationale for the advisory program by stating:

> Students are asked to make many important educational, career, and personal/social decisions, generally without much guidance. In advisement, a team of professionals and paraprofessionals works together to help students on an ongoing basis— the kind of assistance counselors do not have the time to provide (p. 161).

To implement the advisory program, 25 to 40 minutes are set aside each day to fulfill some of the traditional homeroom activities as well as for teachers to give academic and social guidance to students. Students need academic guidance even in middle school because they need to begin making good choices and planning for their futures. Too many students are unaware of the coursework needed to enter a given career path, yet course choices made in middle school and early in high school can influence those outcomes. Guidance counselors often have tremendous loads and are unable to devote the time students need to help them set goals for their future. The teacher advisory programs can fulfill this need as students begin the transition from childhood to adulthood. With the advisory teacher, students can begin to explore career options and determine the courses that will give them the most choices upon graduating from high school.

The advisory program can also be devoted to helping students learn how to assess their own interests, strengths, and areas of need. Students can learn how to access different resources and begin to explore career options. By helping students set attainable short- and long-range goals, students often begin to understand the importance of their current coursework and are more motivated to be successful students. Advisory periods can also be used to boost students' study skills. For students who have learned specific learning strategies, this can be time to review and strengthen these skills. For students who have not had exposure to learning strategies, this would be an ideal time to learn them.

Individual student advisement can also be a component of the advisory program. Traditionally, counselors have been the sole monitors of the academic and behavioral progress of several hundred students. In the STEP Program, the advisory teachers who can be in daily contact with other team teachers can take on the responsibility for monitoring the progress of their own small group of students. The advisory teacher can mentor students, hold them accountable for their actions, and work as an advocate with the guidance counselor to obtain the necessary resources and services to enable students to be successful.

Although the Student Advisory Program is not a substitute for guidance or counseling programs, advisory periods can also be used to teach social and coping skills students will need for the rest of their lives. Two examples of research-based social skills strategies that have been developed for classroom teaching are the SCORE and TEAMS Strategies (Vernon, Schumaker & Deshler, 1996; Vernon, Deshler & Schumaker, 1993). These two strategies teach students the skills for receiving and giving useful feedback and working in small groups, skills that have been identified as necessary for success in the workplace (U.S. Department of Labor, 1992). By learning the skills embedded in these two strategies, students can learn to become valued members of their school, home, and workplace communities.

In developing an advisory program, creating a sense of safety and trust is essential. Students should be encouraged to suggest topics to be covered during advisory periods. As students may be too embarrassed to suggest topics in an open forum, simply having every student turn in a piece of folded paper will enable those who have suggestions to remain anonymous. The range of topics covered during advisory periods can be diverse (see Figure 5). By asking students for suggestions on topics, the discussions can be more student focused. Advisory programs such as these enable transitioning students to feel an immediate sense of community and accountability with a team of students working toward mutual goals and a teacher whose roles include instructor, advisor, and mentor.

The advisory teacher can also take on the role of Parent Liaison in the STEP Program. Parents of students in traditional secondary programs can feel overwhelmed with trying to establish relationships with the numerous teachers serving their son or daughter each semester. Communicating with all of their son's or daughter's teachers, even if the student encourages it, can be a daunting task. In the STEP Program, parents communicate directly with the advisory teacher as the contact person at the school who knows their child well and who can communicate with other school personnel as necessary.

Figure 5
Possible Advisory Topics

- Goal-setting
- Social events
- Relationships
- Study skills
- Sports activities
- Listening skills
- Conflict resolution
- Job expectations
- Accessing resources
- Characteristics of adolescents
- Test-taking
- Service projects
- Peer pressure
- Giving and receiving feedback
- Rap sessions
- Problem-solving
- Self-esteem
- Self-advocacy

The advisory teacher can also conduct parent-teacher conferences. As both students and their parents become known to the advisory teachers in programs like this, parents begin to feel they are true partners with the school in guiding their child's education.

Research on the STEP Program showed that before the program was in place, when teachers began to be concerned about an individual student's progress, they were reluctant to contact the guidance counselor and waited until the problem escalated. After the STEP Program was in place, teachers took action sooner by contacting the advisory teacher after they sensed a problem (Felner et al., 1993). Having a small number of students to advise, advisory teachers were able to address issues quickly and thereby reduce the overall number of referrals, absences, and academic failures. Advisory teachers can prevent students from falling through the cracks as they transition from one level of schooling to the next.

In summary, the STEP model provides a developmentally appropriate and supportive program for transitioning students. Through teacher and student teams and the Advisory Program, which also brings parents into the partnership, the STEP Program reduces the contextual demands placed upon students and fosters a sense of community. The higher academic achievement, attendance, and high school completion rates as well as increased teacher efficacy indicate that the STEP model is an effective, comprehensive program for supporting students as they transition from one level of schooling to the next.

SCHOOL-TO-SCHOOL TRANSITION PLANNING

Every year, tens of thousands of working adults are transferred from one geographic location to another. One of the largest employers in the United States, the military, provides extensive support for individuals transferring between military bases. Besides systems for facilitating transfer of personnel records, the consistency of procedures, expectations, and support systems across bases makes the adjustment to a new base much easier for newly transferred personnel. These same types of support systems can be developed for students who transition from one level of schooling to the next.

Coordinating the transition of students can be a complicated matter for both the sending and receiving schools. On the administrative side, the sending schools have to prepare and send each student's cumulative file and health record. Special education students' IEPs and evaluation reports must be also be sent. At the receiving school, each student must be registered, cumulative files organized, health records updated, IEPs distributed, course rosters developed, buses scheduled, and faculty assigned to teach each class.

These transition activities require much time and energy, but, they should not be the only activities planned for school-to-school transitions. As pointed out throughout this chapter, educators need to move beyond focusing on the logistics of transitions and consider the developmental needs of students. In addition to the strong support that individual teachers and school-wide transition programs can provide for students, the coordinated efforts of the sending and receiving schools can greatly add to the ease of the transition process for students.

By establishing inter-school committees, sending and receiving schools can work together to develop common behavioral and academic standards, as well as work on curriculum articulation. Consistent, clearly stated standards, expectations, and consequences across schools will reduce the ambiguity which transitioning students may otherwise face. In addition, students can be better prepared academically if sending and receiving schools jointly decide upon the grade levels in which specific content as well as learning and social skills strategies should be taught and reinforced. Sending teachers can be assured they are preparing students appropriately for the increasing demands of the next level. Receiving teachers will have a better understanding of what their incoming students should have already learned. In addition, open lines of communication between schools can enable staff members at the receiving schools to learn about and prepare to give more extensive support to those students who have the most severe challenges. The benefits for students and educators are many (see Figure 6).

Transition planning among schools can alleviate much of the worry that teachers like Mrs. Morgan felt when sending students on to the next level. She could be assured she was preparing her students with the skills and knowledge that would enable them to be successful at the middle- and high-school levels. She would know that the students she felt were at-risk for dropping out would be given extra support. In turn, the middle-level teachers would become familiar with and reinforce specific learning or teaching strategies that were emphasized at the elementary level as well as build on them to prepare students for high school. Ultimately, students will benefit greatly from the coordinated efforts that educators put forth to facilitate these transitions.

In summary, major transitions are often difficult, even for adults. The new social groups, expectations, routines, and different demands require newcomers to have high levels of resourcefulness in order to traverse such transitions easily. Adults usually make extensive plans to

---

Figure 6
Benefits of School-to-School Transition Planning

- Students are better prepared with the knowledge and skills necessary to be successful at the next level.
- Redundancies in coursework or materials are reduced.
- The amount of time required for review is lessened as all students are better prepared.
- Teachers can reinforce prior learning (e.g., through teaching learning strategies).
- Students, parents, and teachers understand the flow of courses.
- Academic and behavioral expectations are established early and reinforced.
- School-wide rules are consistent and reinforced (e.g., using a three-ring binder and specific assignment sheets or a *Quality Quest Planner*).

facilitate their own transitions. For adolescents, the transition into a new level of schooling brings the same types of challenges, yet, developmentally, students often do not have the coping skills that are necessary to meet the demands of the traditional secondary setting. The decreases in academic achievement and self-esteem resulting from unsuccessful, unsupported transitions have been linked to high dropout rates. Intentional comprehensive transition plans that include educators, parents, and students can greatly facilitate students' transitions between different levels of schooling. Such programs have been shown to halt and even reverse the common downward spiral that often leads to students dropping out. Educators and families must work together to provide the support students need to successfully traverse this challenging period.

Had Antonio's parents had the opportunity to learn about the courses and expectations that he was about to encounter, they may have been able to help direct his energies and interests in a more positive manner. Had Kindra's parents been able to get information about the career path she envisioned, as well as college and financial aid options, they may have been more willing to support her in her dream.

In the scenarios described earlier, Mrs. Morgan expressed concern about her students as they moved on to middle school. Had she known to set up visits with the middle-school teachers as well as teach learning strategies, she might have felt more comfortable about how well she had prepared her students for the transition. Had Antonio's teachers used the Destinations Portfolio and taught him learning strategies, he would have had a better understanding of the goals and expectations for each course and he would have been better prepared to meet the academic demands of his classes. Antonio might have been a good candidate for an AVID class. What a difference these changes would have made in the life of a boy who was considering dropping out of school! Although Kindra already had successfully developed her own set of learning strategies, the use of the Learning Express-Ways Folder would have helped her introduce herself to her new teachers. With all of her obligations, the last year of high school and the transition to college will be challenging for Kindra. She will need the full support of her teachers and her parents to be able to pursue her dreams. If educators and parents work together to develop comprehensive transition programs, today's and tomorrow's Kindras and Antonios can have much brighter futures.

REFERENCES

Alvidrez, J., & Weinstein, R.S. (1993). The nature of "schooling" in school transitions: A critical re-examination. *Prevention in Human Services, 10* (2), 7-26.

Berry, G. (1998). Personal communication .

Bulgren, J.A., & Schumaker, J.B. (1996). *The paired associates strategy.* Lawrence, KS: The University of Kansas.

Carnegie Council on Adolescent Development, Task Force on Education of Young Adolescents. (1989). *Turning points: Preparing American youth for the 21st century.* Washington, DC: Author.

Christenson, S.L., Hurley, C.M., Hirsch, J.A., Kau, M., Evelo, D., & Bates, W. (1997). Check and connect: The role of monitors in supporting high-risk youth. *Reaching Today's Youth, 2*(1), 18- 21.

Clark, S.N., & Clark, D.C. (1994*). Restructuring the middle level school: Implications for school leaders.* New York: State University of New York Press.

Deppert, P. (1998). Personal communication.

Duffy, G.G., Roehler, L.R., Sivan, E., Rackliffe, G., Book, C., Meloth, M.S., Vavrus, L.G., Wesselman, R., Putnam, J., & Bassiti, D. (1987). Effects of explaining reasoning associated with using reading strategies. *Reading Research Quarterly, 22,* 347-368.

Ellis, E.S. (1995). LINCS: *The vocabulary learning strategy.* Lawrence, KS: Edge Enterprises, Inc.

Ellis, E.S., & Lenz, B.K. (1987). A component analysis of effective learning strategies for LD students. *Learning Disabilities Focus, 2*(2), 94-107.

Epstein, J.L., & McPartland, J.M. (1976). The concept and measurement of the quality of school life. *American Educational Research Journal, 13,* 15-30.

Felner, R.D., Brand, S., Adan, A.M., Mulhall, P.F., Flowers, N., Sartain, B., & DuBois, D.L. (1993). Restructuring the ecology of the school as an approach to prevention during school transitions: Longitudinal follow-ups and extensions of the School transitional Environment Project (STEP). *Prevention in Human Services, 10*(2), 103-137.

Felner, R., Jackson, A.W., Kasak, D., Mulhall, P., Brand, S., & Flowers, N. (1997). The impact of school reform for the middle grades: A longitudinal study of a network engaged in Turning Points- based comprehensive school transformation. In R. Takanishi & D.A. Hamburg (Eds.), *Preparing adolescents for the twenty-first century* (pp. 38-69). New York: Cambridge University Press.

George, P., Lawrence, G., & Bushnell, D. (1998). *Handbook for middle school teaching* (2nd ed.). New York: Longman.

Hirsch, B.J., DuBois, D.L., & Brownell, A.B. (1993). Trajectory analysis of the transition to junior high school: Implications for prevention and policy. *Prevention in Human Services, 10*(2), 83-101.

Horwitz, R.A. (1979). Effects of the open classroom. In H.J. Walberg (Ed.), *Educational environments and effects: Evaluation, policy, and productivity* (pp. 275-292). CA: McCutchan.

Howe, S. (1998). Personal communication.

Hughes, C.A., Schumaker, J.B., Deshler, D.D., & Mercer, C.D. (1988). The test-taking strategy. Lawrence, KS: Edge Enterprises, Inc.

Hughes, C., Ruhl, K., Deshler, D.D., & Schumaker, J.B. (1995a). *The assignment completion strategy*. Lawrence, KS: Edge Enterprises.

Hughes, C., Ruhl, K., Deshler, D.D., & Schumaker, J.B. (1995b). *The quality quest planner*. Lawrence, KS: Edge Enterprises.

Jackson, A.W. (1997). Adapting educational systems to young adolescents. and new conditions. In R. Takanishi & D.A. Hamburg (Eds.), *Preparing adolescents for the 21st century*. Cambridge, UK: Press Syndicate of the University of Cambridge.

Keefe, J.W. (1991). Advisement. In J. Keefe, & J Jenkins (Eds.), *Instructional leadership handbook* (pp. 161-162). Reston, VA: National Association of Secondary School Principles.

Kurita, J.A., & Janzen, H.L. (1996, August). *The role of social support in mediating school transtion stress*. Paper presented at the Annual Meeting of the American Psychological Association, Toronto, Ontario, Canada.

Lacey, C., & Blane, D. (1979). Geographic mobility and school attainment: The confounding variables. *Education Research, 21*, 200-206.

Lenz, B.K. (1994). *Destinations portfolio*. Lawrence, KS: The University of Kansas.

Lenz, B.K., Adams, G., Vance, M., & Kissam, B. (1996). *Communicating with students in secondary schools: How to use the learning expressways folder*. Lawrence, KS: The University of Kansas.

Lenz, B.K., Schumaker, J.B., Deshler, D.D., & Beals, V.L. (1984). *The word identification strategy*. Lawrence, KS: The University of Kansas.

Leonard, C.P., & Elias, M.J. (1993). Entry into middle school: Student factors predicting adaptation to an ecological transition. *Prevention and School Transitions, 10*(2), 39-57.

Lunenburg, F.C., & Schmidt, L.J. (1989). Pupil control ideology, pupil control behavior, and the quality of school life. *Journal of Research and Development in Education, 22*, 36-44.

Lyerla, K.P., & Schumaker, J.B. (1990). *The paragraph writing strategy.* Lawrence, KS: Edge Enterprises, Inc.

Moos, R.H., & Moos, B.S. (1978). Classroom social climate and student absences and grades. *Journal of Educational Psychology, 70*, 263-269.

Nagel, D.R., Schumaker, J.B., & Deshler, D.D. (1986). *The FIRST letter mnemonic strategy.* Lawrence, KS: Edge Enterprises, Inc.

National Center for Educational Statistics. (1996). *Dropout rates in the United States: 1994* (USDE Publication No. CES 94-669). Washington, DC: U.S. Government Printing Office.

Nelson, G. (1984). The relationship between dimensions of classroom and family environments and the self-concept, satisfaction and achievement of grade 7 and 8 students. *Journal of Community Psychology, 12*, 276-287.

Rice, J.K. (1997). *Explaining the negative impact of the transition from middle to high school performance in mathematics and science: An examination of school discontinuity and student background variables.* Paper prepared for the Annual Meeting of the American Education Research Association, Chicago, IL.

Rivera, D.P., & Smith, D.D. (1997). *Teaching students with learning and behavior problems* (3rd ed.). Boston: Allyn & Bacon.

Runzel, D. (1997, January). AVID learners. *Teacher Magazine.*

Schumaker, J.B., & Sheldon, J. (1985). *The sentence writing strategy.* Lawrence, KS: The University of Kansas.

Schumaker, J.B., Denton, P.H., & Deshler, D.D. (1984*). The paraphrasing strategy.* Lawrence, KS: The University of Kansas.

Schumaker, J.B., & Deshler, D.D. (1992). Validation of learning strategy interventions for students with learning disabilities: Results of a programmatic research effort. In B.Y.L. Wong (Ed.), *Contemporary intervention research in learning disabilities: An international perspective.* New York: Springer-Verlag.

Schumaker, J.B., Deshler, D.D., Zemitzsch, A., & Warner, M.M. (1993). *The visual imagery strategy.* Lawrence, KS: The University of Kansas.

Schumaker, J.B., Deshler, D.D., Nolan, S.M., & Alley, G.R. (1994). *The self-questioning strategy.* Lawrence, KS: The University of Kansas.

Schumaker, J.B., Hovell, M.F., & Sherman, J.A. (1988*) The progress program: A teaming technique.* Lawrence, KS: Edge Enterprise.

Schumaker, J.B., Nolan, S.M., & Deshler, D.D. (1985). *The error monitoring strategy.* Lawrence, KS: The University of Kansas.

Simmons, R.G., & Blyth, D.A. (1987). *Moving into adolescence: The impact of pubertal change and school contest.* New York: Aldine de Gruyter.

Simmons, R.B., Blyth, D.A., Van Cleave, E.F., & Bush, D.M. (1979). Entry into early adolescence: The impact of school structure, puberty, and early dating on self-esteem. *American Sociologial Review, 44,* 948-967.

Sinclair, M.F., Christenson, S.L., Hurley, C.M., & Evenlo, D. (1997). Dropout prevention for high-risk youth with disabilities: A longitudinal study. (Submitted for publication.)

Smith, J.B. (1997). Effects of eighth-grade transition programs on high school retention and experiences. *The Journal of Educational Research, 90*(3), 144-152.

Stevenson, C. (1998). *Teaching ten to fourteen year olds* (2nd. ed.). New York: Longman.

U.S. Department of Labor (1992). *Learning a living: A blueprint for high performance. A SCANS report for America 2000.* Washington DC: U.S. Government Printing Office.

Vernon, D.S., Schumaker, J.B., & Deshler, D.D. (1993). *Teamwork strategy.* Lawrence, KS. Edge Enterprises.

Vernon, D.S., Schumaker, J.B., & Deshler, D.D. (1996). *Score skills: Social skills for cooperative groups.* Lawrence, KS: Edge Enterprises.

Williamson, R., & Johnston, J.H. (1991). *Planning for success: Successful implementation of middle level reorganization.* Reston, VA: National Association of Secondary School Principals.

CHAPTER SIX

The Strategies Intervention Model: A Model for Supported Inclusion at the Secondary Level

ROSEMARY TRALLI, BEVERLY COLUMBO,
DONALD D. DESHLER, & JEAN B. SCHUMAKER

Successfully including students with mild disabilities in secondary classrooms is a complex and difficult assignment for classroom teachers and administrators for a variety of reasons, including the following:

- Teachers are under great pressure to cover large amounts of content to meet the demands of the Excellence in Education movement;
- Teaching loads of at least 125 students daily allow little time for individualization and extra support for at-risk students;
- Teachers have limited meaningful planning or collaboration time during the school day;
- Students with mild disabilities lack many of the necessary skills and strategies required to respond successfully to the demands of the secondary setting;
- The prevailing culture in many secondary schools is more supportive of a content-centered than a student-centered orientation toward education. As a result, steps to accommodate the needs of the students with disabilities are not top

priorities of teachers and administrators; and

- For many teachers, raising *overall* class achievement is an important goal, but they may be unwilling to engage in heroic efforts on the behalf of a few students with disabilities in their classes.

Because of these realities, unless classroom teachers receive proper training and support, inclusion of students with mild disabilities (e.g., learning disabilities) within secondary classrooms may be accomplished in name only.

TOWARD A SOLUTION

Clearly, methods for ensuring the success of students with disabilities are needed. In response to this need, the mission of the University of Kansas Center for Research in Learning (KU-CRL) has been to design instructional methods and procedures that enable teachers to address the challenges represented by the realities outlined above. Since 1977, KU-CRL researchers have teamed with teachers to create and validate a variety of interventions to increase the likelihood that students with disabilities can succeed in general education classrooms.

The interventions developed through this research are collectively called the Strategies Intervention Model (SIM; hereafter referred to as "the Model"). They can be grouped into three major categories (Deshler & Schumaker, 1988). The first group of interventions, called *learning strategy interventions,* were developed because many students with disabilities are ineffective learners who lack information-processing skills to cope with the wide range of content and complexity of tasks they encounter in secondary classes. For example, they need to learn how to assess a classroom situation and then use an appropriate learning strategy or a combination of strategies to help them respond to the requirements and demands of that situation. In order to prepare students for the academic demands they will face as lifelong learners, each of the learning strategies constitutes a *strategy system,* a complex set of cognitive strategies to be used in sequence to successfully complete a generic academic task (e.g., to study for a test, take a test, or write a paper). These strategy systems have been designed to be used in a variety of combinations. (See Figure 1 for descriptions of the learning strategies.)

When students with mild disabilities receive intensive instruction in targeted learning strategies in a resource room or other support setting, they can be taught to be strategic learners (see, for example, Schumaker & Deshler, 1992). In addition, they can also learn these strategies to mastery in the general education classroom when classroom teachers devote sufficient instructional time to ensuring that they master the strategy to a point of fluency (Scanlon, Deshler, & Schumaker, in press). The critical features of successful strategy instruction include (a) daily and sustained instruction, (b) multiple opportunities to practice the strategy in a variety of situations, (c) individualized feedback, and (d) required mastery of the strategy (Ellis, Deshler, Lenz, Schumaker, & Clark, 1991).

The second category of interventions, *content enhancement routines,* are instructional routines teachers use to enhance their delivery of content information and improve their students' understanding and recall of the content. Many cognitively and emotionally challenged students have difficulty organizing, understanding, storing, and remembering the information presented during large-group instruction in the general education classroom. KU-CRL research has shown that students' understanding and recall of subject-matter information improve markedly when teachers enhance their delivery of the information by emphasizing critical features of the content (Schumaker, Deshler, & McKnight, 1991). Specifically, when teachers carefully select the content that they are going to teach and then provide students with a well-structured overview of the information at the beginning of a block of instruction (e.g., a unit or lesson), students' understanding and recall of key sets of information improve (Lenz, Alley, & Schumaker, 1987). Additionally, student comprehension and retention of key concepts (e.g., "federalism") in general

Figure 1. The learning strategies curriculum.

ACQUISITION STRATEGIES
Word Identification Strategy: teaches students a problem-solving procedure for quickly attacking and decoding unknown words in reading materials, allowing them to move on quickly for the purpose of comprehending the passage.
Paraphrasing Strategy: directs students to read a limited section of material, ask themselves the main idea and the details of the section, and put that information in their own words. This strategy is designed to improve comprehension by focusing attention on the important information of a passage and by stimulating active involvement with the passage.
Self-Questioning Strategy: aids reading comprehension by having students actively ask questions about key pieces of information in a passage and then read to find the answers for these questions.
Visual Imagery Strategy: is designed to improve students' acquisition, storage, and recall of prose material. Students improve reading comprehension by reading short passages and visualizing the scene which is described, incorporating actors, action, and details.
Interpreting Visuals Strategy: is designed to aid students in the use and interpretation of visuals such as maps, graphs, pictures, and tables to increase their ability to extract needed information from written materials.
Multipass Strategy: involves making three passes through a passage for the purpose of focusing attention on key details and main ideas. Students survey a chapter or passage to get an overview, size up sections of the chapter by systematically scanning to locate relevant information which they note, and sort out important information in the chapter by locatng answers to specific questions.

STORAGE STRATEGIES
FIRST-Letter Mnemonic Strategy: is designed to aid students in memorizing lists of information by teaching them to design mnemonics or memorization aids, and in finding and making lists of crucial information. (Published by Edge Enterprises.)
Paired Associates Strategy: is designed to aid students in memorizing pairs or small groups of information by using visual imagery, matching pertinent information with familiar objects, coding important dates, and a first-syllable technique.
Listening and Notetaking Strategy: is designed to teach students to develop skills which will enhance their ability to learn from listening

Figure 1 (continued).

experiences by identifying the speaker's verbal cues or mannerisms which signal that important information is about to be given, noting key words, and organizing their notes into an outline for future reference or study.

EXPRESSION AND DEMONSTRATION OF COMPETENCE STRATEGIES

Sentence Writing Strategy: is designed to teach students how to recognize and generate four types of sentences: simple, compound, complex, and compound-complex.

Paragraph Writing Strategy: is designed to teach students how to write well-organized, complete paragraphs by outlining ideas, selecting a point of view and tense for the paragraph, sequencing ideas, and checking their work.

Error Monitoring Strategy: is designed to teach students a process for detecting and correcting errors in their writing and for producing a neater written product. Students are taught to locate errors in paragraph organization, sentence structure, capitalization, overall editing and appearance, punctuation, and spelling by asking themselves a series of questions. Students correct their errors and rewrite the passage before submitting it to their teacher.

Theme Writing Strategy: teaches students to write a five-paragraph theme. They learn how to generate ideas for themes and how to organize these ideas into a logical sequence. Then the students learn how to write the paragraphs, monitor errors, and rewrite the theme.

Assignment Completion Strategy: teaches students to monitor their assignments from the time an assignment is gives until it is completed and submitted to the teacher. Students write down assignments; analyze the assignments; schedule various subtasks; complete the subtasks and, ultimately, the entire task; and submit the completed assignment.

Test Taking Strategy: is designed to be used by the student during a test. The student is taught to allocate time and read instructions and questions carefully. A question is either answered or abandoned for later consideration. The obviously wrong answers are eliminated from the abandoned questions, and a reasonable guess is made. The last step is to survey the entire test for unanswered questions.

education classes improve when teachers use graphic devices and *structured teaching routines* to present those key concepts (Bulgren, Schumaker, & Deshler, 1988). (See Figure 2 below for a description of the content enhancement routines.)

Transforming students from ineffective and, in many respects, helpless learners into learners who can compete within demanding secondary school settings requires more than merely teaching them to be strategic learners or enhancing content delivery. The third group of interventions in the Model are the *empowerment interventions,* which are geared toward empowering students to perform at their best and to create positive relationships with others in the school setting. For example, several social and motivational strategies have been developed to enable students to interact in positive ways with peers and teachers as well as to engage in self-advocacy (e.g., Schumaker, Hazel, & Pederson, 1988; Van Reusen, Bos, Schumaker, & Deshler,

---

Figure 2. Content enhancement routines.

ORGANIZATIONAL ROUTINES
Course Organizer Routine: Used to orient students to the "big ideas" of the course and the course plan, including the units to be covered during the course.
Unit Organizer Routine: Used to orient students to a new unit including how it relates to the course plan, previous and future units, and major parts wathin the unit and relationships among those parts.
Chapter Survey Routine: Used lo orient students to a new chapter in the textbook.
Lesson Organizer Routine: Used to orient students to a particularly difficult lesson or group of lessons, including how the lesson(s) relates to previous and future lessons, and the major parts of the lesson.

CONCEPT ROUTINES
Concept Mastery Routine: Used to introduce a major concept like "democracy" to students.
Concept Anchoring Routine: Used to tie a new concept to a a concept students already understand.
Concept Comparison Routine: Used to compare and contrast two or more concepts.

1994; Vernon, Schumaker, & Deshler, 1993).

"One-shot," sporadic interventions have not produced success at average or above-average achievement levels for students with disabilities in inclusive placements (Deshler & Schumaker, 1993). Instead, to significantly impact the performance of students with disabilities in secondary settings, these three groups of interventions must be well coordinated across numerous teachers and classes. Teachers need to plan together and to collaboratively solve problems over sustained periods of time in order for these students to achieve success in school (Knackendoffel, Robinson, Schumaker, & Deshler, 1992).

The essence of the need for comprehensive interventions for this population was underscored recently in findings reported by the Joint Committee on Teacher Planning for Students with Disabilities (1995). The overwhelming consensus of several teams of researchers who studied the inclusion of students with learning disabilities was the following: *"In order for students with disabilities to be successfully included in the general education classroom, educators need to think in terms of* 'supported inclusion,' *not simply* 'inclusion'" (p. 3).

"Supported inclusion" refers to a set of instructional conditions in which classroom teachers

- Are philosophically committed to meeting the needs of all students in the general education classroom, including those of students with mild disabilities;
- Have sufficient time to think about and plan for the diverse needs of students in their class(es);
- Incorporate teaching practices that enable them to better meet the needs of all students in their class(es);
- Work collaboratively with special education teachers to assess student needs, teach in productive ways, and monitor student progress;
- Have the option for their students to receive *short-term,* intensive instructional support from a special education teacher; and

- Have the option for their students to receive *sustained* instruction in basic skills or learning strategies that cannot be
provided in the general education classroom.

The Model incorporates these instructional conditions in such a way
that general and special education teachers work together on behalf
of students with disabilities.

The following accounts describe two efforts to translate the
philosophy and instructional components of the Model into practice.
In the first account, Rosemary Tralli, a special education teacher at
Wethersfield High School in Wethersfield, Connecticut, describes
how the Model is being implemented throughout her district and
how commitment by key administrators and teachers over an extended period has resulted in dramatic changes in the performance of
students with disabilities. In the second account, Bev Columbo, a
secondary special education teacher in Clayton High School in
Clayton, Missouri, describes how components of the Model were
used to address the challenges encountered when her high school
eliminated tracking in an attempt to create an inclusive school.
Common to each of these accounts is the amount of time devoted to
planning and collaboration.

DISTRICT-LEVEL IMPLEMENTATION:
THE WETHERSFIELD PUBLIC SCHOOL SYSTEM

The Model has been implemented in the Wethersfield public school
system since 1988.[1] Prior to this, support services for students with
mild disabilities primarily emphasized tutorial assistance for classroom assignments or remedial instruction in basic skills. Institution-
alization of the Model across multiple teachers and schools required

---

1. The student population of the school district is 3,032, including 864 students at the high
   school level. About 10% of the student population comes from minority groups, approximately 10% have disabilities, and more than 80% of the graduates attend colleges and
   universities.

several years and has involved a deliberate plan to ensure application in both the special and general education programs. After 7 years, the Model is now deeply embedded in the educational system. Thus, the Model has become part of a strategic plan to meet the needs of diverse student populations within general education settings and to ensure more genuine inclusion of students with special education needs.

Factors Contributing to Success

Successful application of the Model in the Wethersfield district has not been happenstance; rather, it is the result of carefully adapting its components to the unique characteristics of school programs and staffs as well as the following factors:

Philosophical Agreement. Foremost, the philosophical underpinnings of the Model reflect the mission statement of the school system. The Model is based on the belief that all students should develop their potential as independent and strategic learners across learning, social, motivational, and executive domains. In keeping with this view, the educational goals of Wethersfield public schools are that each student (a) acquire skills and knowledge for lifetime learning; (b) develop a positive sense of self; (c) develop self-discipline and function as a responsible citizen in society; and (d) understand his or her own ethical, aesthetic, and intellectual values and respect those of others. Additionally, the Model's philosophy emphasizes the shared responsibility of each member of the learning community. Similarly, in Wethersfield, students are recognized as individuals within a learning community that is built to develop strategic and independent learners. Teachers are viewed as facilitators of learning rather than simply as imparters of content knowledge. In short, the strong congruence between the philosophical underpinnings of the Model and those valued by the district has aided the adoption process.

Support Mechanisms. Administrative support (both in the central office and at the building level) has been a critical element in the development and integration of the Model. Support has consisted of providing funding for district-level professional development opportunities; granting release time for teachers to engage in training; purchasing instructional materials; and guiding the creation of a strategic plan that explicitly accommodates the Model across grades, schools, and programs. Administrators have demonstrated their commitment to the Model in several ways: (1) The superintendent frequently speaks of the Model at staff meetings and at each annual orientation session for all district personnel and writes personal letters to staff members who demonstrate implementation success. (2) The assistant superintendent ensures that professional development opportunities for learning how to implement the Model are included in each year's staff development program. (3) The principals use faculty meetings to talk about the program to faculty, publicize the program in school newsletters, and offer insights to visiting administrators about how to integrate the Model in light of site-based reform efforts. (4) The director of pupil personnel and the supervisor of special education frequently publicize information about the Model in the local newspaper.

To further underscore their support of the Model, administrators attend *and actively participate* in staff development sessions with faculty. Their active participation has made it clear that the Model is going to be a central part of the educational process of the Wethersfield school system and that all staff are expected to be engaged and supportive.

Training Opportunities. Ongoing Model training continues to support and expand implementation. Initially, such training was provided by trainers from the KU-CRL. In 1988, however, the district provided funding for a special education faculty member to become a certified Model trainer. Currently, two other faculty members are fulfilling trainer certification requirements so that district-level training initiatives can be expanded. Teachers are trained through formal professional development strands that last from 1 to 3 years. Following initial training on an intervention package, teachers practice implementing the procedure with their students and return to training sessions for debriefing and problem solving. With district support, the training sequence has been arranged so that training strands involve multiple sessions over an extended period of time, thereby affording teachers sufficient opportunities to become comfortable with teaching the new strategy or using a new routine.

Curriculum Development. A scope and sequence of strategies instruction has been developed and is updated continually to ensure that the program responds to the setting demands faced by students at each grade level (see Figure 3). Students are taught only those strategies that are germane to their own needs and that assist them in responding to the demands in their general education classes. Given the shortage of instructional time for skill and strategy instruction, especially at the secondary level, great emphasis is placed on collaboration between general and special educators as well as between personnel at

Figure 3.
Resource implementation sequence—Wethersfield.

Grade Level	Strategies Taught	Content Enhancement
5–6	Sentence Writing (Preskills; Simple & Compound Sentences) Paraphrasing (Preskills) Word Identification	
7–8	Assignment Completion Sentence Writing Error Monitoring Test-Taking LINCs Paraphrasing Visual Imagery SLANT	Concept Mastery
9–12	FIRST-Letter Self-Advocacy Paragraph Writing Theme Writing "Intra-strategy" Integration	Lesson Organizer Unit Organizer Concept Anchoring TRIMS "Intra-strategy" Integration

different schools and grade levels with regard to what strategies a given student will learn. Such collaboration minimizes fragmented interventions that generally do little to improve student performance. Additionally, to make the most of the limited instructional time, 90% of a student's time in the resource room is devoted to strategy instruction. Further, to ensure that current instruction builds systematically on previous instruction, cumulative records are kept of student progress within the Model sequence of instruction and accompany each student from one grade level and/or school to the next.

Strategy instruction applied in Wethersfield resource rooms builds from the simpler strategies to the more complex across grades 5 through 12. Simpler strategies are taught in the upper elementary grades to introduce the concept of strategic learning and to provide students with tools for coping with academic tasks. In grades 7 and 8, at least four additional strategies are taught. Generally, these are strategies that bolster students' ability to respond successfully to advanced reading and writing demands. As students move into high school, the most complex strategies are taught. At each grade level, teachers deliberately prompt students to review and use strategies they have already learned; continual reminders to apply and refine previously learned strategies are critical to developing independent learners and performers. Typically, high school students who have completed this sequence of strategies instruction are able to apply at least 8 to 10 core strategies across a variety of settings.

In addition, general education English, foreign language, and social studies courses at the middle school and high school levels integrate learning strategies instruction and the use of content enhancement routines. For example, strategies are taught in English and foreign language classes to help students master new vocabulary, As students experience strategic learning opportunities across a variety of settings and over multiple years, they become increasingly more independent and proactive as learners. Students who have mastered several strategies achieve higher grades and progress to more advanced course levels more rapidly than do their peers who do not receive strategies instruction.

Parental Support. Parental involvement in and support for the Model has also impacted student growth. When the Model was initially adopted, some parents were apprehensive about shifting from a tutorial model to a strategic model because they were comfortable (yet not always satisfied) with methods that centered on content instruction and tutorial review. During the first few years of implementation, parental support was primarily enlisted through presentations at meetings of the local Learning Disabilities Association. Opportunities for parents to observe the program firsthand were made available through a demonstration site at the middle school level. These measures solidified parental support. Parents now regularly prompt their children to use strategies they have learned to complete homework assignments and insist that the program emphasis across the grades be strategic instruction. Parental involvement has contributed greatly to bringing focus and stabilization to the program.

Focus on the Learning Process. In both special education and general education settings, SIM instruction focuses on *both* process and content. Continual attention is given to exploring the learning process, talking about *how to learn* the content in the class and complete particular tasks, and discussing the benefits of using strategic tools. Additionally, in each class, students are encouraged to determine which parts of the strategies work best for them and to apply them accordingly. Students are also encouraged to create and apply adaptations of the strategies they have learned. For example, they may combine steps from several strategies or several whole strategies to approach a new academic task. Once students identify aspects of the strategies that work best for them and apply them in a variety of situations in a variety of combinations, they become more invested in independently using them.

Collaborative Efforts to Ensure Generalization. Another key to the successful implementation of the Model is the strong emphasis placed on collaboration between special education and general education teachers to maximize student generalization of mastered strategies. Unless explicitly taught, students may not identify those situations where a targeted learning strategy should be applied. Thus, special and general education teachers regularly communicate to ensure that students are taught learning strategies that are applicable to their general education classes. When a student is ready to use a strategy, the general education teacher cues the student to use that strategy when an appropriate situation arises. This teacher also monitors the student's use of the strategy and may provide immediate feedback concerning that application. The general education teacher also provides critical information to the special education teacher about the student's performance. As a result, decisions can be made about aspects of strategy use that need to be bolstered in the resource setting under controlled learning conditions.

The Special Education Component

As described above, instruction within the resource room programs at the upper-elementary, middle, and high school levels is based on a specified scope and sequence of strategies created for each level. All students have mild to moderate learning disabilities and are enrolled in mainstream content courses at low, middle, or high tracking (or difficulty) levels for a majority of the school day. The long-term goal for the majority of these students is to enter postsecondary educational programs.

In order to tie a student's educational experience together at the high school level with regard to coordinated strategy instruction across the grades and to ensure successful transitions to postsecondary settings, students are taught the self-advocacy strategy (Van Reusen, Bos, Schumaker, & Deshler, 1994). This strategy has been found essential to the initiation of a specialized educational program for an individual student as well as subsequent instruction and evaluation of student progress. Use of the self-advocacy strategy affords students an opportunity to inventory their learning strengths and weaknesses, to express goals and expectations, and to take an active role in shaping

their educational programs in team meetings and individual conferences. Instruction in this strategy is based on the idea that before they
can become invested in their individual educational programs, students must understand their own learning characteristics in relation
to the demands present in a variety of educational settings. In short,
since a major goal associated with the Model is to empower students
and to create independent learners and performers, students receive
hands-on experience in thinking about and giving direction to their
programs.

To begin instruction in the self-advocacy strategy, students are
introduced to the concept of self-advocacy and the importance of
being able to effectively talk with others about themselves and about
things that are important to them. Next, they are taught how to
identify and understand their special needs. For example, the meaning of being a student with a learning disability is discussed. Miscon-
ceptions about learning disabilities are dispelled through candid
dialogue and instruction. A concept diagram from the concept
mastery routine (Bulgren, Deshler, & Schumaker, 1993) is filled out
in an interactive process with the students so they can gain a clear
understanding of the essential elements embodied within the learning
disabilities construct (see Figure 4 on the next page).

Students report that they have achieved a new level of self-
awareness and often express relief as a result of this process. Some
students admit they did not want to discuss their special needs for fear
of discovering that a learning disability might be a form of mental
illness or low intelligence. Students have also explained that they are
generally aware that they are different learners than their peers, but
that they think these differences are the equivalent to "something
wrong" since they have been excluded or protected from discussions
about their needs.

Next, students complete the self-advocacy strategy skill inventory
(a device that assists students in thinking about themselves as learners)
and analyze the specific academic, social, vocational, and motivational skills and strategies that they possess. Once students can
identify the strengths they bring to school, the seed of empowerment

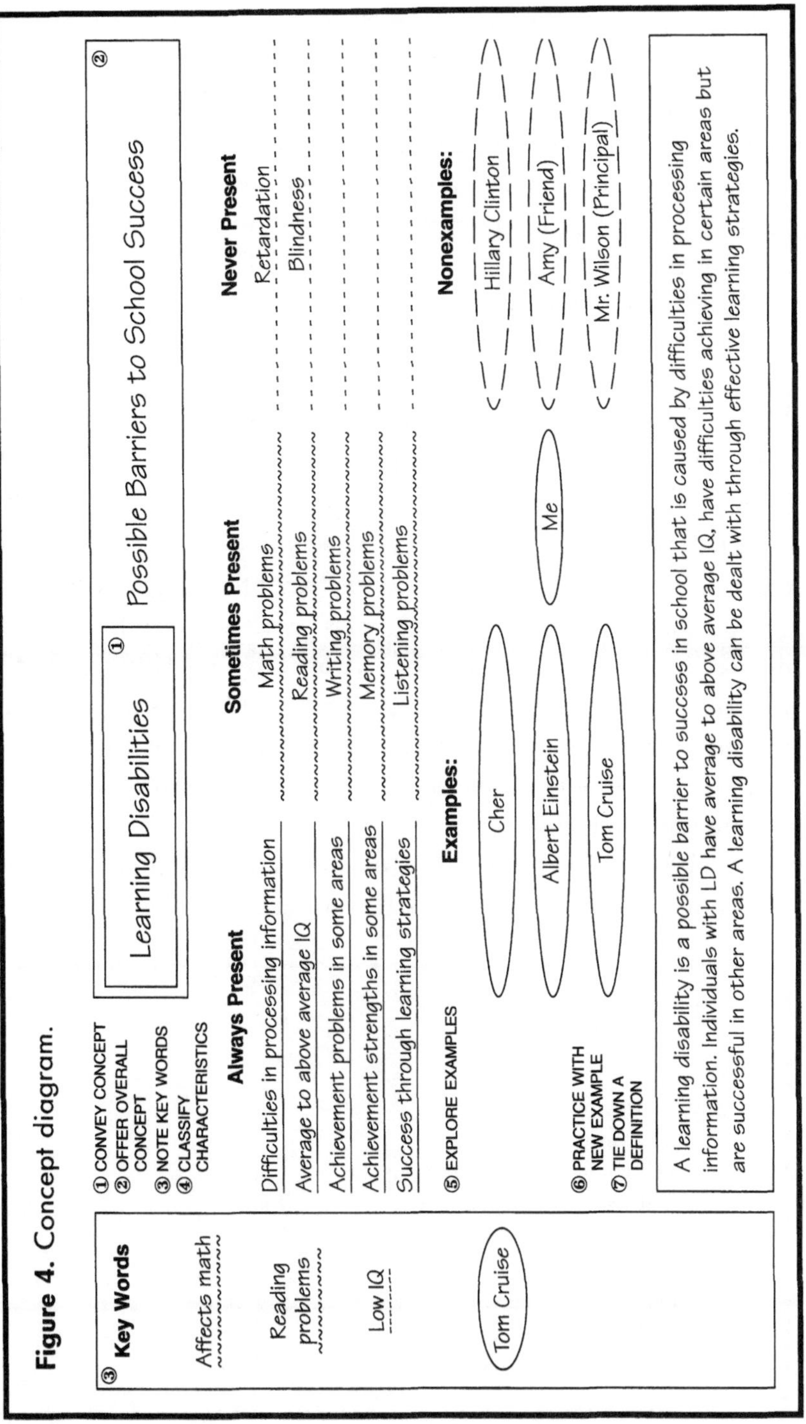

Figure 4. Concept diagram.

③ **Key Words**

Affects math

Reading problems

Low IQ

① CONVEY CONCEPT
② OFFER OVERALL CONCEPT
③ NOTE KEY WORDS
④ CLASSIFY CHARACTERISTICS

| Learning Disabilities ① | Possible Barriers to School Success ② |

Always Present

Difficulties in processing information
Average to above average IQ
Achievement problems in some areas
Achievement strengths in some areas
Success through learning strategies

Sometimes Present

Math problems
Reading problems
Writing problems
Memory problems
Listening problems

Never Present

Retardation
Blindness

⑤ EXPLORE EXAMPLES

Examples:

Tom Cruise

Cher

Albert Einstein

Me

Tom Cruise

Nonexamples:

Hillary Clinton

Amy (Friend)

Mr. Wilson (Principal)

⑥ PRACTICE WITH NEW EXAMPLE
⑦ TIE DOWN A DEFINITION

A learning disability is a possible barrier to success in school that is caused by difficulties in processing information. Individuals with LD have average to above average IQ, have difficulties achieving in certain areas but are successful in other areas. A learning disability can be dealt with through effective learning strategies.

has been planted. By comparing their strengths to the demands present in their classes, students are also able to identify what skills and strategies they need to learn. On the basis of these analyses, each student sets personal learning goals each school quarter and has a major voice in decisions about what strategies will be learned. As new skills and strategies are mastered, students add them to their skills inventories.

Students also learn to use the self-advocacy strategy to prepare for and participate in pupil planning team meetings, transition conferences, and other conferences with teachers. They are taught appropriate communication skills, called the SHARE behaviors (Van Reusen et al., 1994), which are to be used in these conferences (see Figure 5 below). Each student completes a special worksheet to identify expected task demands related to each upcoming course scheduled for the next school year and to list those demands that might be difficult given current strategy and skill levels. These demands are then discussed, and Individualized Education Program (IEP) goals are written related to pertinent strategies that should be learned during the upcoming school year. Students also specify needed instructional modifications as a result of identifying personal learning styles and teaching methods they prefer their teachers to use.

A similar process is used to assist older students in thinking about transitioning from high school to postsecondary life. Using the

Figure 5. SHARE behaviors.

Sit up straight
Have a pleasant tone of voice
Activate your thinking
   • Tell yourself to pay attention
   • Tell yourself to participate
   • Tell yourself to compare
Relax
   • Don't look uptight
   • Tell yourself to stay calm
Engage in eye communication

Transition Planning Inventory (Van Reusen et al., 1994), students identify their strengths and areas that need improvement with regard to postsecondary living. Again, goals and needs are specified.

This information is shared by students at their individual pupil planning team meetings. During the meeting, students actively participate by using their SHARE behaviors to convey their goals and the information that they have prepared on their inventory sheets. The results are powerful. Each year, students take more ownership in developing their programs. As they progress through high school, students become increasingly independent in preparing their unique learning plans for the upcoming school year. Self-motivation, discipline, and commitment are heightened because students "own" their programs.

The General Education Component

General education teachers play a central role in enabling students to be successfully included within the general curriculum. First, they work closely with special education teachers to inform them of the types of curriculum requirements students with disabilities are having difficulty meeting. This information is used to determine the learning strategies that should be taught in the resource room. After students acquire basic fluency on a strategy in the resource room, the general education teacher prompts students to use it in completing assignments in the general classroom. Second, some general education teachers choose a limited number of strategies (i.e., one to three) that they will teach and emphasize to the entire class throughout the school year. Third, some general education teachers use content enhancement routines to facilitate acquisition of the content information they deliver.

For example, several strategies have been included in the curriculum of a high school English class. The sentence-writing strategy (Schumaker & Sheldon, 1985) is taught to develop stronger sentence-writing and grammatical-usage skills. The error-monitoring strategy (Schumaker, Nolan, & Deshler, 1985) is introduced to improve student ability in detecting and correcting errors in written products. Other strategies help students apply study techniques for content mastery. For example, the LINCS Strategy (Ellis, 1992) is introduced early in the school year and is used to assist students in learning content-based vocabulary for weekly tests. The word identification strategy (Lenz, Schumaker, Deshler, & Beals, 1984) is taught to help students pronounce and spell the new vocabulary words. Students' test scores prior to and after strategic interventions are used as pretest and posttest measures of performance and progress is monitored on a weekly basis. Further, peer review of strategy implementation provides opportunities for constructive feedback and peer support. Finally, strategy application is monitored and graded as a part of the coursework.

The content enhancement routines are used to introduce and clarify new concepts across all course levels to elevate learning for students of varying abilities. For example, the concept mastery routine (Bulgren et al., 1993) may be used to introduce a concept such as *feudalism* in a social studies course. Later in the course, the concept comparison routine (Bulgren et al., 1995) may be used to compare and contrast feudalism with another concept, such as *manorialism*. This approach allows students to explore concepts in new and exciting ways. It also allows teachers to present critical aspects of the curriculum in ways from which all students in an academically diverse class can benefit.

Summary

In Wethersfield, adoption of the Model is taking place slowly but steadily. True system change is occurring because key components of the Model have been shaped to meet the unique strengths and needs within the district. The strong and long-term support of administrators and parents, in addition to the commitment of staff to work together in meaningful collaboration within and across school settings, has provided the foundation for successful implementation. However, although this experience has clearly shown that students with mild disabilities can successfully compete in general education course offerings and graduate from high school prepared to enter meaningful postsecondary options, the present results were not achieved by "blindly" including students in the mainstream through administrative fiat. Inclusion has worked in this district only because it is supported inclusion.

SCHOOL-LEVEL IMPLEMENTATION: CLAYTON HIGH SCHOOL

Six freshmen diagnosed as having learning and language disabilities were about to enter Clayton High School[2] in Clayton, Missouri, with a mixture of emotions ranging from hope and optimism to fear and uncertainty. They faced the challenges that confront students with disabilities entering a competitive, college preparatory, public high school in an affluent community. But these students faced an additional challenge: Clayton High School was in the process of restructuring its academic program to reduce tracking. All basic or low-track courses were being eliminated, resulting in heterogeneously grouped classes in all required content courses (with the exception of a few honors or advanced placement courses). The basic classes, offered previously in English, science, and math, had been designed to meet the needs of low-achieving students, including students with disabilities. These classes were generally smaller and slower paced. They were not watered-down classes, but rather an adapted version of the average track classes. In reality, they were as stringent as average classes in other high schools in St. Louis County.

The elimination of these basic classes in the move toward heterogeneous grouping concerned the special and general educators who had taught the basic classes. Although most of the staff philosophi-

---

2. Clayton High School's student enrollment is 800. Approximately 95% of graduates go to college, and 25% of the student body consists of minority students who are voluntary transfer students from inner-city St. Louis. Approximately 10% of the student body has disabilities, and more than 90% of the graduates attend colleges and universities.

cally agreed with the goals associated with eliminating these classes, they shared the fear that many low-achieving students who were struggling in the basic classes would fail in the heterogeneous classes. Given the magnitude of learning problems that many of the students with learning disabilities experienced, the special education teachers were uneasy about all students being included in general education classes during seven periods of an eight-period day. They were particularly concerned about the incoming freshmen and the sopho-mores, whose schedules were packed with required courses they had to pass to satisfy graduation requirements. Traditionally, some stu-dents with more significant learning disabilities had been scheduled into basic classes, while others who were more capable were scheduled into a combination of basic classes and general classes, based on their ability to respond to the demands in the various classes. The special education teachers were worried that the basic-class safety net was being removed with no plan for catching students who might fail. Although the most pressing concern was for the six entering fresh-men, the teachers were also fearful for the sophomores as well as the at-risk students who were not eligible for special education. Given these concerns, the resource teachers and general educators who taught the basic classes formed a planning team and met for a year to formulate a plan of action to accommodate these students.

The Planning Year Experiment

The planning team decided to use the planning year to run an experiment to determine how students with disabilities could best be accommodated within the confines of general education classes. The plan called for resource and general education teachers to co-teach a basic English class to test methods to be used in future heterogeneous English classes. They hoped that the co-teaching arrangement would improve the overall effectiveness of the instruction because the teachers would be able to mediate each other's instruction as well as give extra assistance to students who required help during a class period. The plan included infusing of instruction of some writing strategies into the English class because teachers on the planning team had observed the powerful results of strategy instruction to small groups of students in the resource room during the past 5 years. These results included significant changes in student academic performance as well as in self-esteem and confidence. Many of the students who had learned strategies in the resource room over the course of their 4-year high school career had experienced the "snowball effect" from learning several strategies, exhibiting more growth than anyone had dreamed possible (Deshler, 1990). In light of the changes the planning team had witnessed as a result of intensive strategy instruction in the resource room, team members wanted to determine whether strategies could be taught effectively within the general education classroom.

One of the most significant challenges was designing a way of teaching the learning strategies to large groups of students. Foremost among the challenges were managing the multiple practice opportunities required by each student, providing feedback to students after each practice attempt, maintaining student interest, and ensuring that all students progressed through the instruction at a rapid pace.

To address these challenges, the following steps were implemented. First, an academically diverse English class was divided into two groups, novice and experienced learners. The novice group was assigned to the resource teacher and the experienced group to the general education teacher. Second, the course schedule was organized so that the sentence-writing strategy was taught 3 days per week. This arrangement allowed sufficient flexibility for providing additional practice to those students who were struggling or who had been absent. Third, group instruction techniques were designed that included a thorough review of earlier strategy lessons and a brief model of a new dimension of the strategy. Students were encouraged to take turns leading the group in activities related to completing new practice lessons and to write different types of sentences. In addition, classwide peer tutoring and peer assistance were implemented during various stages of strategy mastery to provide additional opportunities for teachers and others to give individual feedback to students.

All the students in the class learned to use the sentence-writing strategy to write simple, compound, and complex sentences, and several of the students learned to write compound-complex sentences. Moreover, generalization of the strategy to other classes in which the students were enrolled was readily accomplished. The degree of generalization to other settings and situations, which is often a problem when strategies are taught in a special education setting (Schmidt, Deshler, Schumaker, & Alley, 1989), was high in this class. The English teacher, who knew the strategy well, cued its use for writing assignments about the literature the students were studying and prompted them to apply it and self-correct their sentence structure and punctuation during individual writing conferences.

Writing instruction in this class, as in all English classes at Clayton High, was based on the writing process model, in which students learn a prewriting, writing, and revision process and participate in individual conferences with the teacher about their writing. The mechanics of writing are usually not taught directly but are discussed during writing conferences. Thus, direct instruction on sentence structure through the introduction the sentence-writing strategy was a significant departure from the typical holistic style of instruction. As underscored by the success of this experience, direct instruction could be effectively combined with holistic practices, and learning strategy instruction can be successfully infused into a general education course based on a holistic model.

The Implementation Year

Once success became apparent during the planning year, the planning team decided to focus their efforts for the following year on English and science. To prepare, English, science, and special education teachers participated in extensive strategy and co-teaching training and wrote a proposal to become a formal pilot site for state field-testing of the Class-Within-A-Class co-teaching model (Hudson, 1992).

The planning team realized that general education teachers were willing to infuse learning strategy instruction into their courses as long as the time required to do so was "reasonable." That is, these teachers did not think they could sacrifice content to teach strategies because of the pressures they felt to ensure that their students met certain curriculum expectations. They were most willing to incorporate strategy instruction that emphasized organization of time and materials, studying for tests, and task completion. They believed that special educators would be most helpful to all students by providing study skills instruction and by developing supplementary learning activities and materials to help students learn the content.

Even the English teacher, who had been eager to teach the sentence-writing strategy in the basic class during the planning year, placed limits on how much time she was willing to take away from her other teaching objectives to teach the sentence-writing strategy in heterogeneous classes. There were several reasons why she was not willing to spend 4 to 6 weeks teaching the strategy to mastery. First, because the class was a heterogeneous, average to above-average, class, she believed that the content should be the same as that covered in comparable classes. Her previous experiences in these classes had convinced her that most students were very proficient at writing sentences and paragraphs and fairly proficient in writing five-paragraph essays (unlike the students with whom she had worked in the basic class during the planning year). Since the expectation for this course, as well as for all other English courses, was to write six multiparagraph themes per semester, she concluded that sentence and paragraph writing were prerequisite skills students should have mastered. If students lacked those skills, she did not feel she could justify taking time in the general education classroom to teach them.

As a result of hearing her concerns, the resource teachers agreed to assume major responsibility for teaching the sentence-writing strategy and the paragraph-writing strategy (Schumaker & Lyerla, 1991) in the resource room so that students with disabilities would have the option of receiving intensive and extensive instructional support to master these strategies. Through collaborative planning, all the teachers specified that instruction in certain parts of the paragraph-writing strategy and use of various graphic organizers and other prewriting skills would be integrated into writing instruction in the English class. This compromise was accepted because the resource room staff could provide the intensity of instruction and practice that students with disabilities needed and that, in large part, would be absent in the general education classroom.

For the science classes, an agreement was also made on the types of strategic instruction that would take place in the resource room and in the science classes. Specifically, resource teachers agreed to teach parts of the test-taking strategy (Hughes, Schumaker, Deshler, & Mercer, 1988) and various study skills (e.g., outlining) using the principles of strategic instruction (Ellis, Deshler, Lenz, Schumaker, & Clark, 1989).

All of the teachers agreed to use the content enhancement routines. They saw these procedures as being helpful in the identification and delivery of critical content to academically diverse classes. Some teachers used the unit organizer routine (Lenz, Bulgren, Schumaker, Deshler, & Boudah, 1994) to plan and present key blocks of instruction. The content enhancement routine that was used most broadly was the content mastery routine (Bulgren, Deshler, & Schumaker, 1993). This routine enabled teachers to teach critical content that was especially complex or abstract in such a way that all students could understand it. Over the course of the year, the teachers teamed together for the purpose of developing a concept diagram for each important concept in the course (i.e., those foundational concepts that students were expected to know by the end of the year). The literature-based concepts that were taught through the use of the concept mastery routine in the English class included symbolism, analogy, allusion, and theme as well as rhetorical concepts such as narration and exposition. To optimize student involvement, each diagram was co-constructed with the students when the concept was initially introduced. As each new piece of literature was covered in class, relevant concepts were reviewed using the concept diagram and additional examples were added to the examples list, if necessary.

Additionally, teachers modified the tests they used to ensure that they allowed students to demonstrate their competence with critical concepts as opposed to requiring only rote memorization of facts. Test results and the English teacher's evaluation indicated that all the students in the classes (including those with disabilities) not only mastered the critical course concepts but also exhibited a much deeper knowledge and greater ability to apply their knowledge to novel situations than students had in the past.

At the end of the first year, the project was evaluated. Overall, the six freshmen and other students with disabilities were relatively successful. Specifically, all of the students had received credit in English and science. Some received a P grade for "passing" rather than a letter grade, however, indicating that they had met individualized goals but had not met the course objectives at the required level of proficiency. Their level of accomplishment was sufficient, however, to enable them to earn course credit. The students also demonstrated good proficiency with the targeted strategies. Some of them had required additional instruction in the resource room in order to be able to reach a mastery level of performance on strategies taught in the general education classes.

The benefits of knowing strategies were revealed to students with disabilities in several ways in their English classes. For example, as a result of instruction in the sentence-writing strategy, they experienced the pleasure of being the only ones who automatically knew the answers to questions about subordinating conjunctions or who could discuss where and why commas and semicolons were needed! Also, because they knew how to use the paragraph diagram as a result of instruction in the paragraph-writing strategy, they were able to generalize that skill when using other "idea diagrams" that were introduced in their English classes. Learning games developed by the resource teacher such as A Separate Peace, Jeopardy, and Vocabulary Concentration helped students learn the required content and score higher on tests. In science class, they used the test-taking strategy (Hughes et al., 1988) and other study skills to take tests and complete assignments. They received additional support and instruction in the resource room (e.g., reteaching, assistance with writing lab reports, reviewing before tests, etc.). The nondisabled at-risk students experienced a similar level of success, although they often struggled because they did not receive the additional support that the resource room provided.

Overall, teachers indicated that the implementation year was a success. Foremost among the positive outcomes was the marked increase in collaboration among the staff. Specifically, the staff at Clayton High realized the importance of developing a support system for *all* at-risk students to ensure that inclusion would be successful for low-performing students as well as students with disabilities. Therefore, a learning center was conceptualized that would provide learning strategy and study skills instruction and tutoring for all students. The following year, the remedial reading teacher and three teaching interns opened the Mark Twain Learning Center. In addition, during the next year, many Clayton High School teachers began to further reduce the use of objective tests and use more alternative or performance-based assessments (e.g., portfolios, projects, and presentations). These and other changes helped students with disabilities and low-achieving students experience success in heterogeneous classes.

Lessons Learned

What was learned from this journey? First, the six freshmen learned that they could succeed in general classes, as did other at-risk students and students with disabilities. The general and special educators learned several teaching procedures that worked under a co-teaching arrangement. The school staff learned that inclusion would not succeed unless major changes were made in terms of the content that was taught, the methods used to assess competence, and the support provided to teachers and students when difficulties were encountered in the general education classroom.

Second, the planning team learned that general educators at Clayton High were reluctant to give up teaching content for learning strategy instruction, particularly if the class was a heterogeneous class designed for average to above-average students. Although teachers at Clayton High received tremendous latitude in making decisions about curriculum, they still felt pressure to teach certain core skills and competencies and to keep expectations at a very high level. However, they were willing to integrate brief instruction in related study skills and were especially enthusiastic about the use of content enhancement routines.

Third, the teachers found that students with disabilities needed more intensive instruction and many more practice opportunities to master learning strategies than did typical students. This type of instruction requires time that is often not available in general education classes. Given the limitations of the general education classroom, the Clayton High staff now believes that the ideal plan for inclusion is to teach students with disabilities strategies in the resource room and then teach all students a brief, adapted version of relevant strategies in general education classes. This approach provides instruction in strategies for all students, while providing a review for students with disabilities, who are then more likely to use the strategy because it is part of the general education curriculum.

Finally, the teachers discovered — as many other educators and researchers have concluded — that detracking and inclusion of students with mild disabilities in heterogeneous classes requires extensive planning. Clayton High has a history of including students with disabilities in general education classes. Many of these students have had significant learning and behavioral disabilities, including autism, schizophrenia, Tourette's syndrome, mild to moderate retardation, and conduct disorders, as well as learning and language disabilities. The faculty has always been and continues to be a group of hard-working, dedicated, competent professionals who care about students and are willing to make adaptations and modifications for the benefit of students. However, even this group of professionals could not make detracking or inclusion work for everyone without significant changes in teaching and assessment methods and in support systems. Inclusion can work, but only if it is supported inclusion.

CONCLUSIONS

Successfully including students with mild disabilities at the secondary level requires both administrative and instructional adjustments. In the two case studies presented here, teachers received considerable time for planning and ongoing administrative support throughout the change process. Change required considerable time and effort. The instructional program was characterized by a high level of collaboration among general and special education teachers, specifying a scope and sequence of learning strategy instruction across classes and grades, and a commitment to alter what and how content was delivered in the general education classroom through the use of various content enhancement routines. In short, successful inclusion of students with learning disabilities within the general education classroom was realized only when the set of instructional conditions associated with the notion of *supported* inclusion was met.

REFERENCES

Bulgren, J.A., Deshler, D.D., & Schumaker, J.B. (1993). *The concept mastery routine.* Lawrence, KS: Edge Enterprises.

Bulgren, J.A., Deshler, D.D., & Schumaker, J.B. (1995). *The concept comparison routine.* Lawrence, KS: Edge Enterprises.

Bulgren, J., Schumaker, J.B., & Deshler, D.D. (1998). The effectiveness of a concept teaching routine in enhancing the performance of students with learning disabilities in secondary mainstream classes. *Learning Disability Quarterly, 11,* 3-17.

Deshler, D.D. (1990). Lessons from building a snowman. *Strategram, 23*(3), 1-6.

Deshler, D.D., Alley, G.R., Warner, M.M., & Schumaker, J.B. (1981). Instructional practices for promoting skill acquisition and generalization in severely learning disabled adolescents. *Learning Disability Quarterly, 4,* 415-421.

Deshler, D.D., & Schumaker, J.B. (1988). An instructional model for teaching students how to learn. In J.L. Graden, J.E. Zins, & M.L. Curtis (Eds.), *Alternative education delivery systems: Enhancing instructional options for all students* (pp. 391-411). Washington, DC: National Association of School Psychologists.

Deshler, D.D., & Schumaker, J.B. (1993). Strategy mastery by at-risk students: Not a simple matter. *Elementary School Journal, 94,* 153-167.

Ellis, E.S. (1992). The *LINCS Vocabulary Learning Strategy: Instructor's manual.* Lawrence, KS: Edge Enterprises.

Ellis, E.S., Deshler, D.D., Lenz, B.K., Schumaker, J.B., & Clark, F.L. (1991). An instructional model for teaching learning strategies. *Focus on Exceptional Children, 24*(1), 1-14.

Huberman, M. (1993). The model of independent artisan in teachers' professional relations. In J.W. Little & M.W. McLaughlin (Eds.), *Teachers' work: Individuals, colleagues, and context* (pp. 11-50). New York: Teachers College Press.

Hudson, F. (1992, October). *Class within a class: A shared responsibility of regular and special education.* Presentation made at the annual conference of the Council for Learning Disabilities, Kansas City, MO.

Hughes, C., Schumaker, J.B., Deshler, D.D., & Mercer, C. (1988). *Learning strategies curriculum: The test taking strategy.* Lawrence, KS: Edge Enterprises.

Joint Committee on Teacher Planning for Students with Disabilities. (1993). *Planning for academic diversity in America's classrooms: Windows* on *reality, research, change, and practice.* Lawrence, KS: University of Kansas.

Knackendoffel, A., Robinson, S.M., Deshler, D.D., & Schumaker, J.B. (1992). *Collaborative problem solving.* Lawrence, KS: Edge Enterprises.

Lenz, B.K., with Bulgren, J.A., Schumaker, J.B., Deshler, D.D., & Boudah, D.J. (1994). *The unit organizer.* Lawrence, KS: Edge Enterprises.

Lenz, B.K., Schumaker, J.B., Deshler, D.D., & Beals, V.L. (1984). *Learning strategies curriculum:* The *word identification strategy.* Lawrence, KS: University of Kansas.

Scanlon, D.J., Deshler, D.D., & Schumaker, J.B. (in press). Can a strategy be taught and learned in secondary inclusive classrooms? *Learning Disabilities Research and Practice.*

Schmidt, J.L., Deshler, D.D., Schumaker, J.B., & Alley, G.R. (1989). Effects of generalization instruction on the written language performance of adolescents with learning disabilities in the mainstream classroom. *Journal of Reading, Writing, and Learning Disabilities, 4,* 291-309.

Schumaker, J.B., & Deshler, D.D. (1992). An analysis of learning strategies interventions for students with learning disabilities: Results of a programmatic research effort. In B.Y.L. Wong (Ed.), Intervention *research with students with learning disabilities.* New York: Springer-Verlag.

Schumaker, J.B., Deshler, D.D., & McKnight, P.C. (1991). Teaching routines for content areas at the secondary level. In G. Stoner, M.R. Shinn, & H.M. Walker (Eds.), *Interventions for achievement and behavior problems* (pp. 374-395). Washington, DC: National Association of School Psychologists.

Schumaker, J.B., Hazel, J.S., & Pederson, C.S. (1988). *Social skills for daily living: A curriculum.* Circle Pines, MN: American Guidance Service.

Schumaker, J.B., & Lyerla, K.D. (1991). *The paragraph writing strategy: Instructor's manual.* Lawrence: University of Kansas Center for Research on Learning.

Schumaker, J.B., Nolan, S.M., & Deshler, D.D. (1985). *Learning strategies curriculum: The error monitoring strategy.* Lawrence, KS: University of Kansas.

Schumaker, J.B., & Sheldon, J. (1985). *The sentence writing strategy: Instructor's manual.* Lawrence, KS: University of Kansas.

Van Reusen, A.K., Bos, C., Schumaker, J.B., & Deshler, D.D. (1987). *Motivating strategies curriculum: The education planning strategy.* Lawrence, KS: Edge Enterprises.

Vernon, D.S., Deshler, D.D., & Schumaker, J.B. (1993). *The cooperative strategies series: The teamwork strategy.* Lawrence, KS: Edge Enterprises.

This chapter was reprinted with permission, from Remedial and Special Education, 1996, Volume 17, Pages 204-216.

INDEX

Hirsch, B.J., 221
history, big ideas in, 55–56
Hock, Michael F., 9, 10, 25, 27, 33, 34, 54
Hodge, J.P., 34
Hodgkinson, H., 53
Hofmeister, A.M., 60
Hogan, A., 113
Hogan, K., x, 10
Holcutt, A., 155
Hollinger, J., 130
homework assignments, 151, 153–156
   explaining, 183
   modern-age approach to, 156
Horton, S.V., 90–92
Horwitz, R.A., 220
Hovell, M.F., 235
Howell, S.B., 193
Hoy, C., 108
Hudson, F.G., 34, 36, 272
Hudson, P., 5, 91
Hughes, C., 216, 274, 275
Hughes, C.A., 184, 185, 217
Hurley, C.M., 235, 236

imaginative learners, 168
inclusionary education movement, 2. See
   also disabilities
information processors, characteristics of
   good, 9–10
instruction
   acquisition/generalization phases of, 96
   intensity over sustained period of time, 41
   intensive
      essential aspects, 41
      and targeted, 3
   scaffolding, 10
   student-centered, 4
instructional conditions, 37
instructional procedures, standards and
   criteria for successful, viii–ix
instructional strategies, 65
instructional time, 41
Integrated Instruction Model, 99–100
intelligences, theory of multiple, 162–168
intensive personalized instruction, 18–23
   peer tutoring, 34–35
   small-group strategy instruction, 23–25
   strategic tutoring, 25–34

interpersonal cognitive problem solving,
   130–133
interpersonal skills, 109. See also social skills
Irvin, L.K., 128, 137

Jackson, A.W., 210, 212
Jacobs, M., 115
Janzen, H.L., 211
Jenkins, J., 92
Johnson, J., 110
Johnston, J.H., 215
Jones, L.K., 190
Jorgenson, G., 151

Kammeyer, K.C.W., 114
Kantor, R.N., 76
Kasak, D., 212
Kasen, S., 110
Kauffman, J.M., 155
Kavale, K.A., 107, 118, 119
Kazdin, A., 115
Kea, C.D., 193
Keefe, J.W., 239
Keller, C.E., 192
Kelly, B., 60
Kinder, D., 55, 57
kinesthetic learners, 167
Kissam, B., 68, 75, 224
Klamm, 36
Kline, F.M., 192–194
Knackendoffel, A., 256
Knight, J., 39
Kurita, J.A., 211

Lacey, C., 211
Ladd, G., 119
Lakoff, R., 110
Lawrence, G., 238
Lazear, D., 164
learners, expert, 9
   cooperation with novice learners, 9–10
   role in classroom, 10
learning communities, 38–39
learning disabilities construct, concept
   diagram of, 264, 265
learning environment, 65

ABOUT THE AUTHORS

Donald D. Deshler is a professor in the Department of Special Education and Director of the Center for Research on Learning at the University of Kansas. His work has focused on instructional strategies for adolescents who are at-risk for failure in school and work settings.

Jean B. Schumaker is a courtesy professor in the Department of Special Education and the Associate Director of the Center for Research on Learning at the University of Kansas. Her work has emphasized various intervention strategies for teaching at-risk students how to learn and perform in social and academic situations.

Karen R. Harris, Ed.D., is Distinguished Scholar-Teacher and Professor in the Department of Special Education at the University of Maryland, and co-director of the Center to Accelerate Student Learning. Her areas of specialization include development of self-regulation and strategies instruction for students with LD and ADHD.

Steve Graham, Ed.D., is a professor in the Department of Special Education at the University of Maryland and co-director of the Center to Accelerate Student Learning. His research and scholarship focuses on instruction in the area of written language, including the development of teaching strategies designed to improve students' planning, revising, and text production skills.

Beverly Colombo is an instructional facilitator for the Special School District of St. Louis County Missouri. Her development interests are in program design, evaluation, and special adaptations for at-risk adolescents.

Joseph B. Fisher is an assistant professor in the School of Education at Grand Valley State University. His areas of specialization include instuctional practices for inclusive classrooms and the use of technology in teachers' professional development.

Patricia G. Gildroy is an advanced doctoral student in the Department of Special Education at the University of Kansas. Her areas of interest include teacher education, reading instruction, and academic strategies for underachieving students.

Michael F. Hock, Ph.D., is a research associate at the University of Kansas Center for Research on Learning. His area of speciality includes teaching academically underprepared adolescents skills and strategies for independent learning.

Paula Lancaster is a doctoral student in Special Education at the University of Kansas. Her professional interests include effective instruction for adolescents with learning disabilities and the use of technology as a teaching tool.

Joyce Ann Rademacher is an assistant professor in Programs in Special Education, Department of Technology and Cognition, University of North Texas. Her research interests include the development and validation of strategic instructional interventions for underachieving students and issues related to teacher preparation in professional development schools.

Rosemary Tralli is the Director or Special Services in the Enfield Public Schools (Connecticut). Her areas of specialty include system change and learning strategy instruction for at-risk adolescents.

Anthony K. Van Reusen is an associate professor in the Division of Education at the University of Texas at San Antonio. His areas of specilization include academic, cognitive and motivation intervention strategies for underachieving adolescents and young adults.